The Executive's
Accounting Primer

The Executive's Accounting Primer

Robert L. Dixon

Professor of Accounting
Graduate School of Business Administration
University of Michigan

McGRAW-HILL BOOK COMPANY

New York St. Louis San Francisco Düsseldorf Johannesburg
Kuala Lumpur London Mexico Montreal New Delhi
Panama Rio de Janeiro Singapore Sydney Toronto

THE EXECUTIVE'S ACCOUNTING PRIMER

07-017078-9

1234567890   MAMM   754321

This book was set in Intertype Baskerville by The Maple Press Company, and
printed and bound by The Maple Press Company. The editors were Dale L.
Dutton, W. Hodson Mogan, and Linda B. Handler. The designer was Naomi
Auerbach. Teresa F. Leaden supervised production.

Contents

Preface

For Whom Is This Book?

This book is designed for the man or woman who has had little or no formal training or experience in accounting, or who had only a course or two some time ago and has forgotten most of it, and whose current or possible future occupation calls for a breadth of understanding of the financial affairs of a business enterprise. This definition would appear to fit the person who now carries executive responsibilities or who believes his opportunity for promotion to executive levels would benefit from some familiarity with the inner workings and concepts of accounting. Another class of professional people who are prospective readers of this book are members of the legal profession who have had scant training in accounting but who undertake to prepare tax returns and, particularly, those who become involved in litigation which is concerned with such matters as business profit determinations, rates of return, taxes, and financial damages.

What Does It Offer?

The big problems in gaining an understanding of accounting are, first, getting over the threshold with minimum pain; second, choosing, with a certain amount of discrimination and sophistication, specific areas of the field for study; and third, examining these areas enough not only to feel at home with them but, more importantly, to develop an ability to discuss these and other areas with accountants, financial personnel, and lawyers.

In seeking to surmount the threshold, this book starts with the known and heads, at a modest pace, into the unknown. The first five chapters are intended to parade the vocabulary and principal accounting reports and to develop a minimum understanding of the debit-credit structure—or, as I prefer to call it, "the accounting method." Then, the remaining fifteen chapters apply accounting method to the analysis of certain prominent areas of accounting in the belief that one need not suffer through the whole accounting spectrum to achieve only an understanding rather than a pick-and-shovel knowledge of accounting. The third goal comes from achieving the first two. If you "know" some accounting and have exercised your mind a bit in tusseling with some of its favorite problems, you should then be capable of (1) understanding the meaning and significance of the data that come across your path; (2) recognizing your own needs for accounting data as related to the evaluations and decisions you are called upon to make; (3) formulating quite explicitly your requests to the accounting staff for special reports or accounting schedules. In short, this book definitely is not designed to teach you how to be a bookkeeper or to become a CPA, but it should help you very much to be able to understand and communicate with accountants and financial personnel—in short, to be a better manager or executive.

How Should You Read It?

For a person to become a qualified professional accountant requires years of study and accounting experience. This book is fairly short; in fact, a fast reader probably could "read" the entire thing in a day or less. Don't! A good deal of the book is devoted to topics that the best accountants in the world find troublesome, in spite of their years of exposure to accounting. So, please be fair with this book; it is intended for *study* rather than as a bedside reader. Some chapters are quite short and you might do a whole one in a single setting; some chapters are quite long and you certainly should divide these into two or more reading periods. As a rule of thumb, be satisfied to read no more than about eight to ten pages at one time. Study the illustrative examples very carefully and, by all means, do the short tests that appear at the end of most chapters.

Certain chapters, especially Chapters 16 through 19, are somewhat specialized and can be read in any order, or skipped entirely if you wish, but you should be sure to include Chapter 20 on your itinerary. When you have finished this book, if you feel interested in pursuing accounting further, you should find little difficulty in reading any of the widely used textbooks leading into advanced accounting, and you should enjoy reading some of the accounting and finance periodicals such as *The Journal of Accountancy, The Financial Executive,* and *The Wall Street Journal.*

This is my opportunity to express appreciation to two fine colleagues, Professors Harold E. Arnett and Robert H. Arnold who, respectively, wrote the chapters on federal income taxes and computers—subject matter which goes well beyond my personal knowledge horizon.

Robert L. Dixon

The Executive's
Accounting Primer

Chapter One

The Balance Sheet

Why Start with the Balance Sheet?

Even though you have never taken a course in accounting, the probabilities are that you have some notion about what the typical balance sheet looks like. So, we can start with "the known" in the excursion we are about to make into the unknown. More important, the so-called *balance sheet approach* is very commonly used in the popular introductory accounting texts because the balance sheet itself clearly reflects the structure of the accounting mechanism; it's the best possible basis for catching onto the accountant's debit and credit lingo; it's actually at the beginning and end of all accounting activity.

What Is the Balance Sheet's Purpose?

For the moment, let's assert that the purpose of a balance sheet is *to show the financial position* of a given enterprise *at a given point in time*. For example, a balance sheet usually has in it a line labeled "cash," and shows the amount of cash possessed by the enterprise at a particular moment (e.g., at the "close of business," December 31, 19XX). Everything else in that balance sheet should then be reflected (measured) in dollars as they stood at that same point in time. Thus, the *amount* of cash may be shown to be $24,216.47; the amount of machinery, $165,520.01; the amount of merchandise, $45,679; etc. Each of these amounts has at least one thing in common—each has been measured "as of" the same point in time. So, a given balance sheet simply can't show the amount of cash at December 31, the amount of merchandise at November 20, and the amount of machinery at yet some other date.

To repeat, the alleged purpose of a balance sheet is to depict the financial position of the enterprise at a given point in time. The balance sheet does not show how we reached that position (though it may contain some clues), and it does not show where we're heading (though a series of balance sheets on successive dates can be of help in this connection).

Does the Balance Sheet Really Show Financial Position?

Your own financial position is made up of the valuable possessions, or resources, owned by you, *offset by your debts*. The *difference* between the dollar measure of your resources and the dollar measure of your debts is what is commonly called your *net worth*. If we apply the same formula to the company with which you are associated we might, for example, find that the company's balance sheet shows assets totaling $1,000,000 and offsetting debts of $400,000, so that its net worth is $600,000. Accountants, particularly the teacher crowd, are so impressed by the algebra of this situation that they often refer to "the" accounting equation as: *Assets minus liabilities equals net worth, or* $A - L = NW$.

The balance sheet, basically, consists of a reporting of the dollar amount of assets, *on the left-hand side,* and all the existing debts *on the right-hand side;* the two sides are then made equal by filling in enough on the right-hand side to make them equal! The amount of this filler is the net worth. So, if we want to flaunt our mathematical ability a bit, we may point out that, as mentioned above, $A - L = NW$; and this can just as well be written as $A = L + NW$, which is a kind of arithmetic model of the standard balance sheet where the assets on the left equal the sum of the liabilities and net worth on the right.

So far it would appear that financial position means nothing more than a pair of totals (assets and liabilities) offset to show their difference (net worth). As a matter of fact, this arithmetic pattern constitutes only a minor facet of any analysis of a company's financial position. The asset total has some meaning; the liability total has some meaning; and the net worth has some (very limited) meaning; but these are gross concepts, to say the least. Any analysis of a company's financial position will surely take into account, and with considerably greater interest, the relationships (ratios) that exist as between some of the more detailed items within the asset, the liability, and the net worth categories. Financial position, in other words, is not to be construed as a mere difference between the asset and the liability totals. We'll look at more of this later.

Does the Balance Sheet Actually Show What You Think It Does?

We have just been discoursing, with an apparent degree of confidence, on the service of the balance sheet in revealing a company's financial position. Before we become overly enthusiastic, let's slow down a bit and test our premises.

If the balance sheet does, in truth, show the *current value of all* the assets owned by a company and if it also shows all the company's debts, it would apparently qualify as an accurate statement of financial position—if the asset amount is correct and the liability amount is correct, then their difference, the net worth, must be correct. But, now we come to the real hooker. The asset total (as well as many of the details which go to make it up) is *virtually never* equal to the current value of all the assets. If this isn't enough to discourage you, let us add that the *real worth* of a company depends on a great deal more than its list of assets and its list of liabilities. You could probably imagine, in this age of leasing almost everything, a company which *owns* no assets at all, which has some real liabilities, and which, though its accounting net worth would then be a negative figure, might have a great deal of worth in the eyes of the expert investor. In other words, it takes more than tangible assets to make a company worth something— this essential ingredient is management. It would be perfectly ridiculous to expect, for example, that the stock of a company which has an accounting net worth of $100,000, with 10,000 shares outstanding, would have a market value *per share* that is exactly twice as much as that of another company with an accounting net worth also of $100,000 but with 20,000 shares of stock outstanding. The only time this relationship would be likely to hold true would be in case the $100,000 was in hard cash and the companies were about to be dissolved.

How Are Assets Valued?

Early in the preceding paragraph it was pointed out that the balance sheet fails to show true financial position, or true net worth, because the asset total is virtually never equal to the current value of all the assets owned. This admission might come as a surprise to almost everyone who has looked at a balance sheet but who has not had any experience or formal training in accounting.

The fact of the matter is that assets can be divided into two very general categories—the first being *cash and claims to cash* and the second being *assets that have been purchased* for use in the business (such as inventories, plant and equipment). Roughly speaking, the first group is reported in the balance sheet *at the amount of cash funds they represent* (e.g., cash on hand, cash in bank, and amounts due from customers) while the second group is reported *at the amounts we have invested in them*—i.e., *at their cost*. Let's hasten to add that in making up the cost figures one must recognize (1) not only the amounts paid for the assets originally but also (2) the amounts (sometimes estimated) representing the using up of the assets. Thus, we buy a machine for $10,000 and that's its original cost. As the machine is used it depreciates; on successive balance sheets we show that machine (probably combined with other related assets) at lower and lower amounts to reflect its inevitable depreciation or, as someone has phrased it, "its inevitable march to the junk heap."

It should be perfectly obvious that if some of the assets of the company are listed in its balance sheet as cash or near cash (such as accounts receivable) while the remainder are listed at what the company paid for them (in some cases years ago), the sum of these two groups simply won't equal the "present value" of the total assets. For purposes of discussion let's refer to the two groups of assets as (1) the *monetary* assets and (2) the *nonmonetary* assets.

Why Are Nonmonetary Assets Reported at Cost?

Some accountants, particularly some of the folks in the ivory towers, sincerely believe that all nonmonetary assets should be reported in the balance sheet at their *current market values*. It is my personal opinion, however, that it is easier for this group to tell *why* the assets should be so valued than it is for them to tell *how* current market value is to be ascertained. They point out that the asset side of the orthodox balance sheet is a conglomerate mass of dollars representing not only the monetary assets but the nonmonetary at costs that have been incurred sometimes over a span of 25 or more years, and they feel that these cost amounts may be far removed from current reality (the more modern expression is "irrelevant"). Certainly there's a good deal of truth to this accusation. But, we must then examine the alternatives—that is, the utilization of current market value. (Some prefer to use the comparable term "current cost" or, merely, "current value.")

Surely no problem exists in listing cash at its current value because cash (and we're concerned here only with our domestic currency) is, itself, the ultimate measure of value. Similarly, marketable securities, such as the stocks and bonds that are listed on the organized stock exchanges or are quoted in the over-the-counter market, can readily be listed at current values. Next, accounts and notes receivable can quite readily be listed at a close approximation of their current values— that is, at the amounts that will rather surely be collected from them within a reasonable period of time. However, when we move on to assets such as machinery and equipment—especially if these items were tailor-made for our firm—it becomes quite difficult to determine a reasonable market value. Particularly where the machinery is permanently affixed to the plant and would not conceivably be sold, the *relevance* of a current market value becomes pretty hard to recognize. Often the only market would be the secondhand, or the junk market. The land on which our buildings stand may have high potential value in the current real estate market. So what? Does the strength of our company lie in the fact that it could sell its site land for more than it cost, or does its strength lie in the day-to-day operations that it carries on? Needless to say, the market values of most buildings, so often designed for the special purposes for which they are being used, would be quite meaningless even if they were ascertainable. If the company is a going concern, it will not sell its building for the profit that is thus available, unless it is contemplating going out of business. Sometimes structures are appraised by a process of finding the present cost of the kinds of materials and labor that were originally expended in their construction, but such a procedure may result in a very poor representation of the current value of the structure.

Admittedly, this is only a sketchy look at the subject of asset valuation, but it is intended to warn you, if not to soften the blow, that in most cases in dealing with accounting data we will be relying on *historical cost* where nonmonetary assets are concerned. The argument for cost can be expressed quite simply: First, there is no satisfactory means of determining current market value of most nonmonetary assets *economically on a continuous basis;* second, the essence, if not the quintessence, of profit determination lies in the matching of *cost* against *revenue.* Revenue is what we collect from the sale of something; cost is what we paid for something. "Buy low and sell high." In other words, a cardinal principle of accounting is that profit is not earned by mere changes in the value of things; it must be *realized by actual transactions* in which something is literally *sold* for an amount greater than its cost.

All of this leads us to another conclusion. We had better stop using the term *net worth* in our balance sheets; in fact, the principal rule-making body of accountants, the American Institute of Certified Public Accountants, has recommended that other, more meaningful, terms be used. Commonly in the balance sheets one now finds such terms as Stockholders' Equity, or Capital Stock and Retained Earnings, to represent the difference between the total assets and the total liabilities.

Balance Sheet Illustrations

Mainly for purposes of rounding out the present chapter, a few balance sheet illustrations will now be presented. Care is taken to exclude balance sheet items which might be unfamiliar or which might require special explanation at this point in our study. Here we are concerned mostly with the basic concept of the balance sheet, including its content and structure.

Figure 1 is a balance sheet that is condensed beyond all reality, but it is intended to depict the skeleton structure of the orthodox balance sheet. As shown, the balance sheet in Figure 1 is in so-called *account* form. That is, the assets appear on the left-hand side and the liabilities

FIGURE 1
ORANGE PRODUCTS CO.
Balance Sheet as of December 31, 19XX

Assets		Liabilities and Stock Equity		
Current.............	$ 40,000	Liabilities:		
Noncurrent..........	60,000	Current..........	$20,000	
		Noncurrent.......	15,000	$ 35,000
		Stockholders' equity:		
		Capital stock......	$50,000	
		Retained earnings..	15,000	65,000
	$100,000			$100,000

and owners' equities are shown on the right. By the simple process of showing the liabilities and owners' equities below the assets, the form becomes known as the *report* form, as in Figure 2. Quite obviously, it makes little difference whether the balance sheet is presented in account or in report form; the choice may depend solely on page size and convenience.

FIGURE 2
ORANGE PRODUCTS CO.
Balance Sheet as of December 31, 19XX

Assets		
Current.............................		$ 40,000
Noncurrent..........................		60,000
		$100,000

Liabilities and Stock Equity		
Liabilities:		
Current....................	$20,000	
Noncurrent................	15,000	$ 35,000
Stockholders' equity:		
Capital stock...............	$50,000	
Retained earnings...........	15,000	65,000
		$100,000

Figure 3 shows the same data, rearranged a bit more significantly, in "sequence" form. This form has a relatively small following but it is used by some of the big companies. In my estimation the confusion it causes exceeds any merits it may possess.

FIGURE 3
ORANGE PRODUCTS CO.
Balance Sheet as of December 31, 19XX

Current assets..............................	$40,000
Less: Current liabilities......................	20,000
Working capital...........................	$20,000
Noncurrent assets...........................	60,000
	$80,000
Less: Noncurrent liabilities....................	15,000
Stockholders' equity (See Schedule A)...........	$65,000

Schedule A
Stockholders' Equity

Capital stock.................................	$50,000
Retained earnings............................	15,000
	$65,000

Figure 4 shows, in report form, a balance sheet with a few of the more common headings and explanatory notes included. This example might easily represent the balance sheet of a moderately large corporation as it would actually be presented in an annual report, or an interim report, to the company's stockholders.

Balance Sheet Categories

Most people with a nodding acquaintance with accounting would define current assets as those which "can be converted into cash within a year." Such a definition is both out of date and wrong. In the early days, the balance sheet was prepared mainly for use in dealing with creditors—in seeking bank loans or credit from suppliers—who were mainly interested in the "liquidity" of the borrower. Accordingly, current assets have traditionally been displayed ahead of the other assets in the balance sheet; from the creditor's standpoint, assets had to be liquid in order to be current. Now, however, we view the balance sheet as a conveyor of financial information to all parties with a legitimate interest in the company—not only the creditors but especially the owners and, at the same time, potential investors, the tax collectors, and the labor force. So, current assets now include the five classes of assets shown in Figure 4 on the assumption that the balance sheet should show the financial structure of the enterprise—that is, its circulating assets (current) and

FIGURE 4
Orange Products Co.
Balance Sheet as of December 31, 19XX

Assets

Current:

Cash...	$ 5,000	
Marketable securities (at cost; market value is $12,500)....	8,000	
Receivables (after subtracting $1,000 for estimated amount uncollectible)......................................	10,000	
Inventories (at the lower of cost or market).............	15,000	
Prepayments......................................	2,000	$ 40,000

Plant:

Land...		$10,000	
Structures................................	$30,000		
Machinery and equipment...................	40,000		
	$70,000		
Less: Amount charged off as depreciation.......	25,000	45,000	55,000

Intangibles:

Patents (at cost less $1,632 of amortization).............	$ 4,999	
Goodwill (at nominal value).........................	1	5,000
		$100,000

Liabilities and Stock Equity

Current liabilities:

Accounts payable....................................	$12,000	
Taxes payable......................................	4,000	
Dividends payable...................................	2,500	
Miscellaneous......................................	1,500	$ 20,000
Bonds payable, 7%, due in 19XX................................		15,000
Total liabilities.....................................		$ 35,000

Stockholders' equity:

Capital stock, par $10...............................	$50,000	
Retained earnings...................................	15,000	65,000
		$100,000

its relatively permanent plant assets. Thus, we toss out both the one-year rule as well as the "can-be-converted-into-cash" rule. In fact, the latter rule is nonsense from any point of view because land is likely to be salable and in most cases could easily be "converted into cash within a year," but it is usually considered to be a leading example of the noncurrent group.

The noncurrent assets are more commonly called *fixed* assets and placed under that heading.

Current liabilities can safely be defined as those which will come due within a year from the date of the balance sheet, although some exceptions to this rule may occasionally arise.

Balance Sheet Relationships

Almost inevitably when one scans a balance sheet he makes routine note of certain fundamental relationships. First, he is likely to make a rough calculation of the *current ratio*. This is the arithmetic ratio of the total of current assets to the total of current liabilities. (In our example the ratio stands at 40 to 20, or 2 to 1.) He may make a rough determination of the amount of *working capital*, which is the difference between the total current assets and the total current liabilities. (In our example the working capital is $40,000 − $20,000.)

Another rather important relationship is that of owners' equity to total assets. (In the Orange Products Co. example, this relationship, known as the *equity ratio*, is $65,000 to $100,000, or 65 percent).

Financial analysts have invented dozens of "pet" ratios in addition to the three just described. Because this is a book on accounting and not a book on corporation finance or financial analysis, we won't worry about what the various ratios should be in any given case, but you should be warned *not* to settle for any predigested rules or standards. The analysis of any balance sheet rests first and most importantly on a knowledge of what underlies the reported figures, a knowledge of the industry that you are dealing with, a knowledge of what kind of *management* rules the firm (nothing is more important than this), and a lot of other things. At best, the ratios constitute supplementary or confirmatory data and they should *never* be taken as complete answers in themselves.

Balance Sheet Terminology

In concluding this chapter, let's point out that different words are used by different accountants in referring to the same things. Incidentally, the very title, Balance Sheet, is rapidly becoming archaic and is giving way to Statement of Financial Condition, Statement of Financial Position, or simply, Position Statement. A satisfactory heading for the right-hand side of the position statement, to replace the clumsy Liabilities and Stock Equity, is the single word, Equities. In the examples in this chapter only the most common types of position statement items have been mentioned. This is lesson 1; we'll delve into matters such as reserves, LIFO, deferred federal income taxes, consolidated statements, and many other more complex and more exciting subjects as we pass on into our advanced lessons.

Now it's up to you to pull out your pencil and work the exercise that follows. It includes nothing new and you won't know whether you're qualified for reading Chapter 2 until you have passed your first test. You'll find model answers in the appendix but, of course, you won't peek until you have finished working the problem.

TEST PROBLEM

Denton Bread Co. was organized early in 1972, when 10,000 shares of $10 par common stock were issued for cash at par. During the remainder of 1972 the company succeeded in earning $12,000, and it paid dividends of $8,000. Land was purchased for $5,000 cash, a building was erected for $50,000 cash, and machinery and equipment were purchased for $60,000 cash. To finance the fixed asset purchases, a 20-year, 8 percent mortgage note for $30,000 was negotiated with the local bank. At the end of the year 1972 assets, other than those identified thus far, consisted of cash $9,200, accounts receivable with a face value of $12,000, raw materials inventory which cost $5,000, miscellaneous supplies which cost $1,000, and prepayments of $500. Liabilities, in addition to the mortgage, consisted of wages payable $1,600, taxes payable $3,000, and mortgage interest payable $200. Depreciation of the fixed assets (other than land) was recognized in the amount of $3,400, and it was estimated that about $500 of the receivables might prove to be uncollectible.

Required:

In the space provided, prepare a balance sheet in excellent form, as of December 31, 1972.

TEST PROBLEM Solution Space

DENTON BREAD CO.
Balance Sheet as of December 31, 1972

Assets

Current:

Plant:

Equities

Current liabilities:

Stockholders' equity:

{ Chapter Two }

The Income Statement

What Is the Income Statement's Purpose?

If you were to start a business concern by investing $100,000 in cash it is conceivable, but unlikely, that you would be willing to operate it, or assign the job to a manager, and wait until the concern is finally dissolved before any computation of your earnings is made. Actually such a delay in reckoning the earnings would have one virtue—the difference between the amounts of cash *invested* during the lifetime of the enterprise and the amount *finally realized* upon dissolution comes close to being the true profit (or loss) of the venture (assuming that you make proper allowance for any dividends or other withdrawals of funds during the lifetime of the venture). Rather than this, of course, owners and other interested parties demand *periodic* information on the progress of the enterprise; in short, they require a report of net income at least annually and, in a great many cases, quarterly or more often. The space of time covered by such a report is known as an *accounting period*.

It would be difficult to locate any truly authoritative statement of the purpose of the income statement, and it is best perhaps not to focus on any single purpose. If we want to be theoretical, we might state that the leading purpose is to show how much the *net assets of the enterprise have increased (or decreased)* during the accounting period—always with due allowance for any dividends paid or any additional investments or withdrawals by the stockholders.

Net assets and *net worth* are synonymous terms—each refers to the arithmetic difference between total assets and total liabilities. (Remember the equation, $A - L = NW$.) Possibly the term *net assets* is to be preferred because it avoids the word "worth," but it is less likely to be comprehended by nonaccountants.

Unfortunately there is a wide range of opinions on the manner in which the A of the basic equation should be measured—should the net assets reflect current *market* values, current *replacement* costs, historical costs, or historical costs translated into dollars of current purchasing power?

A more fruitful approach, it would seem, is to attribute more than a single purpose to the income statement and set out to prepare income statements that will, in fact, serve multiple purposes. This is achieved, basically, by avoiding overcondensation—*by disclosing the component elements* that go to make up the figure at the bottom of the statement rather than by limiting the report to a half-dozen or fewer figures. Thus, the statement should certainly reveal the total sales and, in keeping with current tendencies, should show the amount of sales made by each of the principal divisions of the enterprise. The expenses, insofar as practicable, should also be shown in some detail—preferably both on a functional basis (or in terms of kinds of expenses) as well as on a divisional basis.

The income statement is often referred to as the *operating statement;* and it should, indeed, portray the ongoing operations of the enterprise to the degree that mere dollar figures can achieve this. The reader should be able to make some assessment of the size, growth, and perhaps the growth potential of the enterprise by analyzing its sales data.

The relationship between the amount of a given expense, for example, and sales for the period may give some insight into the operating efficiency of the company. The relationship between net income and any "fixed charges" for bond interest or leasehold rents may be significant in evaluating the amount of risk inherent in making a stock investment, in lending funds to the enterprise, etc.

As in the case of the balance sheet, the financial analysts have developed a large number of "favorite" ratios relating particular income statement items to others, and also relating certain income statement items with certain balance sheet items. For our purposes, then, let's not think of the income statement as a mere (and possibly frail) measure of financial growth through net income for the period.

What Is Net Income?

As you might guess, the term *net income* means different things to different accountants, so one can safely define it in a number of ways. My choice relates to a possible purpose of the income statement—to show, at some point, *the earnings which management has produced* during the period *for all capital suppliers*. To illustrate, assume that with assets of $100,000 management produces $10,000 of net income during a year; this is an important bit of financial information in itself. Then, a separate question is, who is entitled to this $10,000 of net income? If some of the assets were acquired through the issuance of $40,000 in 8 percent bonds, then 8 percent of $40,000, or $3,200 of the $10,000 net income, goes to the bondholders, which leaves a balance of $6,800 properly termed Earnings of Stockholders. This amount in turn might be subject to cumulative dividend claims of "preferred" stockholders (let's assume an amount of $2,500), leaving a balance to be labeled Earnings of Common Stockholders ($4,300).

Net income cannot really be described clearly without employing other accounting words that we are about to examine. Net income is made up of revenues, as the positive factor, from which are subtracted the negatives, which are the expenses, most losses, and income taxes. Take particular note of the fact that the word "cash" has not been used at any time in this discussion; the reason is that cash has nothing, or at least very little, to do with the determination of net income.

A more popular definition of net income, a variant of the one just presented, holds that it consists of the earnings *after* interest on bonds, etc., has been subtracted. Thus, in the example the net income would be $6,800 rather than $10,000. This is the position taken by the American Institute of Certified Public Accountants through its authoritative Accounting Principles Board in an opinion published under the title, "Reporting the Results of Operations" (December 1966).

What Is Revenue?

First, let's shower you with words: sales revenue, interest revenue, rent revenue, dividend revenue, royalties revenue, and so on. The *total* revenues of a business are the sum of all the revenues from all sources during a given period. An enterprise can have billions of dollars of revenues in a given year and yet report a net loss for that year—because, from the dollars of revenue must be deducted the dollars of expenses, losses, and income taxes before the amount of net income (or net loss) is determined. Thus, the sales revenue is the *total* amount collectible from customers for the delivery (sale) of goods and services during the period. This is *not* income in any proper sense of the word—it is revenue! For example, if we sell for $100 an object that cost us $70, our revenue from the sale is $100; whether or not we earn any *income* on the sale then depends on what are our total costs (including the $70) of the sale. Incidentally, many (perhaps most) accountants, in this simple example, would subtract the $70 from the $100 and call the remaining $30 "gross profit," which is a real corruption of the English language. There simply cannot be any profit until *all* related costs have been deducted from revenue.

Revenue, then, is the total amount obtained by us from the sale of merchandise or other commodities, or from the rendering of services to our customers. By itself, revenue gives no indication of the ultimate *net income*.

Just as revenue must be contrasted with net income, so must it be vigorously contrasted with the *inflow of cash*. Revenue for the period is the amount of revenue "earned" during that period, whether you get paid for it in cash during the same period, during the preceding period, or in the following period. True, if our apparent revenue amounts initially to $100,000 and it later becomes clear that one or more of our customers will fail to pay us a total of $1,000 which they owe us, our revenue can properly be described in two fashions: (1) Our *gross* revenue is $100,000 and (2) our *net* revenue is $99,000. In other words, gross sales revenue for a given period is a summation of all sales for the period, whether for cash or on charge account; and *net* sales revenue is the gross minus any portion deemed to be uncollectible. (Gross sales minus "bad debts" equals net sales.)

Our discussion of revenue leads conveniently to the noting of a word commonly applied to accounting. When a sale is made, cash need not be collected on the spot in order to recognize (record) the revenue. We *accrue* revenue *when the sale is made* or *when the service is rendered*, and this is the revenue that is recognized (reported) in the income statement. The time of collection of cash proceeds from the sale, while by no means unimportant, has no direct bearing on the amount or the timing of the revenue. This is one facet of the *accrual* concept; because the concept is widely applied in business accounting, it is not unusual to hear an accountant speak of *accrual accounting*.

The Accrual Concept

When an accountant says he employs the accrual system it means that he is *not* employing the *cash* system. While accrual accounting, as it is now practiced, is not perfect by a long shot, it is far superior to accounting on a cash basis. Under a thoroughgoing cash system, believe it or not, the existence of nothing is acknowledged formally until cash has been given or received! In other words, receivables and payables are not formally recognized, and neither are the sales of merchandise nor the purchases of merchandise, until the related amounts of cash change hands. There are no revenues except as they flow in in the form of cash; there are no expenses except as they are evidenced by actual outlays of cash. (It might be noted here that most of us, as individuals, employ *cash* accounting in the preparation of our personal income tax returns.)

By way of contrast, now, contemplate accrual accounting. Under this concept revenues are generated by the *delivery* of goods or services to customers (and it matters not that the goods may have been paid for in advance of, at the time of, or sometime after delivery). In short, revenue accrues in the form, and with the generation, of *claims* to dollars on the theory that the claim itself ideally represents culmination of the act of earning. When goods are sold (when title to the goods is transferred to the customers), *revenue is realized*.

Some people, and most economists, might argue that under a *true accrual* system revenue (and income) should be recognized in the records and financial statements even before the goods and services are delivered (sold) to customers; that in an economic sense income accrues as the production activity is being performed since the producer, by definition, is creating utility and corresponding value. Most accountants would find this argument difficult to deny in theory, but "in practice" we generally resort to a doctrine of conservatism which, in essence, says that it isn't safe to assume that all goods produced will automatically be sold at predictable prices. Rather, we insist that revenue cannot be accrued until it is *realized* through the act of sale or its equivalent. (But we don't go so far as to wait until the customer pays his bill.) An equivalent, for example, is found in the accrual of interest receivable on notes receivable, or on bonds owned, *as time passes.* Here no "sale" takes place in the technical sense, but an underlying contract exists and the interest revenue becomes a growing enforceable claim as time passes.

Expenses also are "accrued" rather than being recorded on a cash basis. An expense is accrued in the accounting period that should logically be charged with the expense—although the related cash outlay may or may not occur in whole or in part in that same period.

A worthwhile concept to chew on is that of "matching expenses with revenues." What this means essentially is that we should strive to bring together in the same period the revenues that we earn in that period and the expenses that were incurred to produce those revenues. This will never be accomplished to perfection. It's fairly easy to determine which accounting period should get credit for a given sale or other revenue-producing act, but it's a much tougher job to determine how much of each of the many varieties of expenses should be accrued in the same period. As you may have perceived, revenues tend to dominate the process of income determination; they are "realized" by sale, and expenses are accrued to match.

What Is an Expense?

We've had a good look at revenues and have had a peek at the concept of accrual. This should pave the way for a good introduction to the concept of expense. "Expense" is about as misused by businessmen, as well as accountants, as any term that we'll deal with. Businessmen talk about the expense of constructing a building and cost accountants, especially, frequently speak of factory expense when referring to miscellaneous manufacturing costs other than direct labor and raw materials. Both of these usages are poor if one has any desire whatsoever to speak good accounting. "Expense" is a good word with a perfectly satisfactory spot in the accounting vocabulary, but its use should be restricted to that spot.

"Expense" means (1) that we have given up something of value—either cash (or a promise to pay cash) or a part or all of some other asset such as merchandise, prepaid insurance, machinery, or buildings. Added to this, it means (2) that the something of value given up was given up *intentionally* (though perhaps reluctantly or grudgingly). Added to this, it means (3) that the something of value was given up intentionally *to produce revenue*. In summary, "expense" includes all costs (that is, values given up) incurred intentionally to produce the revenues of the period.

As you should recognize at once, expenses are *good* things—they cause revenues to flow in. You will, nevertheless, (because expenses involve giving up valuable assets) try to be as economical as possible in incurring expenses. That is, if you are incurring an average of $.80 of expense to produce $1.00 of revenue you'll exercise all your management skill to cut the ratio down to $.70 per $1.00 or lower. Incidentally, the ratio of expenses to revenues is used widely by financial analysts in evaluating the operating efficiency of a firm—the ratio is known as the *operating ratio*.

Looked at in yet another way, expenses are the amounts (classified by function or by kind) that are subtracted from revenues on the income statement in working toward *net income*. It's pretty obvious that if you were to construct a building for $1,000,000 during a given year you wouldn't think of treating the full cost as expense of *that year*. The million dollars, as you probably have already recognized, does *become expense* in the future through the depreciation process. That is, the $1,000,000 is "written off" to depreciation expense in some more or less reasonable fashion over the useful life of the building. Also, so-called *factory expense* is not expense at all. It is a *cost of* producing finished goods, which are assets just as definitely as is the building we've just talked about. Costs of buying or making assets are *not* expenses. Such outlays are properly termed "costs of" the assets acquired, and the amounts involved become expenses only in the future as the assets are consumed.

Expenses must, of course, be recorded and reported as subtractions from the revenues of the period to which they *pertain*. It would be wrong, for example, to bunch up your expenses in 1975 in order to be able to understate the expenses in 1976 and thus make the 1976 income statement look better. Such things are being done—often in the name of "conservatism"—but this implies a poor job of matching costs with revenues and can be very misleading to the user of your income statement.

What Is a Loss?

Before you started reading this book, if you thought accounting to be an exact science and if you still think so, you should shed this notion before the end of the present paragraph. We have just been considering expenses and have defined expense as values given up (or costs incurred) to produce revenues. But what if you give up values (i.e., incur costs) intentionally in an effort to produce revenue, and then nothing happens? In other words, your bait simply disappears from the hook. Suppose you create new products and advertise them with a great splash through a television special, and nobody buys them. Obviously, the advertising cost incurred was intended to be an expense—but its end result was a big fat zero. I guess we would agree that the advertising expenditure was a dud or, to be more technical, was a dead *loss*. In this example the conclusion comes easily, but what do we do about gradations in between the dead-loss advertising outlay and the outlay that reaps a bonanza? To be more realistic, can we ever tell just how effective a given advertising outlay has been? In short, if an intended expense misfires, it is theoretically a loss; but in more cases than we like to admit we just can't be sure what the payoff of a given expenditure has been. The typical, practical treatment of outlays in such cases is to classify them as expenses. In other words, the expense category is broadened to cover not only cost outlays that are clearly productive of revenues but, within broad reason, to cover outlays that are *intended* to produce revenues, whether or not we can determine the degree of their effectiveness. Thus, unless the outlay has rather obvious dud characteristics, it will typically be treated as an expense rather than as a loss. Here the accountant exercises judgment, and accounting ceases to be an exact science.

In a related area, when a building or a machine is constructed or when costs are incurred in developing a new product, certain costs may clearly be traceable to the objective and may be set up as assets (building, machinery, development costs); but fairly often costs occur that require judgment in determining their true nature. For example, are the wages that may be paid to employees during brief periods of idleness losses? What about medical costs of employee accidents? A great many examples of similar nature could be listed but, again, it should be obvious that *cost tracing* (that is, the relating of a given cost outlay to its end result) is often problematical and must rest upon the exercise of judgment.

Fairly simple and obvious examples of loss are such transactions as the sale of investments in stocks and bonds at prices that are lower than the original costs, or the sale of a piece of land at less than it cost. An uninsured loss of buildings and equipment through flood damage has none of the earmarks of expense and is easily recognizable as a loss. Costs stemming from vandalism would seem to be losses in most cases. On the other hand, a fire "loss" may not be viewed as a true loss if the owner company is so large that it can afford to carry its own insurance; that is, the company finds it cheaper to sustain its fire damages than to pay fire insurance premiums. In such a situation, assuming that the company's choice is based on expert analysis, routine fire damages may be treated as operating expenses, incurred in lieu of fire insurance expense.

Some Other Offsets to Revenue

Revenues are good, losses are bad, expenses are in between. You always strive to reduce expenses, but you can't prosper unless you incur them, sometimes on a grandiose scale. Another kind of business negative is the *revenue contra*. By this we mean anything that happens which *cancels* out revenue that we have recorded earlier. For a simple example, let's sell merchandise for $100 and record this (even though the customer bought on credit), at the time of sale, as sales revenue; however, within the next week any one of the following four events occurs:

1. The customer brings the goods back and we agree to cancel the charge against him. (This is a *sales return.*)
2. The customer skips the country and we know we'll never collect the $100, so we cancel the account from our records. (This is a *bad debt.*)
3. The customer pays his bill in cash within ten days and we allow him a discount of $2, so our net revenue becomes $98 rather than $100. (The $2 is known as a *sales discount.*)
4. The customer finds the product isn't quite what he wanted and

proposes to return it, but we say, "Keep it and we'll deduct $10 from your bill." (The $10 is known as a *sales allowance*.)

All four of these cases constitute revenue offsets (contras). They are not expenses or losses but are revenue corrections—we had originally recorded $100 of revenue in each case but later events required corrective reductions. On an income statement they are all properly shown as subtractions from gross sales in order to depict net sales. Contras of these kinds arise because at the time of a given sale transaction we can only assume that the customer will pay in due course (even though we know from experience that a certain percentage of our clientele will, for one of the four reasons, fail to pay the amount initially billed).

What Are Income Taxes?

If there's anything that everyone of us has experienced, it's income taxes and we'll skim over the subject here as lightly as possible (with a full chapter on the subject later). The question here is, are income taxes an expense, a loss, a revenue contra, or do they occupy their own unique status? Most accountants would probably classify income taxes as expenses (but I can't see how, by any stretch of the imagination, they produce revenues). Some accountants would classify income taxes as pure loss—but this would deny that government makes any contribution whatsoever to our well-being; and some accountants assert that the government is a sort of partner in every profit-making enterprise and that the income tax claimed by government is, thus, merely its share or division of the earnings. In some cases income taxes take on the appearance of revenue contra where, for example, we make sales of war material to the government and then the government claims a refund in the form of income taxes on the profit from the sales. With all of these views it becomes quite a problem to choose any single one, so I am going to propose simply that income taxes be shown as a separately reported subtraction from the total revenues of the period. You will note this treatment in the illustrative income statement soon to follow.

Interest and Dividends

Most accountants refer to interest as an expense, but it's really a cost of borrowing money and surely in itself does not stimulate revenues as an expense should. In fact, the concept of interest cost is at least related to the concept of dividends. At one extreme, interest on first-mortgage bonds accrues as a contractual liability, with dire consequences in case of default; at the opposite extreme, cash dividends on common stock may be skipped year after year with virtually not a whisper from the stockholders. However, between these extremes is a whole range of securities, all more or less hybrid, which require interest or dividend payments more or less regularly and which constitute a virtual spectrum of financial investment instruments. No one can successfully establish a clear boundary between true debt instruments and true ownership instruments, although we tend to regard the two, respectively, as bonds and stocks. My conclusion is that all interest and all dividends should be treated as *divisions of net income* of the company; that the net income is an amount determined by subtracting expenses, losses, and taxes from the net revenues; and that interest and dividends are then properly displayed as sharers in the net income, in order of their contractual rights. It will be noted in the illustrative income statement to follow that interest expense *and* dividends on preferred stock are both subtracted from the revenue total before income is determined. While, as argued above, income may be said to result before the subtraction of one or both of these items, the statement as presented is designed to emphasize the earnings of the common stockholder, and is in a form that nowadays has considerable authoritative support.

Income Statement Illustrated

There are very few rules to limit experimentation with income statement form; however, only two basic forms are widely used for external reporting purposes. The first, and simplest of these, is usually called the *single-step form*. Highly condensed, the structure is more or less as shown in Figure 1.

Comments on Illustrative Income Statement

1. The statement as shown is in comparative form; that is, two years (or periods) are presented side by side for purposes of comparison and analysis of change. This is quite customary in present-day reporting.

2. Commonly the revenues are presented on two lines, viz., "net sales" and "other income."

FIGURE 1
ALBANY COMPANY
Comparative Income Statements, Years Ended December 31

	1974	1975
Revenues (may list).............................	$xx	$xx
Revenue deductions:		
Expenses (may list)...........................	$xx	$xx
Losses (may list).............................	xx	xx
Interest expense (may explain)..................	xx	xx
Income taxes.................................	xx	xx
Preferred dividends...........................	xx	xx
Income before extraordinary items.................	$xx	$xx
Extraordinary items (if any)....................	xx	xx
Net income....................................	$xx	$xx
Retained earnings at beginning of period............	xx	xx
	$xx	$xx
Common dividends.............................	xx	xx
Retained earnings at end of period.................	$xx	$xx
Earnings per common share:		
Income before extraordinary items...............	$xx	$xx
Extraordinary items (gain or loss)...............	xx	xx
Net income................................	$xx	$xx

3. The expenses are typically displayed on two or more lines, with "cost of goods sold" shown first and "selling and administrative expenses" next (subject to possible detailing either in the body of the statement or in a separate supporting schedule).

4. The expression "single-step form" refers to the fact that the revenue deductions are all added together and then as a group deducted from the revenues, so that an income balance is reached by a single subtraction. This is in contrast with "multiple-step" statements, in which the various expenses are subtracted successively from the revenues, with a resulting sequence of intervening subbalances that may or may not have any worthwhile significance.

5. "Extraordinary items" are gains or losses that occur within a given period which are so unusual, and so unrelated to the regular operations of the enterprise, that their inclusion with the revenues or revenue deductions might seriously becloud the analyst's interpretation of the degree of success with which the enterprise was administered during the period under review. Accordingly, extraordinary items are entered as a separate

element in the statement. Examples of items that have been cited as extraordinary are the sale or abandonment of a significant segment of the business, a major devaluation of a foreign currency, and the lump-sum write-off of goodwill as a result of unusual developments within the period. It follows that the more commonplace losses and gains (such as inventory write-downs and fluctuations in foreign currencies) are listed in the upper portion of the income statement, so that they do affect the amount labeled "income before extraordinary items."

6. It is fairly common practice to terminate the income statement at the point labeled "net income" and then present, as a separate sched-ule, the remaining portion; in this presentation the separated schedule is a Statement of Retained Earnings. Such a presentation has the virtue of emphasizing the net income figures for the year in contrast with the retained earnings, which consist of the accumulated earnings of past years.

7. It now is generally accepted procedure to calculate and report at the foot of the income statement the earnings per share of common stock for the period. Nowadays with the invention of a number of hybrid types of stocks and bonds, as well as stock options and warrants, the determination of earnings per share can become a complex problem in itself. In the illustration it is merely assumed that no complexities exist.

8. Occasionally within a given year a gain or loss becomes apparent that would have been "picked up" (accountants' slang for "recognized" or "reported") in a prior year had sufficient information then been available to determine its nature and amount. When such an item does turn up and its amount is clearly significant, it should be reported as an adjustment of retained earnings (the tail end of our illustrative state-ment) rather than as an element in the determination of net income for the current period. Such items are rare; and the result is that retained earnings is, for all practical purposes, kept "clean"—that is, rarely is its beginning-of-the-year balance modified to reflect currently discovered corrections of prior-year earnings determinations.

TEST PROBLEM

Revenue Data

During the year 19XX Tarrant Co. sold its products for a total of $5,627,483; of this amount, $525,480 had not been collected in cash by the end of the year and $24,000 was estimated to be uncollectible; during the year the company collected $614,240 from sales made in earlier years. In addition to product sales, Tarrant earned $12,220 from dividends on stocks owned, and $1,460 interest on bank deposits.

Expense Data

Assume that the company had no finished goods and no unfinished goods on hand at the beginning of the year. During the year its manufacturing costs consisted of raw materials consumed, totaling $2,420,000; factory labor, $1,115,000; and other factory costs (factory overhead) of $1,247,000. At the end of the year unfinished goods on hand (i.e., the work in process inventory) were valued at $384,000, and finished goods on hand cost $418,000. Selling expenses totaled $592,000, and general administrative expenses were $614,250 for the year. There were no interest expenses and the company has no preferred stock outstanding. Income taxes were $154,000. During the year the company suffered an uninsured flood loss of $125,000 and was required to pay $75,000 in damages resulting from litigation originating 2 years earlier. Retailed earnings at the beginning of the year, according to the accounting records, stood at $1,500,000. Cash dividends paid were $1 per share on 100,000 shares. The common stock outstanding during the year, averaged to reflect fluctuations in number and time outstanding, was 102,000 shares.

Required:

Prepare an income statement based on the data given above; assume that the company employs accrual accounting and enter the data in the blank form provided on page 27.

TEST PROBLEM Solution Space

Tarrant Co.
Income Statement for the Year 19XX

Revenues: $

                                                              $ _____

Revenue deductions:
  Expenses:
                                              $

                                  _____ $

                                                              $ _____
Income before extraordinary item $

Net income $ _____
Retained earnings at beginning of year:
  As previously reported $
  Adjustment for
  As restated $ _____
                                                             $

Cash dividends   _____
Retained earnings at end of year $ _____

Per share of common stock:
  Income before extraordinary item $
  Extraordinary item (flood loss)
  Net income $ _____

Chapter Three

The Flow of Funds Statement

What Are Exhibits and Such Things?

During the 1960s the "financial analysts," whoever they may be, developed a great affection for an analytical tool which goes under quite a number of names; and one can never be sure just what is intended by whatever name the analyst happens to use. Perhaps the most used term for this popularity explosion is *cash flow*—we'll get to that later. All this section seeks to disclose is the fact that accountants use a series of words somewhat interchangeably, and you should be sufficiently familiar with these words to be able to take them in stride when they cross your desk or crop up in conversation with your friendly accountant. An *exhibit* or *statement* is usually a financial report of major rank. Thus, in the annual report to stockholders, your company will invariably present a balance sheet (statement of financial condition) and an income statement. These are the omnipresent, major exhibits or statements.

Your report to stockholders may or may not also include one or more *supporting schedules*. All this means is that typically your major exhibits show very little detail; most of the titles or captions cover broad classes of data, such as "plant," "equipment," and "investment." If you wish to disclose the component *elements* of a given class, you may present such elements in a supporting schedule. Thus, the major statements tend to report the headlines; for the inside details of the story, you must look to supporting schedules (if you feel the need).

Undoubtedly, you already realize that the amount of detail, whether in supporting schedules or otherwise, depends a great deal upon the person to whom the report is directed. If the statements are for internal use by management, supporting schedules should be made available in whatever form and degree of detail are called for by the positions and responsibilities of the individual recipients; on the other hand, the general stockholder of a large corporation is usually content to receive highly condensed data with little by way of supporting schedules. It's sad, but true, that most stockholders know absolutely nothing about financial statements and may look at nothing more than the *footings* (totals) of the balance sheet and the final net income figure of the income sheet plus possibly the reported earnings per share.

So, we have exhibits, or statements, supplemented by schedules. For internal purposes, a supporting schedule is often called a *proof*. Thus if your balance sheet shows accounts receivable of $25,620 and if you have something to do with customer credit problems, you may ask your accountant for a proof of the customer total. Don't be surprised if he gives you a simple list of all the customers who now owe money to your firm; and for each customer the list will show the amount owing as of the date specified in the heading of the proof list. Thus, a proof (which "proves" the accuracy of the total shown in the balance sheet) is just another supporting schedule. Proofs are also prepared in considerable quantities by the auditors for verification purposes.

All this chitchat is designed to lead us to a discussion of cash (or whatever we call it) *flow*. Welcome again to the land of terminological confusion. You may see a *cash flow schedule* which really doesn't report flow of cash at all and which really ranks as an exhibit or statement, rather than as a schedule. In any case, let's work our way into the subject systematically by starting with something you've handled a great deal—cash.

The Cash Receipts and Disbursement Statement

We might call this statement "the clubwoman's delight." Every club, society, and fraternity that I know of has a treasurer of sorts; and the financial report, be it presented monthly, quarterly, semiannually, or once a year, consists of nothing more than a statement of cash receipts and disbursements. In this chapter we hope to start with a quickie look at such a statement and then work upstairs to the technical "funds" statement. There's quite a bit of difference between the two, but the cash statement should provide a good, familiar starting point.

Essentially, a cash receipts and disbursements statement, not too surprisingly, consists of two offsetting lists: (1) the amounts of cash received (receipts), showing the sources in as much detail as is desired, and (2) the amounts disbursed, again in whatever detail is called for. The difference between list (1) and list (2) equals the net increase or decrease in cash during the period covered by the statement. Mechanically, if we show the opening (beginning-of-period) balance of cash at the top of the page, then enter the two lists, one below the other, so that their difference can be computed; the difference is then shown as an addition to, or a subtraction from, the opening balance to give us the final balance (as of the close of the period covered by the report). In the truest sense of the term, this describes a *cash flow statement*.

Without concerning ourselves with the amounts or the captions, we see the basic structure of a true cash flow statement in Figure 1.

Let's make a few observations by reference to the cash flow statement:

1. As far as the Jones Bike and Hike Club is concerned, the statement really serves two purposes: It gives a complete summary of the cash activities of the club for the season (prior to the banquet!); and if anyone really wants the complete details, he can visit the treasurer's house and examine the supporting schedules (or proofs); also, because of the simplicity of the operations, the statement probably serves as an income statement. (This is untrue if there are some dues yet to be collected.)

2. The form, or formula, of the funds flow statement could be used to depict the "flow" of any other balance sheet item. Thus, one might prepare an inventory flow schedule, or a marketable securities flow schedule, or an accounts receivable flow schedule; the possibilities are virtually limitless.

FIGURE 1
JONES BIKE AND HIKE CLUB
Cash Flow Statement for the Summer of 19XX

Cash balance at beginning of season...............................			$ 25.17
Cash receipts:			
Dues (see schedule 1* for details)...............	$175.50		
Picnic lunches sold...........................	87.28	$262.78	
Cash disbursements:			
Food (see schedule 2* for details)..............	$ 75.45		
Park rentals (see schedule 3* for details)........	60.00		
Band-aid adhesive bandages...................	2.00	137.45	
Net increase in cash..			125.33
Cash balance at end of season (before banquet)†....................			$150.50

* These schedules are on file at your treasurer's house.

† The amount of $150.50 is now on deposit in the County Savings Bank.

Now, let's take leave of the Bike and Hike Club and think again in terms of a modern business enterprise. Should the report to stockholders include a cash flow statement which shows every penny collected from every source and every penny spent for whatever purpose? Should the report also include flow statements for receivables, inventories, and all the other assets? In general, the answer is no. Such reports may, in truth, be of service to various levels of management, but to the inactive stockholder (and the general public) this kind of information could be overwhelming and of very limited use. However, as a sort of compromise, accountants have devised a kind of flow statement which does have a major place in the modern financial report and which does bear some relationship to the cash flow statement. What we're leading up to is a form of flow statement that depicts the flow of a *group* of balance sheet items taken together, and the group is given the title of "funds." The composition of this group and the purposes of the *funds flow statement* will be examined in the sections that follow. As you will see, the word "funds," in the present context, is synonymous with another accounting expression, "working capital"—the subject of the next section.

Working Capital Changes

In Chapter 1 we had a brief introduction to the balance sheet terms, current assets and current liabilities, and there we learned that the arithmetic difference between the sums of the current assets and current liabilities is commonly known as *working capital*. One might well believe that the current assets should be known as the working capital of the firm and that if from the current assets we subtract the current liabilities, the difference would be termed *net* working capital. Sure it's logical, but that's not the way it's done. Working capital and net working capital refer to the same quantity—the difference between current assets and current liabilities.

Now for a bit of exercise. What types of events, or transactions, cause (net) working capital to change? Obviously, any transaction that changes the total current assets (without a simultaneously offsetting change in current liabilities) changes the working capital. Obviously, any transaction that changes the total current liabilities (without a simultaneously offsetting change in current assets) changes the working capital. Thus, viewed alone, current assets+ and current assets− transactions, respectively, increase and decrease working capital. Current liabilities+ and current liabilities− transactions, happening alone, respectively, decrease and increase working capital. Samples follow.

Current asset increases (that are not offset by current liability increases) occur when a company issues capital stock for cash and when long-term (not a current liability) bonds are issued for cash; also, when land, buildings, equipment, or other noncurrent assets are disposed of for cash. Most important, current assets flow in when the company sells its goods and services for cash. All the transactions listed so far would also cause increases in working capital were they performed on a credit basis instead of for cash, because accounts receivables, like cash, are current assets. Therefore, most sales and other revenue transactions increase current assets, and increase our working capital, as do most sales of noncurrent assets and issues of capital stock and bonds.

Net decreases in current assets (which means decreases in working capital) occur when we buy noncurrent assets for cash, when we incur expenses for cash, and when we retire bonds or capital stock for cash.

An increase in current liabilities (without compensating increases in current assets) *reduces* working capital in such transactions as when we incur expenses (advertising, wages, etc.) on account, when we declare dividends payable, and when we recognize "accrued" income taxes payable.

A decrease in current liabilities (without offsetting decreases in current assets) occurs only in rare instances, because almost always current liabilities are paid off in cash. Let's skip this one.

Finally, there is *no change* in net working capital when (1) we borrow money on a short-term bank loan and (2) when we buy materials or merchandise on account. Each of these transactions involves current liability and current asset increases of equal amount. Similarly, when we pay off a current bank loan or any other current liability in cash, the working capital remains unchanged in amount, because we have merely subtracted the same amount from each element in the formula, $CA - CL = WC$.

Again, then, "funds" is a synonym for working capital; it follows that a funds flow statement is a statement which portrays the opening balance, the inflows, the outflows, the net change, and the closing balance of working capital or funds.

One final word: In place of "working capital," accountants very often use, as a synonym, the expression "net current assets."

The Funds Statement—Purpose

In recent years the funds statement has begun to appear quite regularly in the published reports of publicly held corporations, and its importance has come to be viewed as on a par with that of the income statement and the position statement. The typical annual reports of companies listed on the New York Stock Exchange include the three major statements (income statement, position statement, and the funds statement) plus various subordinate schedules, such as schedules of amounts of assets located in other parts of the world than the United States, schedules showing the amounts invested in affiliated corporations (subsidiaries), and other special-purpose financial data including, frequently, schedules showing sales and other significant financial data up to 10 years in the past. Apart from these formal accounting presentations, the published report typically includes a message from the company president in which he reviews the operations of the year just past and, maybe, risks a prediction of the company's future.

Does the funds statement serve any particular function other than to show the flow of working capital for the period? Yes. It serves a most important additional function. What it does is to fill in a tremendous gap not provided for by the income statement cum balance sheet.

Typically, the annual report shows not only the current balance sheet but, in a parallel column, the balance sheet of a year ago—so we have "comparative" balance sheets at the beginning and end of the year. The income statement, with its listing of revenues, expenses, losses, taxes, interest, and dividends, serves to link the retained earnings balance at the start of the year with the balance at the year-end. In other words, the income statement more or less explains what brought about the transformation of the retained earnings balance on January 1 into the retained earnings balance one year later, on December 31. But where, then, do we find any information to account for the changes in the other portions of the comparative balance sheets? The answer is, in the funds statement. The funds statement details the changes in working capital (which covers all the current assets and current liabilities) and in so doing tends to reveal the events that account for the changes in all other categories.

Because you are unlikely to become a professional accountant and, therefore, may never again read an essay on the funds statement, we're going to take a fairly complete tour here. We hope you'll stick with it on the assumption that whatever insight you may gain will remain with you and will be useful to you in the future. Later on, we'll take a general view of the whole subject of funds flow and try to determine its uses and limitations.

The Funds Statement—Horseback Version

A quickie estimate of the cash flow of a company for a given period can be made by little more than a glance at the company's income statement. Let's take a look at this "horseback" procedure and then appraise its usefulness.

Assume that you are interested in the financial soundness of a company and your financial advisers have told you that you should be sure to check on its cash flow. (They may say "funds flow," which would be more accurate.) The quick-and-easy method is simply to take the reported net income of the company and to this figure add the amount of depreciation for the period of the income statement. To do this is easy; to understand what you're doing is less easy. (A great many people do it and their lack of understanding is evidenced by the misleading inferences that they derive and proclaim from their quickie analysis.)

Here's an example. Camel Products Co. presents the following condensed income statement for the year:

CAMEL PRODUCTS CO.
Income Statement, Year Ended December 31, 19X1

Sales and other revenues..........................		$256,000
Cost of goods sold*.......................	$120,000	
Selling and administrative expense*..........	85,000	
Interest expense.........................	7,000	
Taxes....................................	15,000	227,000
Net income		$ 29,000

* Depreciation included in these accounts totals $14,000.

By quick arithmetic, one determines the flow of funds to have been $43,000 for the year. Let's examine the mechanics of this determination. First, the gross inflows of funds are probably quite well measured by the $256,000 figure labeled "sales and other revenues." You of course know as well as I do that *revenues are not synonymous with cash,* so immediately you can assume, with no fear of contradiction, that it could be seriously misleading to say the company had gross *cash* inflow of $256,000. Accordingly, unless we modify this amount to exclude sales on a credit basis (and to include collections from the credit sales of the year before), we cannot properly label our quickie calculation a determination of cash flow. Second, the cost of sales (or manufacturing cost of goods sold) should include all outlays, or outflows, of funds incurred in the manufacture of the goods actually sold. Note again—if we stick to the word "funds" we're on fairly safe ground, since a reduction of working capital (or funds) occurs when we pay out either cash or other current assets, or when we increase our current liabilities. Third, the other expenses (selling and administrative, interest, and taxes) as listed should include all funds outflows traceable to these categories of expense. But, fourth, as the footnote indicates, some $14,000 of depreciation is buried in the expense accounts. Let's pay special attention to this depreciation.

Does depreciation expense involve an outflow of funds? Yes, it certainly does—but the outflow occurs *when the depreciable assets are purchased.* In other words, the *purchase* of depreciable assets requires an outflow of funds sooner or later, but the subsequent accounting recognition of the *depreciation* of those assets does not. Depreciation is the "write off" of the cost of assets, systematically, over the lives of the assets; the amounts and timing of the depreciation charges would almost never be related in any way to the timing of the amounts paid for the assets. In other words, the *purchase* of an asset normally involves an outflow of funds while the depreciation of the same asset does not. *Depreciation is a "nonfund" charge.*

What has just been said is intended to convince you that the funds outflow for expenses for the year totaled $227,000 *minus* $14,000 of depreciation. If you accept this as valid, you can then go directly to the conclusion that a quick way to estimate the net funds inflow (or outflow) of a company for any reported period is simply to "add back" the amount of depreciation ($14,000) to the amount of reported net income ($29,000). The flow of funds (usually misnamed "cash flow") of Camel Products Co. for the year was accordingly $43,000. In certain situations there may also be other types of nonfund charges that must be added back.

How to Milk a Co.

Because the $43,000 computed as the funds flow for Camel Products Co. made allowance for increases or decreases in current debt, it would be within the realm of reason to say that those in control of this company have roughly $43,000 of cash at their discretionary disposal ("roughly" because funds and cash are not synonymous). This sum could be used (1) to make payments on any long-term debt that is outstanding and subject to redemption, (2) to purchase items of plant and equipment, or (3) to pay cash dividends, within legal limitations. (We must have at least the same amount of retained earnings.) Let's repeat—the $43,000 does provide a measure of the funds available for discretionary disposition as the result of the operations for the year. *But, it does not represent the earnings of the year!*

The science of milking a company consists simply in using funds flow (rather than net income) as the standard for dividend payment—it consists, in effect, of saying that you can ignore depreciation and can budget your dividend payments without providing for the replacement (and, of course, without providing for any expansion) of the plant assets. An expert milker goes a step farther: he "reduces" his expenses by neglecting the normal maintenance and upkeep of the plant assets. So, the combination of failure to replace and failure to maintain hastens the demise of the corporate victim.

To summarize, then, funds flow has meaning in the minds of those who take the pains to understand it; at the same time, funds flow when misunderstood is susceptible to wicked abuse. Some analysts even go so far as to report the "funds flow per share" of common stock outstanding. This is utter nonsense. As you must surely realize, a company which is declining, in fact a company which is regularly suffering operating net losses, may show a "beautiful" record of funds flow per share!

To conclude this section, here is a quotation from the very authoritative Accounting Principles Board of the American Institute of Certified Public Accountants as expressed in one of their official opinions: "The Board regards computations of 'cash flow per share' as misleading since they ignore the impact of cash expenditures for removal and replacement of facilities and tend to downgrade the significant statistics of 'earnings per share.' "[1] For all practical purposes, this comment by the Board prohibits the display of "cash flow per share" in the published reports of a corporation which are "certified" by a firm of CPAs.

The Funds Statement—Balance Sheet Version

In our example of funds flow by the horseback, or quickie, method did we leave out something? You bet we did! Such a determination completely overlooks some very important sources of funds. Three such sources (none of which would normally be revealed in the income statement) are: (1) issues of capital stock for cash, (2) issues of bonds, or other long-term borrowing, and (3) sale of corporate property, (e.g., land, buildings, and equipment) for cash or on account. Similarly, certain very important outflows of funds are excluded from our income statement version of cash flow. These are: (1) retirements of capital stock for cash, (2) payment of long-term debt (e.g., retirement of bonds), and (3) purchases of noncurrent assets, such as land, buildings, and equipment.

It is evident that, with its omissions, the income statement or horseback quickie version is of limited usefulness—but it does serve to show the amount of funds "generated" by routine current operating activities.

---

[1] *APB Accounting Principles,* par. 2021-15.

And this may be information of importance to the sophisticated analyst since it emphasizes the magnitude of the funds flow from the regular, recurring operation of the company exclusive of its sporadic purchases and disposals of long-term assets, capital stock transactions, and the like.

For a more inclusive portrayal of the company's funds flow, let's see if we can prepare something of a formal funds statement directly from a pair of comparative balance sheets. Again, we'll use the amounts of Camel Products Co. Assume now that our only available information is the following pair of balance sheets, prepared at the end of the year corresponding to the income statement we have been discussing and also at the end of the preceding year.

CAMEL PRODUCTS CO.
Comparative Balance Sheets, December 31

	19X1	19X2	Increase (Decrease)
Current assets.............................	$ 80,000	$ 75,000	$(5,000)
Buildings (after depreciation).................	50,000	63,000	13,000
Equipment (after depreciation)...............	110,000	120,000	10,000
Land.....................................	10,000	12,000	2,000
	$250,000	$270,000	$ 20,000
Current liabilities.........................	$ 40,000	$ 31,000	$(9,000)
Bonds payable.............................	50,000	40,000	(10,000)
Capital stock..............................	100,000	120,000	20,000
Retained earnings..........................	60,000	79,000	19,000
	$250,000	$270,000	$ 20,000

To solve this problem, let's abide by the following rules:

1. Use a formal, two-section form showing (*a*) increases (sources) of funds and (*b*) decreases (dispositions) of funds, and define the net funds flow as the net change in working capital.

2. To account for any change that is not explained by the available data, make an "educated" guess as to the cause of the change.

So we proceed. Our first step might be to prepare a very elementary "schedule of change in working capital" since the amount of working capital change is the target figure of our derived funds statement. The necessary schedule is prepared automatically, and with no difficulty, as follows:

CAMEL PRODUCTS CO.
Schedule of Change in Working Capital, 19X2

	19X1	19X2	Increase (Decrease)
Current assets...............	$80,000	$75,000	$(5,000)
Current liabilities............	40,000	31,000	9,000
Working capital.............	$40,000	$44,000	$ 4,000

Only one point of explanation may be called for. In the comparative balance sheets the decline in current liabilities is shown in parentheses as a *decrease,* but in the working capital schedule the current liability decline is shown as a $9,000 *increase* because, as you may remember, the smaller the amount of your current liabilities, the larger the amount of your working capital—and thus the liability decline, viewed alone, constitutes an increase in working capital. In any case, the target figure for our funds statement is the $4,000 change in working capital, since this figure represents the net result of all funds inflows and funds outflows for the year 19X2.

Our next step is to observe the amounts of the changes of all other items, one at a time, and with our "educated" guesses list these changes as being the contributory factors (the sources and dispositions) that change the net amount of funds. So, let's examine the balance sheet items (excluding the working capital items), in order.

Buildings increased $13,000. We know from our examination of the income statement that the company recorded $14,000 of depreciation, and this could affect both the buildings and the equipment; but we've agreed to prepare our statement from the balance sheets alone, and so we either make an arbitrary guess as to the depreciation, or we ignore it. Let's ignore it. Then, if buildings increased by $13,000 we simply *assume* the company spent $13,000 for new buildings. Thus, we have our first disposition of funds—Purchase of Buildings, $13,000.

Equipment increased $10,000. If we reason as we did with buildings, we will conclude that the company spent $10,000 for equipment. Thus, we have our second disposition of funds—Purchase of Equipment, $10,000.

Land increased $2,000 and our educated guess is another purchase, or disposition of funds—Purchase of Land, $2,000.

This completes the scrutiny of the assets; we proceed to the equity portion of the balance sheets and, after skipping current liabilities, find that bonds payable decreased by $10,000. The decrease in bonds could easily be "guessed" as a payoff of part of the company's debt for cash, which amounts to another disposition of funds—Redemption of Bonds, $10,000.

The capital stock increased $20,000. Our guess should probably be that cash of $20,000 was collected through the issuance of capital stock. This is the first "source" item we've encountered—Issue of Capital Stock, $20,000.

The final balance sheet item, Retained Earnings, increased by $19,000. Under our current artificial restriction against referring to the details of the income statement, we cannot modify this figure for depreciation, as we did when dealing with only the income statement. So, let's just list, as our final item, Net Income (source funds), $19,000.

All that now remains to be done is to organize these data in formal style, as follows:

CAMEL PRODUCTS CO.
Funds Statement, Year Ended December 31,
19XX

Source of funds:	
Issue of capital stock...............	$20,000
Net income......................	19,000
	$39,000
Disposition of funds:	
Purchase of buildings...............	$13,000
Purchase of equipment..............	10,000
Purchase of land..................	2,000
Redemption of bonds...............	10,000
Added to working capital............	4,000
	$39,000

Comments on Balance Sheet Version

The income statement version merely computed a final total of cash flow from operations for the year, $43,000. Obviously, this is a far cry from the balance sheet version, which attempts to reveal not only the flow from operations (net income) plus all other sources, but also the dispositions that were made of the funds collected. This form, though loaded with inaccuracies resulting from educated guesses based on very sketchy information, comes much closer to the aim of the funds statement set forth earlier in this chapter—including, broadly, an analysis of the changes in major balance sheet items for the period under review.

The Funds Statement—Complete Version

Finally, let us remove the blinders and prepare a funds statement on the basis of the internal records of our company. In other words, assume that we have not only the income statement and comparative balance sheets but also all the information needed to account for the changes in the major balance sheet items.

To keep our illustration within bounds, assume that the "additional information" consists of the following:

1. No equipment or buildings were disposed of. Of the $14,000 of depreciation, $2,000 was deducted from buildings and $12,000 from equipment. A building was purchased for $15,000 and equipment was purchased for $22,000.
2. Land was purchased for $2,000.
3. Bonds were retired at par, $10,000.
4. Capital stock was issued for $20,000.
5. Dividends of $10,000 were paid.

With this much information to keep track of, the best procedure in developing a solution consists of setting up a skeleton form with plenty of space to record the various sources and the dispositions. Then, directly in the skeleton form, start making the entries that you can discern, first, from the "additional" information; second, from the income statement; and, finally, from the balance sheet. The combined form is shown as Figure 2.

Comments on Complete Version

The version of the funds statement that is based on free access to all accounting information is, of course, superior to all others. What it does is to incorporate the "horseback" version as the lead-off entry in the source section, thus providing, for whatever it may be worth, the financial analyst's desired computation of cash flow for the year; however,

FIGURE 2
CAMEL PRODUCTS CO.
Funds Statement, Year Ended December 31, 19XX

Sources of funds:

Net income (per income statement)....................	$29,000	
Add back all nonfund charges: Depreciation..............	14,000	
"Cash flow" from operations..................................		$43,000
Capital stock issued (details)..................................		20,000
Total funds acquired.......................................		$63,000

Disposition of funds:

Purchase of building...	$15,000
Purchase of equipment..	22,000
Purchase of land...	2,000
Retirement of bonds (details)..................................	10,000
Cash dividends paid..	10,000
Net addition to working capital (see schedule)....................	4,000
	$63,000

the form, by also detailing the balance sheet changes for the year, makes the statement a complete report of the financial activities of the year insofar as they went through the working capital funnel.

As stated earlier, the funds statement in recent years has greatly gained in prominence, to the point where many consider its importance equivalent to that of the income statement and the position statement. The layout of the data follows no prescribed form, as you will note upon examining the financial reports of a number of corporations, and the choice of title remains open. My preference, to go along with "income statement" and "position statement," is "funds statement," but very commonly the statement is called a *statement of sources and applications of funds,* or merely a *statement of changes in working capital.*

If we seek to have the funds statement fully achieve the purpose of bridging the gaps between comparative balance sheets, and there's much to be said in support of this ideal, then it would be necessary at times to include transactions that do not actually change the amount of working capital. (Some accountants say a funds statement, strictly speaking, is an "analysis of changes in working capital.") Thus, if a corporation were to issue capital stock to someone in exchange for land or buildings or equipment, such an exchange would be omitted from the strictly prescribed funds statement. But, it would seem that no harm would be done were we to adopt a new title for the funds statement—

e.g., call it a statement of "financial changes"—and then proceed to include in it not only matters that affected net working capital but also significant events that did not. I believe this will be a natural, future development in statement presentation.

TEST PROBLEM

The following data are from the accounting records of Decatur Co. covering the calendar year 19X2.

Income Statement, 19X2

Sales		$300,000
Expenses:		
Cost of goods sold	$170,000	
Selling and administrative	75,000	
Interest	4,000	
Taxes	21,000	270,000
Net income		$ 30,000

NOTE: Depreciation of $10,000 was accrued in 19X2.

Comparative Position Statements

	19X1	19X2
Current assets	$ 80,000	$100,000
Plant (after depreciation)	300,000	340,000
Land	20,000	10,000
	$400,000	$450,000
Current liabilities	$ 40,000	$ 40,000
Mortgage payable	60,000	50,000
Capital stock	200,000	250,000
Retained earnings	100,000	110,000
	$400,000	$450,000

Additional Data:

Cash dividends of $25,000 were paid in 19X2.
Plant was purchased in the amount of $50,000.
Land which cost $10,000 was sold for $15,000 cash.
Mortgage principal payments of $10,000 were made.
The increase in capital stock resulted from the issue of new shares for cash.

Required:

Prepare a funds statement in the following blank form.

TEST PROBLEM Solution Space

DECATUR CO.
Funds Statement, Year Ended December 31, 19X2

Sources of funds:

$

_____

$

$ _____

Applications of funds:

$

$ _____

Schedule of Working Capital Changes

	19X1	19X2	Increase (Decrease)
	$	$	$
Current assets			
Current liabilities			
Working capital	$	$	$

Chapter Four

The Accounting Structure

Management Decisions

As "boss," whether at the top, middle, or side, you qualify for your title only because of the faith that one or more persons (including yourself) must have in your ability to make rational decisions. Bossing is essentially a combination of leadership and decision making or, if you prefer, leadership and the acceptance of responsibility. Some bosses are ultracautious, to the point where they literally trust no one to make subdecisions or to assist the boss by supplying him with the right information for his decision-making responsibilities. These bosses finally get bogged down at their desks. Other bosses blithely delegate most of their decision making to their subordinates and concentrate on their golf handicaps and martini formulas. The better bosses, and let's hope they constitute the majority, fit in between these two extremes.

Decisions, by definition, all relate to the future—they invariably involve *judgments* as to the results of choice among alternative courses of action. When a decision situation arises, the good boss knows what kind of information he needs to guide him in applying his *judgments* to the problem. Good bosses develop the necessary supportive personnel to be able to call for, and get, the relevant information in a hurry. The good boss does not *develop* the information (with some exceptions); he *delegates* this job. But he should know what his information providers are doing with their time; he must understand what their information means, *so that he can call for it as needed* rather than depend passively on his helpers to decide what he needs. He will never allow his accountants to set up their own private, impenetrable empire.

Accounting data are essential to a wide range of decisions, but the data that are stored by accountants are almost entirely the details of transactions, or events, that have occurred in the past. The well-trained accountant is capable of doing much more than performing the mere function of collecting and storing information for your use; he is also capable of "interpreting" the information for you; and, with the historical records plus current and probable future data, he should be of great help to you in your *planning* activities. Needless to say, planning covers a major portion of all executive activity and we can merely mention it here.

However, the whole point of this section is to urge you, as an executive, to know what your accountants are doing so that you can call on them for information not only on a routine basis but, whenever necessary, on an emergency basis, and so that you can sensibly evaluate the information which they supply in response to your calls. To achieve this requires that you be able to talk the accountant's language. Perhaps that's the whole purpose of this book. Each chapter may involve getting you "over a hump"; we hope that you'll take the humps in stride. A major hump comes in the remainder of this chapter as we get down to the absolute elements of accounting, including the debit-and-credit lingo. We're going to review the elements of the typical accounting system—the forms, the journals, the ledgers, etc.

Business Forms

Basic to all accounting is something we all view as unpalatable—the red tape. This is the deadly job of making notations on *business forms*. If you have good internal accounting help, they have designed the forms that are needed. Business forms are the seeds that produce the valuable crops—the decision-supporting reports. Probably it's a good thing for executives to keep the form producers in the company constantly on the defensive. You must respect the concept of business forms, but don't allow them to spring up and flourish like weeds around you. If, as an executive, you find that basic business documents are routinely flowing across your desk, the chances are you're being put upon by somebody. Business forms are designed for *routine processing.* This means they should flow automatically to accountants, clerks, or other individuals who (1) may merely file them; (2) may examine them and prepare a report to you of any "exceptional" items that call for action on your part; (3) may summarize them in the form of a routine report (headlines only) for you as an executive; and (4) may make accounting entries from them.

Business forms, in the accounting sense, constitute "underlying" documents. They are the raw materials of the formal accounting records. The documents that record transactions or events that will affect your financial statements and supporting schedules all flow to the accounting department. (Carbon copies, of course, may go to other departments as needed.) And, most important, where computers are used for processing the accounting data, the forms must be designed to act as effective "input" media. This we'll cover in a later chapter.

The Business Diary

In logical sequence, the preparation of underlying documents comes first. These documents are sorted in systematic order for accounting record purposes. In some cases a single document, or a single bit of information from a single document, is copied into the formal accounting records; in most cases totals obtained from the various classes of sorted documents are entered into the formal accounting records. In some cases, the details of the sorted documents are recorded in one area of the accounting records while their totals are recorded elsewhere.

To record, in the formal accounting sense, means to *make an entry* in an accounting *journal* or in an accounting *ledger* (often in both places).

The *journal* is the financial diary of the business. It is a chronological record of the transactions that affect the enterprise. (We'll look into computer data processing later.)

As an executive you may never have occasion to look at the accounting journal, because it is two stages removed from the accounting reports that you should receive. But a business enterprise, no matter how small, cannot safely depend on someone's memory to supply details of transactions that occurred last week, last month, or last year. The journal is a business memory in formal dress. The so-called *journal entry* will prove invaluable for our purposes in examining the anatomy of any given transaction; so, later in this chapter, you'll be given the full treatment—you'll be urged to learn how to make a journal entry!

The Accounting Ledger

The journal, often referred to as a *book of original entry,* serves as a diary in which each transaction, or batch of similar transactions, is recorded intact. The next step is to take precisely these same transactions and record them over again in the ledgers, or *books of final entry.* The difference is that each piece of the entry recorded first in the journal is copied ("posted") in its own ledger account. So, if a journal entry is composed of, say, five pieces, these five pieces will each be posted to a separate ledger account. The journal is organized as a chronological record of transactions, as units, in the order of their occurrence; the ledger is organized into as many different pages (or "accounts") as are needed to accumulate the pieces posted (copied) from the journal, but classified according to significant financial elements.

To illustrate. We borrow $1,000 from the bank. This is a transaction. It is recorded ("journalized") in the journal in technical form to show, together, the two financial changes caused by the bank loan: (1) The bank added $1,000 to our checking account, which is to say that our Cash in Bank increased by $1,000; and (2) counterbalancing the $1,000 addition to our bank account is an addition of $1,000 to our liabilities, under the technical heading of Bank Loans Payable. In the journal these two effects are recorded as a matched pair—a whole transaction, journalized as a unit. Next, the $1,000 increase of Cash in Bank is copied from the journal entry to a ledger page headed Cash in Bank, and the $1,000 increase of Bank Loans Payable is copied (posted) to a special ledger sheet (set up a sheet if we don't already have one) labeled Bank Loans Payable.

The ledger, then, consists of as many sheets (accounts) as we feel we need to keep track of the many financial elements of the business. As a starter, let's assume that in our ledger we would, at least, have a separate account for each of the items to be listed in our balance sheet, our income statement, and our funds statement. In fact, the ledger sheets (the ledger accounts) will be in loose-leaf form and will be filed in the same order as they appear in the financial statements. You see, the amounts shown in the financial statements are found by merely copying the balances of the ledger accounts into the arrangements chosen for the financial statements.

The Ledger Account

It is quite common for companies to have their ledger pages printed according to their own prescription, but the fundamental structure remains the same. The classical account has two sides—left and right— separated by a vertical line; and the account is topped by a horizontal line on which the account's name (and an assigned account number) is written. We cannot afford to be concerned about bookkeeping details so we'll ignore the various forms in which the account may be designed and stick to the fundamental shape, which is that of a capital letter T. Just visualize a page divided down the middle, representing the stem of the T, with a horizontal line about an inch from the top of the page, representing the crossbar of the T, on which the title (e.g., Cash in Bank) and the reference number (e.g., 101) are written.

Now, how do we use this gadget? You're going to have to memorize the formula and then we'll use it throughout the book; when you get through, it should have become second nature to you.

Here's the plan. One side of each account will be used to record *increases* in the content of that account and the opposite side will be used for *decreases*. The first thing to remember is that all asset and all expense accounts follow the same rule—to record an *increase in any asset or any expense* make an entry in the *left-hand* side of that asset's or that expense's account. To remember this shouldn't be too tough for you because, as I hope you recall, in Chapter 1 (and throughout American practice) assets are displayed on the left-hand side of the balance sheet. Remember? Thus, assets may be thought of as "left-handed" items.

It's a bit harder to explain why expense accounts are operated the same as asset accounts but, if you'll go along with me, think of expenses as "expired assets" and then show *increases in expenses by left-hand entries* (the same as assets).

Now, if increases in assets and increases in expenses are recorded by left-hand entries, their decreases will have to be recorded on the right-hand side of their Ts.

Asset and Expense Accounts

In Figure 1 you see a T account for Cash in Bank to which a number of postings have been made. (We could call it a "skeleton ledger account" because it's stripped down to bare bones.) You should be able to read this account as follows: The company had a bank balance of $1,242.50 at the beginning of the year, January 1. Their deposits, posted as summary totals for each month, (asset additions are shown on the left-hand side of an asset account) were $6,857.28 for January, $7,142.86 for February, $4,125.19 for March, and $5,147.31 for April. The accountant has informally "footed" this column in small pencil figures showing a total of $24,515.14 on the left-hand side. The withdrawals from the bank account, also shown in the form of monthly totals, are recorded on the right-hand side of the account. Again informally totaled, the withdrawals footing is $22,297.45 for the period, leaving a left-hand balance of $24,515.14 — $22,297.45, or $2,217.69. This should be the amount of cash in bank as of April 30, and this is the amount that would appear in the company's balance sheet dated April 30 were one to be prepared "as of" that date.

FIGURE 1

				Cash in Bank		101
Jan. 1, Bal.			1,242.50	Jan. 31		7,214.20
Jan. 31			6,857.28	Feb. 28		4,114.18
Feb. 28			7,142.86	Mar. 31		7,212.15
Mar. 31			4,125.19	Apr. 30		3,756.92
Apr. 30			5,147.31			*22,297.45*
	2,217.69		*24,515.14*			

In Figure 2 you see a T account for Miscellaneous Office Expenses. Like asset accounts, the T accounts for all expenses are "left-handed." There's one big difference, however. At the end of an accounting period the closing balance then existing in each asset account (after any corrections, updatings, or adjustments that may be required) is "carried forward" as the beginning balance of the next period. Note again the January 1 balance shown in Figure 1. This is the "opening" balance for the current year which, of course, began as the final stroke of midnight closed out the preceding year; thus, the closing balance of one year (or other accounting period) becomes the opening balance of the adjoining year *in those cases where the amounts are actually carried forward from one period to the next.* But, the expenses of one period pertain to that period only (if we've done a good job of accounting for our expenses). Thus, we speak of the advertising expense, the depreciation expense, etc., of last year as compared with the advertising expense of this year. What this signifies is that each expense account *starts out each year with a zero balance.* The expense for one year is the expense for that year—it cannot at the same time be the expense for some other year. To repeat, all expense accounts have beginning-of-year (opening) balances of zero. During the year we make left-hand entries in them to keep track of each kind of expense as it builds up. Then at the end of the year we again empty the account (by simply making a right-hand entry in it sufficient to reduce its balance to zero) and we're ready to repeat the expense-recording process for the next period. These emptying-out entries are known as *closing entries.* Now note in Figure 2 that a number of entries have been made to record Miscellaneous Office Expenses as they were incurred throughout the year, but there was no opening balance; and we've made a closing entry (right-hand) equal to the sum of the left-hand entries and, thus, ended up with a zero balance—the account is swept clean in readiness for next year's "charges." The number of left-hand entries in Figure 2 in our case has no particular significance; only a few are needed to exemplify the accounting treatment of expenses.

To review, then, expenses (like assets) are recorded by entries on the left-hand side of each expense account involved; at the end of each accounting period (usually a year), a right-hand (closing) entry is made which reduces the account's balance to zero in readiness for the next period's entries to be made as a continuation of the same account. Note how the two sides of the expense accout are footed and ruled to provide a clean start for the next year (Figure 2).

FIGURE 2

Miscellaneous Office Expenses			
Jan. 12, 19X1	175.20	Dec. 31 (to close)	720.63
Mar. 26	214.18		
Sept. 19	129.20		
Dec. 7	202.05		
	720.63		720.63

Equity and Revenue Accounts

In order to use the terms debit and credit as accountants do, we must apply the rules just illustrated for assets and expenses to the opposite side of the coin—that is, to the equity accounts and the revenue accounts, where they work exactly in reverse. To record asset increases you make left-hand entries, but to record increases in liabilities you make right-hand entries. We consider the liabilities and the accounts showing the owner's equities both to be forms of equities; the rule for increasing owners' equity accounts is the same as that for liabilities—increases are recorded by right-hand entries. In short, any equity account (liability or ownership) is increased by a right-hand entry. This is perfectly logical because on the balance sheet, as you have seen, all the equities are reported on the right-hand side. And, to wrap it all up, revenues are positive factors with respect to ownership accounts. That is, your sales revenue, your interest revenue, your dividend revenue, and your rent revenue all have the effect of increasing your ownership equity; so *revenue accounts* (the exact opposite of expense accounts in effect) also *are increased by right-hand entries.*

Figure 3 shows an important liability account, Accounts Payable, and an important revenue account, Sales Revenue, with illustrative entries

FIGURE 3

Accounts Payable			
Jan. 31	27,380	Jan. 1, Bal.	20,267
Feb. 28	36,120	Jan. 31	35,200
Mar. 31	39,170	Feb. 28	29,600
Mar. 31, Bal.	24,537	Mar. 31	42,140
	127,207		127,207
		Apr. 1, Bal.	24,537

Sales Revenue			
Mar. 31 (to close)	138,790	Jan. 31	43,010
		Feb. 28	39,640
		Mar. 31	56,140
	138,790		138,790

which bear out what has just been said. Note that Accounts Payable, a balance sheet account, has an opening and a closing balance (just like Cash in Bank), while Sales Revenue starts each year at zero, builds up as sales are made, and is "closed out" at the end of the year just as expense accounts are closed out.

You should now have no trouble interpreting the entries in the accounts shown in Figure 3. Accounts Payable shows six amounts on the right-hand side. To keep the illustration short, it has been assumed that the accounting period is 3 months rather than a year; so the right-hand items consist of the opening balance of $20,267 carried forward from December 31, plus a lump-sum addition at the end of each month. The left-hand side shows three lump-sum entries representing amounts of accounts payable paid off (decreases) and a "plug" figure which is the *balance* at the end of our assumed 3-month accounting period. This plug figure makes the two sides equal; after footing and ruling both sides in fancy accounting style, the balancing figure is "brought down" on the right-hand side as the net amount owed at the start of the new period on April 1. Thus, the closing balance on March 31 becomes the opening balance on April 1.

The Sales Revenue account is easier to interpret. As in the case of expense accounts, there's never an opening balance in a revenue account at the start of a period; after entries are made on the right-hand side to record the revenue of each month, the whole amount is canceled out by a left-hand closing entry. To repeat, asset and equity accounts (balance sheet accounts) generally have opening and closing balances— amounts carried forward from one period to the next; expense and revenue accounts have no opening or closing balances because they are swept clean at the end of each period by closing entries.

Figure 4 summarizes the rules that we have been examining.

FIGURE 4

Any Asset Account		Any Equity (Liability or Ownership)	
Increases	Decreases	Decreases	Increases

Any Expense Account		Any Revenue Account	
Increases	Decreases	Decreases	Increases

The Process of Recording
Complete Transactions

Now for the first, very basic rule: *At all times the sum of all amounts accumulated by left-hand entries must be kept equal to the sum of all amounts accumulated by right-hand entries.* This is the secret of the balance sheet—this is why the total of the asset side always equals the total of the equity side.

And now for the second basic rule: *Whenever any transaction is recorded, the accountant must make left-hand and right-hand entries that are equal in amount* (so that the first basic rule is not violated).

Let's accustom ourselves to these rules by the process of making a few fundamental entries.

Assume (1) that a corporation is established by the issuance of common stock for cash in the amount of $100,000. To record this (pretending that it is all a single transaction) we must recognize the increase in the asset, Cash in Bank, by setting up a ledger account with that title and making a left-hand (increase) entry in the amount of $100,000; *and,* concurrently, we must record the creation of the owners' equity (they invested $100,000) by setting up a ledger account entitled Capital Stock and making a right-hand (increase) entry in it. Figure 5 shows the entire ledger of our new company after the first transaction has been recorded:

FIGURE 5

	Cash in Bank			Capital Stock	
(1)	100,000			(1)	100,000

Could we prepare a balance sheet now by using the data in the ledger accounts? Certainly. The asset side would show a total of $100,000, consisting entirely of cash in bank, and the equities side would show a total of $100,000, consisting entirely of the owner's equity, capital stock.

Let's try another. Assume (2) that the company spends $40,000 of cash to purchase a building worth $30,000 on land worth $10,000. Here our balanced transaction is made up of left-hand entries of $30,000 to Building and $10,000 to Land, offset by a right-hand entry of $40,000 to Cash in Bank. The accounts now stand as in Figure 6.

FIGURE 6

Cash in Bank				Capital Stock		
(1)	100,000	(2)	40,000		(1)	100,000

Building	
(2)	30,000

Land	
(2)	10,000

Were we now to produce a balance sheet, it would show three assets totaling $100,000 and one equity with a balance of $100,000.

Now try some more basic entries. Assume that the following transactions occur—starting with (3) to carry on our illustration:

3. The company borrows $10,000 by giving the bank a 6 percent, 60-day, note payable. (See entry 3 in Figure 7.)

4. The company buys merchandise on account for $20,000. (See entry 4 in Figure 7.)

5. The company sells merchandise on account for $30,000. (See entry 5 in Figure 7.)

6. Cash is paid for miscellaneous operating expenses, $8,000. (See entry 6 in Figure 7.)

7. A count (inventory) is made of the amount and cost of merchandise remaining on hand at the end of the period, and it is found to be $5,000. This signifies that all the rest of the merchandise must have been transferred to customers in the sales transactions summarized in (5) above. In other words, the merchandise asset which cost $20,000 has been reduced to $5,000; that is, of the $20,000 of merchandise asset, $15,000 has been given up and constitutes an *expense* known as Merchandise Cost of Sales. (Many accountants call this Cost

FIGURE 7

Cash in Bank					Capital Stock		
(1)	100,000	(2)	40,000			(1)	100,000
(3)	10,000	(6)	8,000				
		√Bal.	62,000				
	110,000		110,000				
√Bal.	62,000						

Building				Retained Earnings			
(2)	30,000			(8a)	8,000	(8c)	30,000
				(8b)	15,000		
				√Bal.	7,000		
					30,000		30,000
						√Bal.	7,000

Land				Bank Loan Payable			
(2)	10,000					(3)	10,000

Merchandise				Accounts Payable			
(4)	20,000	(7)	15,000			(4)	20,000
		√Bal	5,000				
	20,000		·20,000				
√Bal.	5,000						

Accounts Receivable				Sales Revenue			
(5)	30,000			(8c)	30,000	(5)	30,000

Miscellaneous Operating Expenses				Merchandise Cost of Sales			
(6)	8,000	(8a)	8,000	(7)	15,000	(8b)	15,000

of Goods Sold.) So, entry (7) consists of a a right-hand entry of $15,000 in the Merchandise account and a left-hand entry to Merchandise Cost of Sales.

8. *Closing entries* are made. To do this, as you will recall, we must reduce the balance of each expense account and each revenue account

to zero by making offsetting (closing) entries on the "reducing" side
of each account sufficient to reduce the balance to zero. Query: When
we make a right-hand entry to Miscellaneous Operating Expense to
close that account, where do we make our required, equal left-hand
entry? Try Retained Earnings. Note that similar entries are made to
close the other expense account, Merchandise Cost of Sales. And our
only revenue account, Sales, is closed by a left-hand entry which is
accompanied by a right-hand entry of the same amount to Retained
Earnings. So, essentially, expenses end up on the left-hand (reducing)
side of Retained Earnings and revenues end up on the right-hand side;
and the expense and revenue accounts are left in a zero (closed) condition in readiness for the operations of the next accounting period.

The General Journal

It would appear that we're not getting first things first. Earlier it was
said that entries should be recorded first in the journal, from which
the items are posted to ledger accounts. That's true, but it's easier to
depict the left and right sides of a ledger account; so we just skipped
the journal for the time being. Now, in Figure 8 you'll find all the
entries as they would appear in formal, chronological order in a simple
journal form. Note that to symbolize left-hand entries, we merely write
the account title as far to the left as we can and put the corresponding
dollar amount in the left-hand money column on the same line. Right-
hand titles are simply indented a half-inch or so, and their corresponding
dollar amounts are entered in the right-hand money column. Dates (in
our case transaction numbers) are inserted in a column on the left-hand
edge; and a brief explanation is written after each journal entry. The
complete journal appears in Figure 8.

Comments on Figures 7 and 8

From the illustration that you have just traced through, you should
now recognize that in the journal (which we should have prepared
first as the book of original entry) each transaction (or summary of
a group of similar transactions such as sales) is recorded as a unit so
that you can see all aspects of it in one place. Next, each left-hand
entry and each right-hand entry is posted to a ledger account that carries
precisely the same title as is used in the journal entry. At the end of

FIGURE 8
The General Journal

Dates		LF	Left	Right
1	Cash in Bank	√	100,000	
	Capital Stock	√		100,000
	To launch the corporation, $100,000 of capital stock is issued at par for cash.			
2	Building	√	30,000	
	Land	√	10,000	
	Cash in Bank	√		40,000
	A building costing $30,000 on land, valued at $10,000, is purchased for cash.			
3	Cash in Bank	√	10,000	
	Bank Loan Payable	√		10,000
	Borrowed $10,000 from bank on 6%, 60-day note.			
4	Merchandise	√	20,000	
	Accounts Payable	√		20,000
	Purchase of merchandise on account.			
5	Accounts Receivable	√	30,000	
	Sales Revenue	√		30,000
	Sales of merchandise on account.			
6	Miscellaneous Operating Expenses	√	8,000	
	Cash in Bank	√		8,000
7	Merchandise Cost of Sales	√	15,000	
	Merchandise	√		15,000
	Cost of merchandise asset given up in sales recorded in (5) above.			
8a	Retained Earnings	√	8,000	
	Miscellaneous Operating Expenses	√		8,000
	To close Miscellaneous Operating Expenses to Retained Earnings.			
8b	Retained Earnings	√	15,000	
	Merchandise Cost of Sales	√		15,000
	To close Merchandise Cost of Sales.			
8c	Sales Revenue	√	30,000	
	Retained Earnings	√		30,000
	To close Sales Revenue.			

the accounting period, journal entries are made to close the revenue and expense accounts, so that their net effect is reflected in Retained Earnings. The revenue and expense accounts now have zero balances and are ready for similar entries in the next period, while the balance sheet accounts are left open, so that their balances will carry forward into the next period. Note that the balances to be carried forward are singled out by the formal ruling and balancing procedure.

Closing Entries Revisited

Instead of closing each expense account and each revenue account directly to Retained Earnings, it is customary to close them first to a temporary summary account called Income Summary, or Profit and Loss; then the net balance of that account is closed to Retained Earnings. This keeps Retained Earnings from becoming cluttered up with hundreds of entries. Closing entries performed this way are shown in Figure 9.

FIGURE 9

8a	Income Summary (instead of Retained Earnings)		8,000	
	Miscellaneous Operating Expenses			8,000
	To close miscellaneous expenses to Income Summary.			
8b	Income Summary (instead of Retained Earnings)		15,000	
	Merchandise Cost of Sales			15,000
	To close cost of goods sold.			
8c	Sales Revenue		30,000	
	Income Summary (instead of Retained Earnings)			30,000
8d	Income Summary		7,000	
	Retained Earnings (finally, for net income only)			7,000
	To close Income Summary to Retained Earnings.			

The Trial Balance

What should happen if we were now to make a list of all the ledger accounts and, opposite each, show the net balance of each as it now stands? Answer: We would have prepared a *trial balance* and the dumb thing had better balance!

Fortunately our illustration is a simple one and, because we made no mistakes, our trial balance does balance. See Figure 10.

Note that we have listed all accounts, though some have no balances. Customarily accounts with zero balances are not listed. However,

FIGURE 10
Trial Balance After Closing

| | Balances | |
	Left	Right
Cash in bank............................	$ 62,000	
Building................................	30,000	
Land...................................	10,000	
Merchandise............................	5,000	
Accounts receivable......................	30,000	
Accounts payable........................		$ 20,000
Bank loan payable.......................		10,000
Capital stock...........................		100,000
Retained earnings.......................		7,000
Sales revenue...........................		—
Merchandise cost of sales.................	—	
Miscellaneous operating expenses...........	—	
	$137,000	$137,000

a trial balance can be prepared any time that you want one; so let's see how ours would look had it been prepared *before* the closing entries (8*a, b, c,* and *d*) were made. See Figure 11.

Note that this trial balance shows no balance for Retained Earnings because (1) this is the first year of operation for our company and (2) the revenue and expense accounts have not yet been closed to Income Summary and to Retained Earnings.

FIGURE 11
Trial Balance Before Closing

	Left	Right
Cash in bank............................	$ 62,000	
Accounts receivable......................	30,000	
Merchandise............................	5,000	
Land...................................	10,000	
Building................................	30,000	
Accounts payable........................		$ 20,000
Bank loan...............................		10,000
Capital stock...........................		100,000
Retained earnings.......................		—
Sales revenue...........................		30,000
Merchandise cost of sales.................	15,000	
Miscellaneous operating expenses...........	8,000	
	$160,000	$160,000

It is customary to prepare a trial balance at the end of each month (1) to reveal the existence of bookkeeping errors which would "throw the trial balance out of balance" and (2) to aid in preparation of monthly financial statements.

The Financial Statements

Quite obviously an income statement and a position statement can easily be prepared by copying the figures from Figure 11 (or from Figure 10) in the proper forms. Note, however, that we are for present purposes ignoring the fact that the building would have depreciated a bit during the year and we would owe some interest on the bank loan and some income taxes. The resulting income statement is shown as Figure 12 and the position statement as Figure 13.

FIGURE 12
OUR COMPANY
Income Statement for the Year Ended December 31, 19XX

Sales......................................		$30,000
Expenses:		
Merchandise cost of sales..................	$15,000	
Miscellaneous operating expenses...........	8,000	
Depreciation (omitted).....................	—	
Interest on bank loan (omitted)............	—	
Income taxes (omitted)....................	—	23,000
Net income (to retained earnings)....................		$ 7,000

FIGURE 13
OUR COMPANY
Position Statement, December 31, 19XX

Assets			*Equities*		
Current:			Current liabilities:		
Cash in bank...	$62,000		Accounts payable.......	$ 20,000	
Accounts			Bank loan.............	10,000	
receivable....	30,000			$ 30,000	
Merchandise...	5,000	$ 97,000			
Noncurrent:			Stock equity:		
Land.........	$10,000		Capital stock..	$100,000	
Building.......	30,000	40,000	Retained		
		$137,000	earnings.....	7,000	107,000
					$137,000

Conclusion

Now you have had a glimpse at the traditional accounting financial statements and at all the traditional accounting routines except one. We have mentioned the need for making *adjusting entries* at the end of each accounting period, but these entries deserve more than a passing glance so we'll examine them in the next chapter. It should be noted, however, that entry 7, which recorded the cost of merchandise sold, is an adjusting entry; and adjusting entries would be needed to recognize depreciation of the building and the end-of-period liability for income taxes. These financial developments, as was pointed out earlier in our book, occurred in a "flow" rather than "on-the-spot" form.

For your chapterly exercise, a set of data and forms appear below for you to use in performing the accounting tasks described in this chapter. Formal solutions, as usual, are presented in the appendix.

TEST PROBLEM

The problem that follows is designed to include only the barest essentials of the accounting cycle—a skeleton on which we can build, in logical sequence, to the end that we should be able to unravel the most perplexing of the problems of modern-day financial reporting and analysis. To solve this problem you are asked merely to record a few basic transactions directly in skeleton ledger accounts, prepare a trial balance, statements, and closing entries. The assumed transaction data follow:

Transaction Data (Month of July):

(1) Empire Corp. is established and 10,000 shares of $10 par common stock are issued for cash which is deposited directly in the bank.

(2) A building is rented for $1,000 per month and July rent is paid. (Treat the rent as a miscellaneous expense.)

(3) Store equipment is purchased for cash, $30,000.

(4) Merchandise is purchased on account, $50,000.

(5) Sales, all on account, total $60,000.

(6) Miscellaneous expenses, all paid in cash, total $10,000.

(7) At the end of July, an inventory is taken and it is determined that of the $50,000 of merchandise purchased, $15,000 remains on hand; that is, the merchandise inventory on July 31 is determined to be $15,000.

(8) The estimated useful life of the equipment is 20 years with no significant salvage value likely at the end of the life. Accordingly, the depreciation expense for July is determined to be one-twentieth of the cost divided by 12, or $1,500 ÷ 12, or $125. (Treat as a miscellaneous expense.)

(9) A trial balance is prepared.

(10) An income statement is prepared.

(11) A position statement is prepared.

(12) Closing entries are made.

TEST PROBLEM Solution Space

Cash in Bank

Capital Stock

Accounts Receivable

Retained Earnings

Merchandise

Sales

Store Equipment

Merchandise Cost of Sales

Accounts Payable

Miscellaneous Expenses

Income Summary

(9) EMPIRE CORP.
Trial Balance (before closing), July 31, 19XX

	Balances	
Account Title	*Left*	*Right*
	$	
		$
	$	$

(10) EMPIRE CORP.
Income Statement for July, 19XX

Sales	$
Expenses:	
Merchandise cost of sales	$
Miscellaneous	
Net income (and earnings retained)	$

(11) EMPIRE CORP.
Position Statement, July 31, 19XX

Assets		*Equities*	
Current:		Current liabilities:	
Cash in bank	$	Accounts Payable	$
Accounts		Stock equity:	
receivable		Capital stock	$
Merchandise		Retained	
inventory	$	earnings	
Store equipment			
	$		$

{ Chapter Five }

The Accounting Cycle

Elements of the Accounting Cycle

No matter what kind of an accounting system the individual business enterprise maintains, the so-called *cycle of accounting activities* will be basically the same. The word "cycle" should not be defined too precisely, however.

Although a specific "bit" of accounting data will typically flow through the various stages of the cycle in consecutive order, such bits of data are being introduced into the accounting system at all times throughout the period and thus, within the business as a whole, several parts of the cycle will be undergoing activity simultaneously.

In the order of their classical sequence, the stages of the accounting cycle are:

1. *Underlying documents.* Transaction data are recorded (noted) on underlying documents.

2. *Journalizing.* The transaction data on the underlying documents are sorted and entered in the *journal*(s) either individually, or in batches as summarized lists.

3. *Posting.* The transaction data are posted from the journal(s) to the ledgers. In some cases individual journal items may be posted; in other cases, the journals are so designed that much of the journal data can be summed and posted in total to the ledger. (Thus much posting time is saved, and accuracy is improved.)

4. *Trial balance.* A trial balance is prepared to test bookkeeping accuracy and to aid in preparation of the work sheet and statements. (Step 5 might well be labeled "Hunt for Errors," but we'll assume the trial balance did balance immediately.)

5. *Work sheet.* A work sheet may be prepared at the end of the period, before adjusting entries are made. The work sheet will be explained and illustrated later in this chapter.

6. *Adjusting entries.* The end-of-period adjusting entries are made. This means that they are (*a*) journalized and (*b*) posted to ledger accounts just as regular transaction entries are handled.

7. *Closing entries.* There's not much to be said about closing entries except that their purpose is, at the end of an accounting period, to sweep clean the income statement accounts (all revenue, expense, loss, tax, and interest accounts) to make them ready for the accumulation of similar information in the next period. The net result of the sweeping operation is entered in the Retained Earnings account as the net income for the year. (Here you can see why we must emphasize the need for care in the process of "matching" costs or expenses with revenues each period—to arrive at a sensible *net income* for the period.) The routine closing entry procedure was illustrated in Chapter 4.

8. *Financial statements.* After everything is ship shape, with all accounts adjusted up to date, with all liabilities determined, etc., financial statements are drafted. Fundamentally this operation involves no more than the copying of amounts, accumulated in the ledger accounts, into whatever forms the management elects to use in the structure of the income statement, the position statement, and the funds statement.

9. *Independent audit.* When all the above steps have been taken, it may be appropriate (or mandatory) to engage a firm of CPA's to perform an "independent" audit. What this means in essence is that outside, professional auditors examine your financial statements and, to the extent deemed necessary, your accounting records, the supporting documents, and whatever else is needed, and express their opinion (the so-called *accountants' certificate*) that your statements are prepared in accordance with generally accepted accounting principles. In recent

years the CPA firms have expanded their activities to include tax-return preparation, accounting systems design, budgeting, and a wide range of management consulting services.

What Is Meant by the Accounting Period?

We generally think of the accounting period as a year—a 12-month passage of time—whether the year be a regular calendar year ending on December 31 or a so-called *fiscal year* which closes at the end of whatever month suits our business. However, if 12 months is the formal accounting period, we must recognize that for the effective management of the business, as well as for effective disclosure of operations to absentee owners, financial reports are inevitably needed more frequently. Such reports are known as *interim* statements; and, though the term is not too commonly used, we might refer to the time spanned by any report that covers less than a year as an *interim period*.

In the preceding section appears a list of the basic procedures that constitute a complete accounting cycle. From such a list it might be inferred that the only accounting activity within an accounting period is the accumulation of financial data on underlying documents followed by journalizing and posting of the data. However, depending upon the size and needs of the organization, the accounting staff may devote a substantial amount of time to what is known as *internal auditing* and to the preparation of routine as well as special-purpose reports for the various levels of management. Essentially, internal auditing consists of systematically checking the data that flow into the accounting records to assure their accuracy. In many situations, it involves the continuous testing of the organizational controls that have been set up to prevent the commission of recording errors or thefts of cash or other valuable resources. The nature of routine and special-purpose reports for internal management will be discussed in Chapter 14.

Again, referring to the list of activities that constitute the formal accounting cycle, let me point out that some of the steps can be omitted or abridged when we are dealing with an interim period. For example, closing entries will *not* be made at the end of each month or each calendar quarter; and adjusting entries (which are necessary for any interim period no matter how short) may be made on a work sheet, which is then used directly for the preparation of the interim financial statements.

The balance of this chapter is devoted mainly to the nature of adjusting entries and the use of the work sheet.

What and Why Are Adjusting Entries?

If we do a good, thorough job of recording transactions as they occur, why should it ever be necessary to make adjusting entries at the end of the regular or interim period? The answer is that what we have earlier termed flow transactions simply cannot be kept up to date; and for certain types of "spot" transactions, where they are repetitive and individually relatively insignificant, it is more efficient to allow the data to accumulate and record them in periodic batches (that is, by periodic adjusting entries which, in effect, treat the stream of spot transactions as if they constitute a continuous flow). A true flow-type transaction, of course, is something such as depreciation or interest expense or interest revenue, all of which "flow" continuously.

By merely scanning the list of accounts that make up a typical trial balance, you'll readily understand the inevitability of adjusting entries. Now let's look at a few as samples.

Start with cash in bank. If we have carefully recorded every collection or other receipt of cash, every deposit in the bank, and every check that we've written, should any end-of-period adjustment ever be called for? The answer is, yes. Banks have the habit of making service charges (which may depend upon the number of checks, deposits, or other transactions handled, in relation to the average balance maintained). Banks may make collections for you and report the collections via monthly statements. In short, any additions or reductions that the bank records with respect to your deposit account must be duplicated in your own accounting records, and the information for such "adjustments" may not be known to you until you receive the monthly bank statement.

Your company may hold temporary investments of marketable securities, or other dividend- or interest-bearing investments, as a means of obtaining some income on funds that are temporarily in excess of current operating needs. At the end of any accounting period, these investments must be reviewed to determine what interest and dividends may have been earned but have not yet been collected in the form of a spot-cash transaction. Adjusting entries are thus required to "accrue" interest and dividends receivable.

Accounts receivable are not always "good"—that is, almost every business is bound to have some deadbeats among its clientele. The recognition of so-called *bad debts* may be recorded on a spot basis (that is, whenever a specific account is determined to be uncollectible, it may be written off as a bad debt "expense"), or a periodic *blanket provision* may be made to reflect management's estimate of the portion of sales revenue that will never be collected. The latter procedure, which is the more common among larger companies, involves periodic adjustment to accrue the amount of bad debts estimated to have been accumulated within a given period. Typically this accrual adjustment is measured as a flat percentage (e.g., ½ percent) of the total credit sales for the period. Because the total is unknown until the end of the period, an end-of-period adjustment is required.

Next, consider merchandise. When an item of merchandise is sold the event is, of course, a spot transaction. If you're a retailer of automobiles it's likely that when each sale is made you'll not only record the revenue (remember, a left-hand entry to Cash or Accounts Receivable, and a right-hand entry to Sales Revenue), but you'll also record the merchandise cost of the sale on the spot (by a left-hand entry to the expense account, Merchandise Cost of Sales, and a right-hand entry to Merchandise or Car Inventory). But entries to record the individual costs of merchandise sold become highly impractical under many circumstances. Could an electric power company record the cost of each kilowatthour as the current flows through the customer's meter? Could the variety store record the cost of merchandise sold each time that it sells a lead pencil? Could a department store make a cost of goods sold entry whenever it sells a yard of cloth? You can think of more examples ad infinitum. The solution, of course, is to record only the revenue (and even this may be done in batches rather than individually) and *at the end of the period* make one big adjusting entry to record the cost of goods sold for the entire month (or longer period).

Almost every company pays in advance for various types of insurance. The moment the prepayment is made, it begins to expire. We can't possibly record the expiration on a continuous basis—though we could make an accounting entry each day, or each week, or each month. Usually, we settle for the once-a-month solution. This, again, illustrates the fact that the real purpose of adjusting entries is to update all accounts that have been allowed to lag as a practical necessity.

The examples given so far should suffice as a demonstration of the *need* for periodic adjusting entries. Next, let's go through an illustrative problem dealing with adjusting entries and, at the same time, we'll introduce the accountants' work sheet.

Problem Data

Tuesday Co. uses the calendar year as its formal accounting period, and management has asked the accounting staff to provide an income statement and a statement of financial position at the end of each month. Accordingly, at the end of January the accounting staff takes a trial balance of the accounts as they stand before any adjusting entries have been made. The trial balance is as follows:

	Account Balances	
	Left	Right
Cash in bank...................	$ 5,000	
Marketable securities..............	20,000	
Accounts receivable...............	40,000	
Merchandise...................	60,000	
Prepaid insurance................	3,000	
Land.........................	8,000	
Equipment....................	60,000	
Buildings.....................	80,000	
Allowance for depreciation..........		$ 30,000
Accounts payable................		35,000
Notes payable..................		25,000
Capital stock..................		100,000
Retained earnings...............		21,000
Sales........................		85,000
Selling expenses................	10,000	
Administrative expenses...........	10,000	
	$296,000	$296,000

It is determined that adjusting entries must be made for the following reasons:

1. Bank service charges, in the amount of $72 for the month of January, are shown on the monthly bank statement which has just been received. The required adjusting entry must record a $72 reduction of Cash in Bank (this calls for a right-hand entry) and a recognition of $72 of expense which, for our purposes, we'll classify as administrative expense (a left-hand entry). The entry, in skeleton form, is:

Administrative Expenses...........................	72	
Cash in Bank....................................		72

2. The marketable securities consist entirely of government, industrial, and public utility bonds. The interest earned in January (on an accrual basis) is determined to total $130. The required adjusting entry, to show the receivable of $130 and the corresponding interest revenue, is:

Interest Accrued Receivable......................	130	
Interest Revenue.............................		130

Note that this entry depicts an increase in the asset Interest Accrued Receivable by a left-hand entry, and an increase in the revenue account, Interest Revenue, by a right-hand entry.

3. This company's experience has shown that the bad debt rate has tended to be about 1 percent of total sales. Since any uncollectible receivables that came into being during January would still be "on the books," an adjusting entry must be made to show that receivables totaling approximately 1 percent of sales for the month of January are *probably* uncollectibles. The entry to record this adjustment is made as follows:

Bad Debts.......................................	850	
Allowance for Bad Debts.....................		850

The left-hand entry, the charge to Bad Debts, represents not really an expense but a cancellation (offset or reduction) of the month's recorded revenue of $85,000. The accounts receivable must also be reduced by $850, but this is just an estimate; we don't yet know which specific accounts are uncollectible. We perform an accounting trick; we make the right-hand entry not to Accounts Receivable but to an offsetting account, which is named Allowance for Bad Debts. You should note that this is the practical equivalent of making a direct reduction of the accounts receivable balance, but since the accounts receivable are made up of accounts with, perhaps, hundreds of customers, we *achieve the effect* of a reduction by using what all accountants call a *contra* account—Allowance for Bad Debts. On the balance sheet this account shows up as follows:

Current assets:		
Cash in bank.....................................		$ 4,928
Accounts receivable......................	$40,000	
Less: Allowance for bad debts............	850	39,150

By the procedure just demonstrated, we are able to keep the (so far unidentified) uncollectible accounts receivable on the books and, at the same time, achieve the financial effects of recognizing their worthlessness. (We'll soon see other uses for contra accounts.)

4. The $60,000 balance in the merchandise account consists of $20,000 carried over from last year plus $40,000 purchased in January. We now determine, either by physical count or by estimate, that the cost of merchandise remaining on hand on January 31 is $10,000. This means that $50,000 has disappeared, we hope as the result of sale. Needless to say the $50,000 may also include disappearance by theft, spoilage, and other forms of shrinkage. For the present we'll be charitable and pretend the whole $50,000 represents cost of goods sold. Then our required adjusting entry is to reduce the merchandise (asset) account to $10,000 by a right-hand entry and increase Cost of Goods Sold, an expense account, by a left-hand entry, as follows:

Cost of Goods Sold.........................	50,000	
Merchandise............................		50,000

5. It is determined that the balance of Prepaid Insurance (often termed Unexpired Insurance) should be reduced by $100 to represent the amount that expired during January. A right-hand entry is made to reduce the asset, Prepaid Insurance, and a left-hand entry is made to increase our administrative expense, thus:

Administrative Expenses.........................	100	
Prepaid Insurance...........................		100

6. Equipment and buildings depreciate through use and the passage of time. We'll look into this phenomenon later, but for the present let's assume that the depreciation for January totals $800. Now, rather than subtract the $800 from the numerous accounts that our company keeps for the various categories of equipment plus an account for the building, we again use the offset technique—the contra account—and make our right-hand entry to Allowance for Depreciation, while we split the left-hand entry (we'll assume it's a reasonable split) 80 percent to Selling Expenses and 20 percent to Administrative Expenses. Here's the entry in journal form:

Selling Expenses................................	640	
Administrative Expenses.........................	160	
Allowance for Depreciation...................		800
To record equipment and building depreciation of $800, charging 80% to selling and 20% to administrative expenses.		

7. Our salesclerks are paid weekly; and because January ended in the middle of a week, we must recognize "accrued wages payable" of

$1,000, as follows:

Selling Expenses............................ 1,000
Wages Accrued Payable.................   1,000

You'll recognize the effects of this event—to increase Selling Expense by $1,000 and to increase a liability, Wages Accrued Payable, by $1,000. Note again that the word "accrued" is used to indicate an interim recognition of a liability that is growing through time and is to be paid later.

8. Interest on our notes payable was paid on last December 31, but by the end of January we must recognize the accrual of (assume) $200 of fresh interest expense. The entry is:

Interest Expense................................ 200
Interest Accrued Payable.....................   200

9. To round out our adjusting entries, we must recognize that we'll probably owe some income taxes. It's not easy to make a reliable estimate of the amount attributable to the first month of the year, but let's accept $2,500 as a reasonable guess. Our adjusting entry then is:

Income Tax Expense.......................... 2,500
Income Tax Accrued Payable...............   2,500

Now if we can safely assume that there are no more adjusting entries to be made, we are ready to post entries 1 through 9 in our ledger accounts and prepare our monthly statements. But, purely for educational purposes, let's now demonstrate the use of a work sheet as an instrument for the preparation of interim statements.

The Work Sheet

The accountant's work sheet is a most useful gadget and it's something you are now well-equipped to handle. Here's the concept. We start with a sheet of columnar paper—one with a wide column at the left for the listing of our account titles, followed by from a half-dozen to a dozen narrower money columns to the right. In the first pair of money columns, we list the amounts which make up our unadjusted trial balance as of any given date. In the next pair of columns we make left- and right-hand entries (adjusting entries) to adjust the raw trial balance figures; then, we copy the trial balance figures, *as modified by the adjusting entries,* into the third pair of columns (which are headed Income

Statement) or into the final pair (which are headed Balance Sheet). Whether a given item is copied in an income statement column or a balance sheet column depends simply on whether the item is to appear in the income statement or in the balance sheet. Thus, the adjusted amount for Cash in Bank would be carried to the left-hand (asset) column under the heading, Balance Sheet, while the amount for Sales and for each class of expenses would be entered in the Income Statement columns. Then, all that remains to be done is to copy the sorted amounts into your regular income statement and balance sheet formats, and there you have your financial statements all done.

Let's illustrate this procedure with the example in the preceding section on adjusting entries. Figure 1 is an eight-column work sheet in finished form. Note the trial balance in the first pair of columns, the adjusting entries in the second pair, the income statement amounts (as adjusted) in the third pair, and the balance sheet amounts (as adjusted) in the fourth pair.

The Work Sheet—Comments

In order to be thoroughly familiar with work sheet procedure, you ought to follow through the details in Figure 1. For example, note that Cash in Bank, on the first line, had a balance of $5,000, but that in adjusting entry (1) we made a right-hand entry of $72 to record the reduction caused by the bank's service charges. This same adjusting entry is shown in the right-hand adjusting entry column and then, after all other adjusting entries have been entered in the work sheet, Cash in Bank, as adjusted by $72, is carried way over to the left-hand balance sheet column (because Cash in Bank is an asset). Exactly the same procedure was followed through the whole illustration.

But note two technical matters. First, each left-hand column is headed "Debit," and each right-hand column is headed "Credit." It's as simple as that—these two words mean nothing more than "left" and "right," and don't let anybody try to convince you otherwise. So, from now on instead of saying that we're going to make a left-hand entry in a journal entry or in an account, we're going to say that *we're making a debit entry.* Instead of right-hand we'll say *credit.*

Second, please note how the last two pairs of columns are "balanced." Obviously if you carry the adjusted revenue balances to the credit (right) side of the income statement and carry the expenses to the debit side,

FIGURE 1
Tuesday Co.
8-column Work Sheet, as of January 31

	Trial balance		Adjusting entries		Income statement		Balance sheet	
	Debit	Credit	Debit	Credit	Debit	Credit	Debit	Credit
Cash in bank	5,000			(1) 72			4,928	
Marketable securities	20,000						20,000	
Interest accrued receivable			(2) 130				130	
Accounts receivable	40,000						40,000	
Allowance for bad debts				(3) 850				850
Merchandise	60,000			(4) 50,000			10,000	
Prepaid insurance	3,000			(5) 100			2,900	
Land	8,000						8,000	
Equipment	60,000						60,000	
Building	80,000						80,000	
Allowance for depreciation		30,000		(6) 800				30,800
Accounts payable		35,000						35,000
Notes payable		25,000						25,000
Interest accrued payable				(8) 200				200
Wages accrued payable				(7) 1,000				1,000
Income tax accrued payable				(9) 2,500				2,500
Capital stock		100,000						100,000
Retained earnings		21,000						21,000
Sales		85,000				85,000		
Interest revenue				(2) 130		130		
Bad debts			(3) 850		850			
Cost of goods sold			(4) 50,000		50,000			
Selling expenses	10,000		(6) 640 (7) 1,000		11,640			
Administrative expenses	10,000		(1) 72 (5) 100 (6) 160		10,332			
Interest expense			(8) 200		200			
Income taxes			(9) 2,500		2,500			
Net income					9,608			9,608
	296,000	296,000	55,652	55,652	85,130	85,130	225,958	225,958

the two sides won't be equal—you have to *plug* them to make them equal, and the amount of that plug is your net income (or loss). Also, if you carry the assets, the liabilities, the capital stock, and the retained earnings to the balance sheet columns, they won't have equal totals until you plug them for the net income (addition to retained earnings) for the period. You see, the retained earnings balance in the raw trial balance is the amount carried forward from December, and it is brought up to date as of the end of January only when you add January's net income to it.

Financial Statements

The financial statements for Tuesday Co. are prepared by properly organizing the data in the last four columns of the work sheet. They appear as Figures 2 and 3.

FIGURE 2
Tuesday Co.
Income Statement, January, 19XX

Sales (less bad debts of $850).................		$84,150	
Interest revenue............................		130	$84,280
Expenses:			
Cost of goods sold................	$50,000		
Selling.........................	11,640		
Administrative...................	10,332	$71,972	
Interest......................................		200	
Income taxes................................		2,500	74,672
Net income.....................................			$ 9,608

Are Interim Statements Dependable?

The extent to which interim balance sheets and income statements are dependable is arguable. One thing is certain: They do have their weaknesses. Business executives, who should be making use of such statements, should certainly know enough about them to be aware of these weaknesses—in other words, don't make decisions on the basis of unreliable data, at least without knowing that minor, or even major, weaknesses exist.

It's too early in the game for us to explore the weaknesses of interim statements in detail but, if you're willing temporarily to take an opinion

FIGURE 3
TUESDAY CO.
Balance Sheet, January 31, 19XX

Assets

Current:
Cash in bank...................................		$ 4,928
Marketable securities.............................		20,000
Interest accrued receivable........................		130
Accounts receivable....................... $ 40,000		
Less: Allowance for bad debts..............	850	39,150
Merchandise......................................		10,000
Prepaid insurance................................		2,900

$ 77,108

Noncurrent:
Land...		$ 8,000	
Equipment.............................. $ 60,000			
Building...............................	80,000		
	$140,000		
Less: Allowance for depreciation..............	30,800	109,200	117,200

$194,308

Equities

Current liabilities:
Accounts payable..................................		$ 35,000
Notes payable.....................................		25,000
Interest accrued payable...........................		200
Wages accrued payable............................		1,000
Income taxes accrued payable......................		2,500

$ 63,700

Stockholders' equity:
Capital stock.....................................		$100,000	
Retained earnings, January 1................ $21,000			
Earnings retained, January..................	9,608	30,608	130,608

$194,308

on faith, a couple of observations will be presented now and we'll examine the question of reliability more thoroughly later.

First, if we are going to divide the total lifetime of the enterprise into segments for financial reporting purposes, the most natural segment length would appear to be the year—whether or not December 31 is chosen as the annual cutoff date. However, statements prepared to report the results of operations even for a whole year (as well as balance sheets at year-ends) inevitably involve the exercise of judgment, the making of estimates, and some arbitrary decisions. To cut the year, in turn, into two, four, or even twelve segments for reporting purposes amplifies the level of uncertainty for a number of reasons; and it may well be contended that reports for periods shorter than a year should be prepared on a special-purpose basis only—that is, they should contain only data that pass the test of reliability. Data that do not pass this test should be clearly labeled as conjectural or speculative.

Conclusion

If you're still with us, you have now suffered through just about all of the mechanical details (call it bookkeeping if you wish) that we're going to deal with. No apologies are offered for the amount of book-keeping that we have analyzed because it will help us immeasurably in the discussion of the sequence of topics that follow. If you will apply your pencil to the summary test problem on the following pages and if you find that it presents no major difficulties, you should be all set to explore some of the more interesting aspects of accounting—particularly the ways in which it should be useful to you in your work.

TEST PROBLEM

The trial balance of Blitz Co. on December 31, before adjustments, is shown in the first two columns of the work sheet on page 80. Data on which end-of-year adjusting entries are to be based are as follows. (Assume that the company did not make interim adjusting entries in its formal records.)

(1) Unrecorded bank service charges amount to $25.
(2) The $100 balance in Allowance for Bad Debts is the amount remaining from last year's provision. The proper increment for this year is estimated to be 1 percent of total sales for the year.
(3) The inventory of merchandise at year-end is determined to be $10,000.
(4) Depreciation for the year is determined to total $4,000, of which 90 percent is selling expense and 10 percent is administrative.
(5) Interest accrued payable on the bonds at the end of the year is $1,000.
(6) Income taxes are to be accrued in the amount of $650.

Required:

In the spaces provided, prepare a complete work sheet, an income statement, and a balance sheet.

TEST PROBLEM Solution Space

Blitz Co.
Work Sheet for the Year Ended December 31, 19XX

	Trial balance		Adjusting entries		Income statement		Balance sheet	
	Debit	Credit	Debit	Credit	Debit	Credit	Debit	Credit
Cash in bank	2,500							
Accounts receivable	40,000							
Allowance for bad debts		100						
Merchandise	40,000							
Plant	100,000							
Allowance for depreciation		35,000						
Accounts payable		20,000						
Interest accrued payable								
Income tax accrued payable								
Bonds payable		25,000						
Capital stock		50,000						
Retained earnings		13,400						
Sales		60,000						
Bad debts								
Cost of goods sold	10,000							
Selling expenses	11,000							
Administrative expenses								
Interest expense								
Income taxes								
Net income for year								
Totals	203,500	203,500						

BLITZ Co.
Income Statement, Year Ended December 31, 19XX

Sales		$
Less: Bad debts		
Net sales		$
Expenses:		
Cost of goods sold	$	
Selling		
Administrative		
	$	
Interest expense		
Income taxes		
Net income (and earnings retained)		$

BLITZ Co.
Balance Sheet, December 31, 19XX

Assets

Current:			
Cash in bank		$	
Accounts receivable	$		
Less: Allowance for bad debts			
Merchandise			$
Plant (cost)		$	
Less: Allowance for depreciation			
			$

Equities

Current liabilities:			
Accounts payable		$	
Interest accrued payable			
Income tax accrued payable			$
Bonds payable			
Total liabilities			$
Stockholders' equity:			
Capital stock		$	
Retained earnings, January 1	$		
Earnings retained, 19XX			
			$

Chapter Six

Working Capital

What Is Working Capital?

By now you must be well aware of the fact that when the accountant speaks of working capital (or net working capital), he means the algebraic difference between the total of the current assets and the total of the current liabilities. The term is used a great deal and, as a business executive, you should be quite familiar with it. In fact, I think you should be able to tell your accountant a thing or two about working capital.

As a starter, the term is a poor one because it simply doesn't convey its real meaning. "Capital" has several different meanings (e.g., the invested capital of the company, and capital assets—the noncurrent assets), and to put the word "working" in front of "capital" doesn't seem to add much. But, as the saying goes, we must see it "like it is" and that means "current assets minus current liabilities equals working capital."

To add to our difficulties, it is not unheard of for the banker, or other lender, to insist that you maintain a certain specified amount of working capital at all times. This not only leads to occasional arguments over what should be included in working capital, but it may also require you to be stingy with dividend payments to your stockholders and perhaps to accumulate more working capital than you can use economically.

Now let's spend the next several paragraphs on simple illustrations of the more common transactions that affect our working capital. Just for practice in the use of accounting language and form, for each common working capital element we'll run through a few typical transactions. Part of the reason for this exercise will be to build up your familiarity with "debit" and "credit." Our aim in each case will be to list the more common transactions and show how they are recorded in simple journal form.

Cash Receipts Transactions

Cash comes from many sources. The more common are depicted in the journal entries (with their explanations) that follow. Because the dollar amounts involved are of no importance to us at this point, in most cases, we'll just use x's in place of assumed figures.

(1)

Cash on Hand..	xxx	
Capital Stock.......................................		xxx

To record the issue of capital stock when a corporation is formed. A debit (left-hand) entry is made in the Cash account as an asset increase, and a credit (right-hand) entry is made in the Capital Stock account as an equity increase.

(2)

Cash on Hand..	xxx	
Bonds Payable.......................................		xxx

We borrow money by issuing bonds. Bonds Payable is a liability and we must make a credit to record the increase.

(3)

Cash in Bank..	xxx	
Bank Loan (Notes Payable)...........................		xxx

We borrow money from a bank. Our bank account (an asset) is increased (debit) and a current liability (Bank Loan Payable) is increased (by a credit).

(4)

Cash on Hand..	xxx	
Sales Revenue.......................................		xxx

When we sell merchandise for cash, in addition to debiting cash we must record the *increase in revenue* by a credit.

(5)

Cash on Hand...	xxx	
Accounts Receivable.................................		xxx

This entry records the collection of cash from a customer who at an earlier time purchased merchandise from us "on account."

(6)

Cash on Hand...	1,200	
Marketable Securities.................................		1,000
Gain on Sale of Marketable Securities.................		200

We sell for $1,200 securities that cost us $1,000, and we realize a gain of $200 (which is shown as a credit because the gain constitutes an *increase* in the owner's equity).

(7)

Cash on Hand...	800	
Loss on Sale of Marketable Securities.....................	200	
Marketable Securities.................................		1,000

We sell for $800 some securities that cost us $1,000, and we incur a loss of $200 (which is shown as a debit because the loss constitutes a *decrease* in the owner's equity).

(8)

Cash on Hand...	3,000	
Allowance for Depreciation...............................	6,000	
Retirement Loss..	1,000	
Machinery..		10,000

We sell for $3,000 machinery which some time ago cost us $10,000 but which has been depreciated down to $4,000, and our apparent loss is the $1,000. Note that the accumulated depreciation over the years had been recorded in a "contra" account (as an offset to the machinery account), and when we dispose of the machinery our contra account must be reduced along with the reduction of the machinery account. (We'll spend more time on this later.)

(9)

Cash in Bank...	xxx	
Cash on Hand..		xxx

To record a bank deposit.

Cash Disbursement Transactions

Although statistical evidence of cash disbursement transactions is hard to find, it is likely that the bulk of all purchases of merchandise, raw materials, supplies, and services made by business firms are made on credit—that is, on account. As a matter of fact, when the company employs the so-called *voucher system* in formal fashion, even its cash purchases are recorded initially as if they were on account; this means that, at least theoretically, every cash disbursement is a payoff of an account payable. To illustrate, assume that our company buys $100 of merchandise for cash. The entry in journal form would be:

Merchandise....................................	100	
Cash in Bank...............................		100

But, if the voucher system is in operation, this entry would be recorded in two steps. First, as the assumed incurrence of an account payable when title to merchandise is received:

(1)

Merchandise....................................	100	
Vouchers Payable...........................		100

Second, the follow-up entry eliminates the account payable (voucher payable) by a debit, with a corresponding credit to Cash in Bank.

(2)

Vouchers Payable.............................	100	
Cash in Bank...............................		100

Two observations are pertinent at this point. First, good business practice dictates that *every* disbursement be made by check. This assures us of a formal record of the payment. Second, a voucher is *any document* that serves as evidence of a given transaction. Thus, if every check we issue is documented by an invoice (bill) or other piece of documentary evidence, we are likely to be in pretty good shape when the auditors come around to check up on our records. As documentary support of a cash disbursement, a voucher consists of one or more business forms detailing the transaction and, as a rule, at some point some or all of the forms may bear signatures of vendors, officers of our company, or other parties. Such signatures constitute authorization for the issuance of a check. The use of the voucher system (with disbursements by check only) constitutes part of what is known as a system of *internal check and control.* We'll develop this more later.

To repeat. Under a strict voucher system, *since every payment is preceded by the setting up of a liability* (which may be a very temporary one) called *vouchers payable,* then Vouchers Payable is the only account that can be debited when we make a credit to Cash in Bank.

In the absence of a voucher system, we will, of course, have credits to Cash in Bank accompanied by debits to whatever thing or service was acquired for cash. Thus, in addition to debits to Merchandise, we might make cash purchases of materials (debit Raw Materials), public utility services (debit Heat, Light and Power), labor services (debit Labor Services), and so on. Also, we might have cash payments for dividends, interest, income taxes, or the payment of long-term debt. In each case Cash in Bank would be credited and the appropriate account (Dividends, Interest, Income Taxes, Bonds Payable) debited.

Marketable Securities

Only four transactions are common with respect to marketable securities. They are (1) purchase, (2) collection of interest and dividends, (3) resale at a gain or loss, and (4) end-of-period markdown to reflect loss of value. These may be illustrated in simple journal entries as follows (with assumed amounts):

(1)

Marketable Securities—Cost	12,000	
Vouchers Payable		12,000

We purchase nonspeculative, marketable securities to be paid for out of excess of cash currently on hand during lull in business activity and to build up a fund for payment of income taxes at a later date.

(2)

Cash	600	
Interest Revenue		400
Dividends Revenue		200

To record receipt of interest and dividends earned on marketable securities.

(3)

Cash	9,300	
Marketable Securities—Cost		8,750
Gain on Sale of Marketable Securities		550

To record sale, for $9,300, of securities that cost $8,750.

(4)

Loss from Decline in Value of Marketable Securities	400	
Marketable Securities—Cost		400

Entry made at end of accounting period so balance sheet will show marketable securities at *the lower* of their cost or their current market value, per accounting convention of conservatism.

Accounts Receivable

Only three transactions commonly involve accounts receivable: (1) their origination at time of sale, (2) collection, and (3) charge-offs when found uncollectible. To illustrate each of these, observe the following:

(1)

Accounts Receivable..	10,000	
Sales Revenue...		10,000

To record our sales of merchandise for given dates, all subject to terms 2/10, *n*/30.

In the explanation to entry (1), note the terms, 2/10, *n*/30. This simply means that a 2 percent discount will be allowed if the bill is paid within 10 days and that in any case the whole bill is due within 30 days. Such terms vary. Thus, we could have 3/10, 2/30, *n*/60, which means the *face* of the bill is "net" if the customer waits more than 30 days, but the net amount is 3 percent smaller if the bill is paid within 10 days and is 2 percent smaller if paid between 10 and 30 days from the date of the invoice (bill).

(2)

Cash..	89,000	
Sale Discounts...	1,000	
Accounts Receivable..................................		90,000

To record collections from customers of invoices totaling $90,000 face, less discounts totaling $1,000.

With respect to the elements of entry (2), note that we have collected $1,000 *less* than the amount originally charged to the customers. Since the original charge was recorded by a debit to Accounts Receivable and a credit to Sales Revenue of $90,000, we must now reduce the recorded revenue by $1,000 because we are permitting the customers to pay off this debt *in full* by remitting only $89,000. In other words, when we sell goods or services with the understanding that the customer can take a cash discount if he pays, say, within 10 days, our initial recording of sales revenue (at gross) must be revised if we collect a smaller amount. We could simply debit Sales Revenue for the $1,000 but, for purposes of keeping management informed on the amount of discounts the customers are actually taking, it may be better to make the debit to a contra account, Sales Discounts, which is treated as a subtraction from Sales in our income statement.

In Chapter 5 one of the end-of-period adjusting entries that was used for illustration showed how we recognize the probability that some of your accounts receivable will turn out to be uncollectible. To refresh your memory, the adjusting entry shown there was:

```
Bad Debts......................................   850
    Allowance for Bad Debts.....................        850
```

As was explained, the allowance constitutes an estimated blanket *offset* to your accounts receivable—a substitute for making a credit to Accounts Receivable—at a time when you are sure some of your receivables will not pay off but since you don't yet know which ones, you can't make a direct credit to the receivables; therefore, you employ the bookkeeping trick of using a *contra* account.

Now let's assume that after the lapse of a few weeks we become certain that John Doe, who owes us $150, will never pay his bill. This means that $150 of the $850 is now identifiable with a specific account receivable, so we can transfer $150 from the blanket contra account to the credit side of Accounts Receivable. Our entry is:

```
Allowance for Bad Debts........................   150
    Accounts Receivable.........................        150
```

The balance of the allowance account now stands at $700, which means that we expect to have additional write-offs of approximately $700 from sales made in the past period.

Inventories

The routine transactions involving inventory items (such as merchandise, raw materials, work in process, and finished goods) consist of their acquisition (by purchase or by manufacture) and their consumption (by sale or by internal usage). Following are illustrative entries:

(1)

```
Merchandise....................................   xxx
    Accounts Payable............................        xxx
To record purchase of merchandise.
```

(2)

```
Raw Materials..................................   xxx
    Accounts Payable............................        xxx
To record purchase of raw materials.
```

(3)

Supplies.. xxx
    Accounts Payable... xxx
To record purchases of supplies.

(4)

Cost of Goods Sold.. xxx
    Merchandise... xxx
A physical inventory of goods remaining on hand is taken in order to determine the cost of goods that have been sold.

(5)

Work in Process.. xxx
    Raw Materials... xxx
To record cost of raw materials requisitioned for processing into finished goods.

(6)

Work in Process.. xxx
    Factor Labor.. xxx
To transfer cost of factor labor into the account representing the cost of making finished goods.

(7)

Work in Process.. xxx
    Factory Overhead.. xxx
To transfer miscellaneous factory costs into the account representing the cost of making finished goods.

(8)

Finished Goods... xxx
    Work in Process... xxx
To transfer from the work in process account to the finished goods account the cost of goods actually finished this period.

(9)

Cost of Goods Sold... xxx
    Finished Goods.. xxx
To recognize the cost of finished goods that have been sold during the period.

Prepayments

To round out the accounts that make up the current asset sector of working capital, we must mention various kinds of prepayments.

In general, prepayments (commonly called *prepaid expenses*) consist of amounts that have been paid in advance to suppliers of services. The most common examples are prepaid insurance, prepaid rent, and prepaid property taxes. Under normal circumstances only two common transactions affect the prepayment accounts: (1) the payment made in advance and (2) the amortization of the prepayment as it expires. To save space and your time, the first of these will be illustrated in a single bundle.

(1)

Prepaid Insurance.. xxx
Prepaid Rent... xxx
Prepaid Property Taxes... xxx
    Cash in Bank...   xxx
To record payments in advance for services to be received over various periods of time in the future. Entries made later to record the expiration of each of these follow.

(2)

Insurance Expense.. xxx
    Prepaid Insurance..   xxx
To record expiration of the portion of prepaid insurance allotable to post period.

(3)

Rent Expense... xxx
    Prepaid Rent...   xxx
To record expiration of prepaid rent.

(4)

Property Tax Expense... xxx
    Prepaid Property Tax...   xxx
To record expiration of prepaid property tax.

Current Liabilities

The negative element in working capital is made up of all the current liabilities. Although the cash needed to pay them may not always be easy to find, the accounting entries for current liabilities present no significant difficulties. Examples are:

(1)

Merchandise... xxx
Raw Materials... xxx
Telephone Expenses.. xxx
    Accounts Payable..   xxx
To record amounts owed for purchases of merchandise, materials, and telephone services.

(2)

Accounts Payable.. xxx
    Cash in Bank..   xxx
To record payment of accounts payable.

(3)

Interest Expense... xxx
    Interest Payable.. xxx
To record amount of interest payable as of end of period.

(4)

Labor Services... xxx
    Wages (Payroll) Payable.................................. xxx
To record liability for unpaid wages as of end of accounting period.

(5)

Dividends Charge.. xxx
    Dividends Payable.. xxx
To record the declaration of a dividend to be paid on (date).

Entries to record payment of each of the illustrated current liabilities are the same—simply debit the liability account (to show that you are reducing it) and credit Cash in Bank.

These examples do not by any means exhaust the possible kinds of current liabilities; however, you should have no trouble in applying the same pattern of entries to any other current liabilities that come to your attention.

What Can Your Accountants Do for You?

So far in this chapter we have really been doing nothing more than drill on the technique of depicting a transaction in journal entry form. By now, you should begin to feel more or less at home with the notion of debit and credit.

Essentially, what we have done so far is to study the procedure followed in recording *historical events*. This is the accountant's data-storage function, and by no means should it be sneered at. In order to know how much cash you have in the bank, you must keep some kind of record; in order to be able to send bills to your customers, you must keep accounting records of their purchases and their payments; in order to keep track of merchandise, raw materials, and other inventories, you need a record of your purchases; and you either keep perpetual inventory records or take periodic physical inventories. All of this the accountant takes for granted and it's done in the regular course of business.

On the other hand, your accounting staff should stand ready to supply you with special-purpose studies and reports whenever you need them, as well as with other reports of a more or less routine nature. We'll hope to tick off quite a number of such reports as we progress from chapter to chapter. They should give you a fairly good acquaintance with the things your accounting staff is capable of doing to assist you in the performance of your managerial functions; on the other hand, *you should never make the mistake of relying solely on accounting information when making a decision which should actually rest on information from additional sources as well.* Such a mistake is altogether too common in business practice.

Two examples of routine accounting schedules that commonly prove useful to management are the cash budget and the accounts receivable aging schedule. A brief section will now be devoted to each.

The Budget

While this is by no means intended to be a book on corporation finance, it is inevitable that certain aspects of financial management will crop up as we progress from one aspect of accounting to another.

A budget stands midway between the accounting function and the financial management function in an enterprise. Usually you would expect the accountants to perform the actual task of *compiling* the budget. If your company, however, is large enough to have any job specialization whatsoever, the raw data that are to be fed into the budget must come from a variety of sources (including, for example, the treasurer, the sales manager, the production manager, and all others who are in a position to have a significant influence on financial affairs). Often the budgeting process is performed by a budget committee which may begin its work 3 months or more before the start of the year for which the budget is being prepared.

Let there be no misunderstanding—*budgeting is absolutely essential to the welfare of the enterprise.* In case you don't share this enthusiasm for budgets, contemplate the following quotation from someone unknown: "Not to budget is not to plan." Do you believe in planning?

Budgets take various forms and are often prepared in segments prior to being brought together to form a "comprehensive" budget. One very important segment is the *cash budget,* which we'll now explain.

The Cash Budget

The portion of the comprehensive budget which "plans" the *outflows, inflows,* and *balances* of cash as it stands at various points throughout the period is covered by the cash budget. Opinions vary as to the most satisfactory budget period, but one scheme, which perhaps is the most popular, develops fairly detailed plans for a full year in advance, with the budget schedule showing the flows and balances for each month. Visualize a 13-column schedule, with a column for each of the 12 months and a thirteenth column for aggregates and planned end-of-year balance.

The generalized form of the budget schedule is the essence of simplicity. If we assume a year starting on January 1, the first figure in the first column should be the amount of cash held at the beginning of the year; this is the opening balance. For budgeting purposes the opening balance includes both cash on hand and cash in bank.

Following the opening balance, we list the various sources from which we plan to receive cash during the month of January and also list the anticipated amount from each source. Naturally, we next list the planned amounts to be disbursed during January. Needless to say, the formula Opening Balance + Receipts − Disbursements gives us a resulting end-of-month balance. This balance is of course automatically the start-of-month balance for February, and the adding and subtracting process is repeated. So it goes throughout the 12-month period. The form of the cash budget is illustrated in Figure 1 for the first quarter of a year, with a total column appended.

Certainly a most important reason for the *forward-looking* cash budget is to detect possible future cash stringencies, and to make arrangements well ahead of time for coping with such shortcomings. Bankers insist upon copies of up-to-date financial statements which they will want to analyze carefully before agreeing to make a loan; but nothing is more useful than a detailed cash budget which shows the proposed loan, as a cash receipt within a given month, and then proceeds to show the repayment of the loan with interest, on schedule, among the disbursements of one or more later months. You will note that both a borrowing and a repaying transaction are illustrated in Figure 1, along with the routine cash flows, in and out, from collections as well as various types of payments. Also, note that the schedule has a line for minimum operating cash balance. Such a balance may be formally decided upon by your company, and its introduction in the budget schedule works out well mechanically if it is added to the disbursements. (Money set aside or held as reserve is, in a rather farfetched sense, a sort of internal disbursement.) This treatment complicates the schedule a bit, but it soon becomes routine.

FIGURE 1
Pseudo Co.
Cash Budget, First Quarter, 19X1

	January	February	March	Summary
Cash balance, first of month..........	$ 5,000	$ 5,400	$10,165	$ 5,000
Cash receipts, routine:				
Collections on account.............	$28,000	$30,000	$27,000	$ 85,000
Cash sales......................	8,000	9,000	7,500	24,500
Miscellaneous...................	1,400	1,800	1,500	4,700
Total receipts.....................	$37,400	$40,800	$36,000	$114,200
Total available (before financing).....	$42,400	$46,200	$46,165	$119,200
Cash disbursements, routine:				
Payments for:				
Merchandise, materials, and sup-				
plies........................	$30,000	$20,000	$23,000	$ 73,000
Advertising...................	1,500	1,000	1,000	3,500
Utilities......................	300	350	350	1,000
Other outside services...........	1,200	1,200	1,200	3,600
Wages and salaries.............	6,000	6,000	6,000	18,000
Property taxes.................	—	—	2,000	2,000
Rent.........................	500	500	500	1,500
Income taxes..................	—	—	3,500	3,500
Land purchase contract..........	1,000	1,000	1,000	3,000
Miscellaneous.................	1,500	950	550	3,000
Total disbursements................	$42,000	$31,000	$39,100	$112,100
Minimum operating cash balance.....	5,000	5,000	5,000	—
Total cash requirement.............	$47,000	$36,000	$44,100	$ —
Anticipated cash excess or (deficiency)..	$(4,600)	$10,200	$ 2,065	$ —
Financing:				
Short-term bank loans.............	$ 5,000			$ 5,000
Loan repayments................		$(5,000)		(5,000)
Interest payments...............		(35)		(35)
Total financing....................	$ 5,000	$(5,035)	$ —	$ (35)
Cash balance, end of month..........	$ 5,400	$10,165	$ 7,065	$ 7,065

Comments on Cash Budget Illustration

Note first that the amounts used in our budget illustration are purely
hypothetical. In your own situation you must be supplied with acceptable
predictions (plans) of sales for each month and a calculation of probable
cash flow resulting from cash sales and collections from sales that are
made on account. Past experience, the market outlook, and *plans for*

improvement go into the preparation of the budgeted figures. Similar considerations govern the various classes of disbursements. Isn't it amazing, the number of newly formed businesses that fail before they ever get off the ground? If everyone who contemplates setting up in business could somehow be required to prepare in detail a comprehensive budget for the first year or two, and in rough form for the first five years, what a lot of business failures would be avoided simply because they would not be started in the first place! Wouldn't you agree that, in general, a profitable business is an asset to society because it puts together raw materials and labor and management and converts them into something of *greater value* to society? An unprofitable (loss) enterprise is a detriment to society because it consumes materials and labor, but its output is worth *less* than the materials and labor consumed! The loss enterprise, in effect, wastes valuable resources. All hail the budget as a means of avoiding losses by advance planning.

One more word about cash. It's very poor business practice to have too much of it around for too long. Unused cash is nonproductive and, worst of all, it actually shrinks in value as that old bugaboo *inflation* eats its way into our economy. If the general price level goes up 6 percent in a year, it means that any cash that we've held throughout that year has lost approximately 6 percent of its power to buy goods and services. Also, claims to cash (accounts receivable) suffer the same shrinkage as does cash itself. So, it's of real importance that we plan our cash flows in such a way as to minimize any cash balances in excess of current working-capital needs. Obviously, the cash budget is a prime tool in accomplishing this aim.

Control of Receivables

As we progress in this book, we should be able to present new topics with lesser amounts of introductory explanation because you are accumulating a fundamental understanding of the rituals and concepts of accounting. You should soon need only to see a journal entry or an accounting report in order to understand it with minimal explanation.

Let's try this approach with another valuable accounting schedule, the widely used accounts receivable aging schedule. As in all cases, the scope, the detail, etc., must be adapted to the size and complexity of your company, but whether your accounting system is operated strictly

FIGURE 2
Pseudo Co. Customer Accounts
Aging Schedule, March 31, 19XX

Customer (or number)	Present balance	Under 31	31–60	61–90	91–180	181–360	Comment
				Age of balances, days			
A. A. Adams	$ 100	$ 100					
B. B. Black	50			$ 50			
C. A. Cream	70	30	$ 20	20			Paid in full on April 10
D. C. Duke	150					$ 150	Can't locate customer
Z. A. Zohn	220	220					
Totals	$58,120	$27,170	$16,420	$7,160	$5,400	$1,970	
Percentage of total	100%	47%	28%	12%	9%	4%	

by pen and ink or is thoroughly computerized, an aging schedule is a great device for control of receivables.

The accounts receivable aging schedule lists the name of each customer and, in a series of columns after his name, shows (1) the total amount that he owes you and (2) a breakdown of that amount in terms of the length of time it has been owing. Space at the right-hand end of the schedule may be provided for comments, which may include references to communications with the customer, recommendations for actions to be taken, etc. In very abbreviated form such a schedule is shown in Figure 2.

Comments on Aging Schedule

If the company is small enough for such attention, the aging schedule may be useful in providing management with details that lead to managerial (or legal) action with respect to individual customers. In all situations the column totals should prove useful in determining the quality of the accounts receivable total. What portion is in the older categories and in risk of becoming uncollectible? Are the proportions in the older, or more recent, categories changing for the better or for the worse? Should credit terms and credit pressure be modified? Is our present allowance for bad debts adequate? The schedule is commonly used to check out these questions by making estimates of the portion of each column total that is likely to be uncollectible. For example,

FIGURE 3
Test of Adequacy of Bad Debt Allowance
March 31, 19XX

Age group, days	Total	Estimated uncollectible, %	Estimates
1–30	$27,170	1	$ 270
31–60	16,420	3	500
61–90	7,160	5	350
91–180	5,400	10	540
180–1 year	1,970	50	1,000
Total	$58,120		$2,660
Present allowance			1,600
Addition needed			$1,060

we might derive the schedule shown in Figure 3 from the details shown in the aging schedule.

The aging schedule can be prepared as often as necessary to assist the credit manager, or other manager, to "keep on top" of the accounts receivable situation.

TEST PROBLEM

In the space provided for your solution, make simple journal entries to record the following transactions, all of which involve working-capital items:

(1) Sales of merchandise for $500 cash
(2) Sales of merchandise for $600 on account
(3) Collection of $196 from customers after allowing $4 of sales discount
(4) Borrowing $5,000 from the bank by giving a 90-day, 8 percent note payable
(5) Payment of the note in (4) at maturity
(6) Sale, for $800 cash, of a machine which originally cost $2,000 and on which we have so far recorded (accrued) depreciation of $1,100
(7) Provision for $500 of estimated bad debts
(8) Write-off of an account receivable, $120
(9) Recognition of end-of-year merchandise cost of goods sold based on opening inventory of $1,000, purchases of $10,000, and final inventory of $2,000
(10) Recognition of insurance expiration of $300

TEST PROBLEM Solution Space

Debits   *Credits*

(1)

(2)

(3)

(4)

(5)

(6)

(7)

(8)

(9)

(10)

{ Chapter Seven }

Inventories

What Are Inventories?

The term *inventories,* like so many words that we find in accounting, is widely used in ordinary conversation. It tends to refer to our "supply" of almost anything; thus, we might refer to our inventory of battleships, houses, etc. Let's be more precise for accounting purposes; the best example of inventories is our stock of merchandise held for sale to customers, i.e., our merchandise inventory (often referred to as our *stock in trade*). And if we're connected with a manufacturing company, the term inventories embraces our raw materials, our semifinished goods (work in process, or "in progress"), and our finished goods. A dealer in marketable securities, such as stocks and bonds, would have a marketable securities inventory. Added to this, we generally allow the inclusion of various kinds of consumable supplies under the inventory heading. Supplies (not to be confused with *equipment,* which means more or less permanent assets) include auxiliary goods such as stationery, fuel, lumber, repair parts, and the like. Technically we should not include as inventories stores of lumber and building supplies that we may have purchased for use in the construction of our own buildings or manufacturing plant, because inventories are limited to those stocks of goods which qualify as current assets and which are part of working capital. Public utility companies regularly err in their balance sheet presentation of construction materials and supplies by showing them as a current asset.

Typical Inventory Transactions

Without paying much attention to reasons or theory, let's now skim through a series of unrelated transactions represented in the form of simple journal entries. As in the series of journal entries presented in Chapter 6, no dollar amounts will be assumed in most cases because they would not be of significance to the illustrations.

(1)

Merchandise..	1,000	
Accounts Payable....................................		1,000

Purchase of merchandise at invoice price of $1,000, terms 2/10 eom.

The notation 2/10 eom means that if the account payable ($1,000) is paid within 10 days after the end of the month (eom), the buyer is granted a cash discount of 2 percent. Often you'll see terms such as 2/10, *n*/30 or 3/20, *n*/60. The first means that the bill is due in 30 days but the buyer can deduct 2 percent if he pays within 10 days from the date appearing on the invoice. The second example is similar—3 percent off if paid within 20 days, but if delayed beyond 20 days the face of the invoice becomes the net price. Thus, in the case of our $1,000 account payable, the net price is $980 until the tenth of the next month; after that, the net price becomes $1,000. Where no discount is offered, the bill may merely bear the notation "terms net."

(2)

Accounts Payable...	1,000	
Cash in Bank.......................................		980
Merchandise Discount................................		20

To record payment of account within 10 days after end of month, to take advantage of cash discount.

How would you classify the account Merchandise Discount? Your logical conclusion should be that this credit constitutes a *correction* of the overstated $1,000 original debit to Merchandise. We recorded the purchase of merchandise at "gross," or $1,000, but as things turned out our cost of merchandise was only $980; so, we could make a $20 credit directly to the merchandise account or (you guessed it) use a *contra* account to reflect the reduction in recorded cost. In the old days most accounting texts said, incorrectly, that a cash discount is a form of gain or revenue.

A better way to record the two transactions is to debit merchandise for the *net amount* initially, showing accounts payable also at net. Surely under the terms of the purchase *we owe only $980* until the tenth of next month has passed. If you want to debate this point with your accountant, the proper "buzz" words are gross versus net. Barring some peculiar set of circumstances which make recording at net impractical, the net method is far superior, as the following entries show.

(1*a*)

Merchandise...	980	
Accounts Payable..		980

Purchase of merchandise at invoice price of $1,000 less 2% if paid by 10 eom.

(2*a*)

Accounts Payable...	980	
Cash in Bank...		980

Payment of invoice within discount period.

To add to your side of the argument, let's assume that payment of the bill is delayed until the discount period has expired. Then we must pay the entire $1,000, of which $20 is a *penalty* for waiting until the last minute. As the accounts will show, under the net method we now will pay off a debt that we recorded at $980 by giving up $1,000 for a *loss* of $20; let's label that loss Loss from Lapsed Discounts. The entry is:

(2*b*)

Accounts Payable...	980	
Loss from Lapsed Discounts...	20	
Cash in Bank...		1,000

Wouldn't you argue that the accounts should show discounts that have been lost through neglect rather than to emphasize, as the gross method does, the routine "taking" of cash discounts? Do you realize that with terms 2/10, *n*/30 the 2 percent amounts to an annual rate of 36 percent? (Payment 20 days earlier than necessary saves you 2 percent of the face of the bill. A 360-day year contains eighteen 20-day periods, and 18 times 2 percent is 36 percent.)

(3)

Accounts Payable.......................................	xxx	
Merchandise Return and Allowances..................		xxx

To record returns of merchandise for credit and to record reductions in price (allowances) granted by the suppliers on goods found to be defective or not in accord with specifications.

(4)

Merchandise..	xxx	
Accounts Payable..................................		xxx

To record freight and transportation charges as an added cost of merchandise purchased.

(5)

Merchandise Inventory................................	27,000	
Cost of Goods Sold...................................	116,000	
Merchandise......................................		143,000

To allocate cost of merchandise pool between goods left over (inventory) at the end of the period and the goods sold.

The amounts in (5) are determined by taking a physical inventory at the end of the period, finding its cost, and assigning the remainder of the total cost pool (opening inventory plus purchases) to Cost of Goods Sold. This is known as the physical, or periodic inventory method. When we are dealing with items that are individually significant, we may use the continuous (or perpetual) inventory procedure. Then, each time that a sale is recorded the corresponding cost of goods sold is recorded simultaneously.

(6)

Supplies...	xxx	
Accounts Payable..................................		xxx

To record purchases of various kinds of supplies.

(7)

Selling Expenses.....................................	xxx	
Administrative Expenses..............................	xxx	
Supplies...		xxx

To record consumption of various kinds of supplies for various purposes as measured by amounts recorded on requisitions (underlying documents).

(8)

Factory Overhead....................................	xxx	
Supplies...		xxx

To record consumption of supplies by various factory departments, with the cost charged to Factory Overhead because it cannot be traced directly to units of product manufactured.

(9)

Raw Materials...	xxx	
Accounts Payable......................................		xxx

Purchase of various kinds of raw materials for use in production in our factory.

(10)

Work in Process..	xxx	
Raw Materials.......................................		xxx

To record cost of raw materials used in production, as measured by amounts shown on requisitions issued and traceable directly to specific jobs in process.

(11)

Work in Process..	xxx	
Payroll Payable......................................		xxx
Factory Overhead....................................		xxx

To recognize direct labor and factory overhead costs chargeable to work in process.

(12)

Finished Goods...	xxx	
Work in Process.....................................		xxx

To recognize cost of goods finished during the accounting period.

(13)

Cost of Goods Sold.....................................	xxx	
Finished Goods......................................		xxx

To record the factory cost of goods sold during the period.

Inventory Valuation

The values at which the inventories of merchandise, materials, work in process, finished goods, etc., are recorded have a dual significance in financial reporting. First, the amount shown in the balance sheet as a current asset is likely to be a significant working-capital component. Statement analysts may be expected to pay considerable attention to your working-capital position, and special attention to the proportion of your current assets that consists of inventories. Thus, to the degree of choice that you have in reporting a valuation figure for your inventories, you will be in a position to influence the decisions of creditors and investors who look to your financial statements as a prime source of financial information. Second, and perhaps even more important, the accounting valuation which you place on your inventories directly affects the amount of net income for the period. Recall the following formula:

```
Inventory at start of period.............................  xxx
Add: Cost of goods purchased (or manufactured)..........  xxx
Total goods to be accounted for.........................  xxx
Less: Inventory at end of period........................  xxx
Cost of goods sold......................................  xxx
```

Quite obviously, the amount shown as inventory at end of period directly affects the final amount, cost of goods sold. The greater the cost of goods sold, the lesser is the net income; the lesser the cost of goods sold, the greater the net income. Or, to get right to the point, the greater the amount shown as ending inventory, the greater the net income; the lower the ending inventory, the lower the net income.

The fact is that you do have substantial leeway in the valuation of your ending inventory; this leeway is derived from the variety of choices available to you in your expressed assumption as to the manner in which the goods flow through your establishment. Let's examine these flow assumptions one by one but, first, let's acknowledge one cardinal rule: Basic to all good accounting is *the rule of consistency;* we cannot shift back and forth from one flow assumption to another as suits our wishes or whims each year. This is a real handicap for anyone who wants to manipulate the reported net income figures of his company.

Identified Cost

It is almost universally acknowledged that inventories should be reported at their cost (with due allowance for physical shrinkage, wear and tear, and shrinkage in value). If we acknowledge that cost is the appropriate target for inventory valuation, we may next ask, cost of what? The amount would seem to be *the cost of the goods on hand.* This is our inventory at any point in time. Many people overlook the fact that, carried to its logical conclusion, the expression "cost of the goods on hand" must mean *the amount that we paid for the specific goods* that remain unsold at the end of the period. Now, we may have bought several batches of certain items; and the prices that we paid per unit may have been different for each batch. Suppose at the end of the year we have on hand a few units from each batch. Because these units (though otherwise identical) cost different amounts, the identified cost concept requires that we inventory them at their respective costs. Thus, if we have on hand five units of material X and know that we paid $2 each for two of them, $3 each for two of them, and $4 for the fifth, our identified cost inventory of material X is $14. Some people like to argue that it is perfectly ridiculous to list a series of identical items at different values. Yes, this would be ridiculous if our balance sheet were intended to show the *current values* of all our assets, but the balance sheet makes no such pretense. The general rule for nonmonetary assets is to record them *at their cost*. Under this view, the identified cost method is absolutely great—except for one thing, *it's usually not practical!* Surely, if you're a speculator in real estate you can easily keep track of the cost of each lot, each house, or each farm that you buy, but it's just not feasible to identify the specific costs that attach to specific gallons of gasoline, cubic feet of gas, pounds of flour, barrels of cement, or yards of cloth.

What do we do, then, when we want to apply the identified cost concept but find it totally impractical? Answer: We make a whopping big assumption as to the order in which the goods *flow* through our business and we price our inventory on the basis of our chosen flow assumption. Let's examine the popular assumptions.

First-in, First-out

As a matter of physical fact, all goods, unless they are allowed to rot or rust in the storage bins, flow through the business in a first-in, first-out (FIFO) procession. Of course the flow is not perfect—some goods never become used or sold and are finally discarded or sold as scrap; some goods are slower moving than others. But the realistic assumption is that your raw materials, your supplies, your work in process, and your finished goods pass through your hands in an orderly first-in, first-out parade. The oldest goods of a given category are constantly cleared from the shelves, and the inventory at any date may reliably *be assumed* to consist of the most recent purchases.

The first-in, first-out assumption has no magic significance in itself; it is an assumption for the sake of convenience. It is a convenient way to *simulate* identified cost. Let's demonstrate the method by a simple example.

At the end of the year our company has on hand 1,000 units of a particular item left over from a beginning-of-year inventory of 800 plus 9,000 that were purchased during the year. Clearly a total of 8,800 have disappeared if we can now find only 1,000 of the 800 plus 9,000 to be accounted for. If the 800 units on hand at the beginning of the year cost $1 each and we bought the 9,000 units in three batches of 3,000 each, costing $1.10, $1.20, and $1.40 per unit, respectively, what is the FIFO (first-in, first-out) cost of the 1,000 in the final inventory? The answer is, 1,000 at $1.40, the invoice price of the most recent purchase. The cost of goods sold is then the difference between $1,400 (1,000 at $1.40) and the grand total cost ($11,900) of all units to be accounted for, or $10,500. The details may be displayed in schedule form as follows:

	Units	Per Unit	Total
Initial inventory......................	800	$1.00	$ 800
Purchase 1...........................	3,000	1.10	3,300
Purchase 2...........................	3,000	1.20	3,600
Purchase 3...........................	3,000	1.40	4,200
Total to be accounted for..............			$11,900
Final inventory at FIFO..............	1,000	1.40	1,400
Cost of goods sold (or used)...........			$10,500

If it had been feasible to mark the cost on each unit as we purchased it, we could have totaled up the costs of the 1,000 left over at the end by examining each one and running an adding machine tape to get the total. But if we followed good housekeeping practice during the year, the likelihood is strong that almost all of the 1,000 remaining on hand at the year-end came from purchase 3; and, note this, if our assumption creates no material error, we should employ it rather than go through the clerical process of marking and identifying each item as if it were an important individual.

What Are Inventory Profits and Holding Gains?

A great many articles have been written in which the authors point out that net income is often affected significantly by the fact that the replacement costs and the selling prices of goods may rise (or fall) while they are being held in stock by the company. Such a development, so it is argued, creates *holding gains* or, as they are more commonly termed, *inventory profits*. The concept is more elusive than you might think. Let's dive into it with a mini-example.

Our company buys one unit of an item for $100, wholesale, when the retail price is $130. This specific item is not sold until later when the wholesale price has risen to $120 and, obediently, the retail price has gone to $156 (30 percent over cost). By traditional accounting, on a strict cost basis, our company would show a gross margin of $56 on the sale ($156 − 100) which, of course, would be offset in the determination of net income by various operating expenses and taxes. The point is that $20 of the gross margin (and a corresponding portion of the net income) could be attributed solely to the wholesale and retail price rises that occurred while we were "holding" the item. Out of this phenomenom have evolved three distinct schools of accounting thought. Let's take a look.

THE HOLDING GAIN SCHOOL: This crowd says that holding gains are quite different from "trading" gains, which are the result of normal buy-and-sell transactions. (Trading gains are deemed to represent the fruits of managerial effectiveness—they are the real "operating" gains.) Our income statements should divide the gross margin into two parts: (1) holding gain and (2) trading gain. In our example, this school would report the gross margin as follows:

Sales.	$156
Cost of goods sold, on replacement-cost basis.	120
Gross trading margin.	$ 36
Add: Given holding gain ($120 − 100).	20
Gross margin.	$ 56

THE INVENTORY PROFITS SCHOOL: This crowd says that inventory profits are illusory. To them the *real* cost of goods sold is not the identi-fied (or FIFO) historical cost of the goods sold but, rather, the current, *or near-current,* replacement cost as *measured by the amounts we have actually paid most recently for identical goods.* To illustrate this notion we must make an added assumption; assume that our company did buy a second item for $118 not long *before* it sold the first one. This group does not want to abandon the hallowed historical cost principle; so as a substitute for the current $120 replacement cost employed by the holding gain school, cost of goods sold is calculated as being made up of the actual cost(s) of the goods most recently purchased. In other words, these folks would avoid the need for showing holding gain (which they consider to be a mirage) by making the highly artificial assumption that we didn't really sell the old $100 item—what was actually sold was the latest one we bought, the $118 item. This assumption is the reverse of FIFO and is known as LIFO (last-in, first-out); it should be known as *artificial* LIFO because, actually, goods don't flow through a company in this cock-eyed order. In our example, the anti-inventory profits (LIFO) school would report their gross margin as follows:

Sales...	$156
Cost of goods sold, on LIFO basis.......................	118
Gross margin.......................................	$ 38

THE IDENTIFIED COST SCHOOL: Now let's get back to basics. Most businesses are constantly buying, fabricating, and selling goods. Under the most common circumstances the stock of goods is maintained at minimum levels (to minimize costs of storage, protection, interest on investment, deterioration, and obsolescence); in other words, most enterprises are in business to trade, in the normal sense of the word, rather than to speculate on price increases. Fluctuations, up and down, in wholesale and retail prices are part of the economic environment and there seems to be little reason for undertaking the complicated bookkeeping procedures that would be required to determine with any precision the amount of gross margin that is caused by holding gains, nor would the reporting of such information often be of any real service to the statement analyst; on the other hand, it is totally wrong to deny that such gains have occurred and to repress their recognition (by use of LIFO). The identified cost group, then, would report as follows:

Sales...	$156
Cost of goods sold, on FIFO basis.......................	100
Gross margin.......................................	$ 56

COMMENTARY: Now that you've had a glimpse at three interesting schools, I'd like to convince you that the third would be best *if they would only adjust their historical dollar costs to reflect changes in the value of our measuring unit—the dollar.* Unfortunately, we must delay full explanation of the problem of our shaky dollar until Chapter 20; therefore, please keep in mind the underlined words in the preceding sentence.

Last-in, First-out

Although LIFO was touched upon in the preceding section, it's much too prominent in current usage to be dropped so quickly. The LIFO inventory valuation procedure is completely acceptable for income tax purposes and has the endorsement of the prestigious American Institute of Certified Public Accountants. We must at least scan the highlights of LIFO.

During periods of persistent inflation (which seems to be almost constant), our costs and selling prices tend to rise in parallel fashion. As was demonstrated in the preceding section in simplified form, use of the FIFO flow assumption, realistic as it may be, matches costs that may have been incurred days, weeks, or months ago, against revenues from current sales—simply because, as each sale is made, the accountant checks off against that sale the cost of the unit of inventory that has been on the shelves for the longest time. The result is a gross margin determination that includes the full amount of holding gain (or, as we'll see later, the *illusory* gain from deterioration of the purchasing power of our currency).

LIFO, on the other hand, artificially assumes that the oldest goods remain on the shelves (forever?). In fact, some refer to LIFO as FINO—first-in, never-out! If, for example, our company begins to use LIFO at a time when it has 100 tons of steel on hand that cost $100 per ton, and if its ending inventory of steel for the next 20 or more years never goes below 100 tons, on its balance sheet for every one of those years the same 100 tons at $100 will be included in the inventory.

In favor of LIFO, it may be admitted that it tends to suppress recognition of illusory gains from inflation, but at best this is done in a makeshift fashion since prices of steel and other specific commodities do not move in concert with changes in the purchasing power of the dollar. Strongly in favor of LIFO is the possibility of stalling off payment of income tax on illusory gains, since LIFO is an allowable procedure for income tax purpose.

In very strong opposition to LIFO is the fact that the FINO inventory figures, which appear as current assets in the balance sheet, are farcical. Unfortunately tied to the privilege of using LIFO for tax purposes is the absolute requirement that LIFO must also be used in financial reports.

Let's look at one more example. Assume that a newly formed company makes the following purchases of a given item during its first year of existence:

Date	Quantity	Price per Unit	Amount
Jan. 1	1,000	$2.00	$ 2,000
Feb. 10	3,000	2.40	7,200
June 15	4,000	3.00	12,000
Nov. 5	3,500	3.50	12,250
Totals	11,500		$33,450

Also assume that sales of this item during the period, when price varied from $3.00 to $4.50 per unit, amounted to $40,000, and that on hand on December 31 there remain 1,500 unsold units. First, let's see what our gross margin would be were we to use FIFO. Following is the FIFO schedule.

Sales...		$40,000
Cost of goods sold:		
Purchases..	$33,450	
Inventory, December 31 (1,500 @ $3.50).................	5,250	28,200
Gross margin..		$11,800

Next, the same schedule shows the gross margin if LIFO is employed.

Sales...		$40,000
Cost of goods sold:		
Purchases..	$33,450	
Inventory, December 31 ($2,000 + $1,200)..............	3,200	30,250
Gross margin..		$ 9,750

As you should recognize, the LIFO procedure shows $2,050 less gross margin. This difference is equal to the difference in the amount assigned to the 1,500 units of closing inventory. Under LIFO procedure the 1,500 units will constitute the beginning inventory for the following year, at the same $3,200 valuation; and these same units and same value could, theoretically, remain in the financial statements for all time. FIFO procedure, on the other hand, tends to provide inventory costs that are continuously up to date.

Dollar Value LIFO

It does not seem appropriate here to explore the intricacies of so-called *dollar value LIFO* but its rationale should be noted. For companies that handle standard materials or standard merchandise year after year, the LIFO procedure that we have just scanned is entirely feasible. However, many companies, especially retail stores, have more or less constant changes in the variety of goods handled, and LIFO would be of little use to them since they are persistently "selling out" their complete stock of items that are dropped from their line. In short, as originally conceived, a somewhat limited number of taxpayers could employ LIFO and all others were in a true sense being discriminated against. To remedy the discrimination, dollar value LIFO was invented. Essentially, dollar value LIFO treats a complex variety of materials or merchandise as a pool of dollars rather than as a quantity of physical units; by use of a series of price index numbers, goods on hand at the end of each year are valued at costs which are translated into earlier years, with an end result which simulates LIFO on a physical unit basis.

Average Cost

To round out the discussion of inventory valuation procedures, it must be noted that some companies value their ending inventories on a moving average cost basis. This may mean that, for each class of materials or merchandise, the cost of the purchases for the year is added to the cost of the opening inventory, and the sum is divided by the corresponding total number of units to obtain an average unit cost. This average unit cost is then applied to the number of units remaining on hand at year-end to determine the dollar valuation of the ending inventory. Where continuous (perpetual) inventory procedure is used, the average cost per unit may be changed whenever a new batch of a given item is purchased, and then the final inventory is priced at the average cost in effect at the year's end. Needless to say, the use of an average cost procedure is bound to result in a cost of goods sold figure (and a gross margin) that lies somewhere in between the corresponding amounts resulting from FIFO and LIFO.

Cost or Market, the Lower

Let's face it. Businessmen in general, and almost all accountants, are conservative in their financial affairs. An old-time guiding principle of accounting goes somewhat as follows: Recognize all losses, anticipate no gains. As translated, this means, "Write assets down and liabilities up, whenever any glimmer of doubt appears, but don't ever acknowledge any gain until it has been unquestionably realized in the form of cash (or claim-to-cash) proceeds." We could debate the doctrine of conservatism for hours, but this would be inappropriate here. Rather, as we pass from one area to another, we'll simply take note of the implications of conservatism as they are reflected in the current "generally accepted" practice.

For a prime example of accounting (and business) conservatism, the "opinions" of the Accounting Principles Board of the American Institute of Certified Public Accountants require that unless inventories are valued at LIFO they must be valued at *the lower of cost or market*. The bulletin which prescribes the rules for determining this valuation is too technically complex for our detailed consideration, but in simplified terms the rule boils down to a requirement that if the goods on hand at the end of the period could be replaced (in customary quantities and through customary channels) at prices that are lower than those that were actually paid, the recorded costs of the goods on hand should be written down to their replacement costs (and a corresponding loss shown). The theory is that if your buying price for goods has dropped, it is likely that your resale price for the goods will drop also. Many comments (not all flattering) could be made about this rule, but one point stands out. If the replacement cost (market price) of goods has *fallen,* we must accrue a corresponding assumed loss; should the reverse occur—forget it! It should be added that income tax rules do not permit the use of cost or market if the taxpayer is "on LIFO."

Inventory Turnover

One of the relationships which financial analysts frequently use in appraising the financial quality of a firm is the ratio of the cost of goods on hand (inventory) to the cost of goods sold for an entire year. If, for example, the company now has on hand goods inventoried at $20,000, while the cost of all goods sold during the past year was $240,000, the ratio of 20 to 240 (1 to 12) indicates that the company's inventory approximates the needs for a month's sales. The relationship may be reported as a "30-day supply" (since accountants usually assume a 360-day year for ease in quoting such approximate relationships), or the term *turnover* may be used. In our example the evidence indicates an inventory turnover rate of 12 times per year. Turnover is computed by dividing cost of goods sold for the year by the amount of inventory at year-end or, better, by the average of the initial and ending inventories (or even by the average of the inventory quantities at the ends of all 12 months). In general, of course, the higher the turnover rate, the better. If a company can operate successfully with a 10- or 20-day inventory, this means fewer funds tied up in merchandise and materials and, accordingly, lower costs. Needless to say, one important function of management is to seek and to maintain *optimum* inventory levels. Overstocking means excessive interest costs, obsolescence, and high storage costs, while understocking leads to loss of customers and loss of sales. The buzz word for understocking is "outages," and our current crop of management scientists delight in seeking to measure the cost of outages.

Inventory Reports for Management

If perpetual inventory records are kept or if inventory records are computerized, accountants should be able to keep management currently apprised of the firm's inventory position not only in terms of inventory totals but also in reports of significant over- or understock of specific items that are important to the welfare of the company. Quite a bit of research has been done by the operations research (OR) folks with respect to inventory management, including, for example, the development of formulas for determining the optimum quantity of goods to be purchased at a time.

TEST PROBLEM

On January 1 the raw materials inventory of a company, valued at FIFO cost, is $12,000, consisting of 20,000 pounds of material. The company buys 25,000 pounds at 80 cents per pound on January 10 (terms 2/10, n/30) and pays for them on January 19; the company buys 20,000 pounds at 90 cents per pound on January 20, under the same terms, and pays for them on January 31. All raw material purchases are recorded at net prices. Perpetual inventory records show a balance of 22,000 pounds of the material on hand on January 31.

Required:

In simple journal form record the purchases, the payments, and the usage during January, with respect to the raw materials.

TEST PROBLEM Solution Space

JAN. 10

JAN. 19

JAN. 20

JAN. 31

Chapter Eight

Fixed Assets and Depreciation

Classes of Fixed Assets

In a very broad sense accountants divide assets into two major groups—current and noncurrent. By tradition the noncurrent assets have come to be termed *fixed assets,* a term which is not particularly apt since, with the possible exception of land, no asset is permanently fixed or permanently attached to a particular owner. There is no established rule as to terminology; you may take your choice.

In the noncurrent category five principal subdivisions stand out. A corporation, a partnership, or a person for that matter may acquire the capital stock, bonds, notes receivable, or mortgages issued by other companies or persons; and the intent may be to hold these "securities" for a considerable period of time for their investment value—that is, for the interest and dividends, or possible value growth, that will be obtained. In contrast with purchases of marketable securities for the short-term employment of temporarily excessive cash funds, these securities are *long-term investments,* and are properly classified as fixed assets in the balance sheet. Because we will be looking at these same securities from the standpoint of their issuers later, we will give them no special consideration in this chapter.

A second major category of fixed assets consists of all types of *natural resources*. Most commonly in this category we think of the land on which our buildings rest—site land—but this group also includes agricultural land, mining land, rights-of-way, etc. For most companies these assets present no major accounting problems and we'll touch on them only lightly in this chapter.

The third category includes all types of *depreciable structures,* of which buildings constitute the principal subgroup. We'll concern ourselves with the questions of the valuation of structures when they're first acquired and as they age.

The fourth category consists of *machinery and equipment* of all types. As with structures, we'll be concerned with both the initial and the subsequent valuation of items in this group.

The fifth category is made up of all kinds of so-called *intangible assets*. It is very difficult to concoct a satisfactory accounting definition of intangibles because accounts receivable and cash in bank, for example, are both intangible, but neither is included within the technical accounting category of intangibles. So, the best way out seems to be just to list the things that accountants usually classify as intangibles. They are goodwill, patents, trademarks, trade names, franchises, secret processes, and, possibly, leaseholds and long-term prepayments. You may think of others. In any case, we'll devote no more time to this category here but will take a closer look at goodwill at a later point in the book. Essentially, then, this chapter will be concerned with the initial and subsequent valuations of structures, machinery, and equipment.

Initial Valuation of Fixed Assets

There tends to be very little disagreement as to the proper initial accounting for depreciable and nondepreciable fixed assets of all types. "Cost" has almost universal acceptance. (A few of my friends believe there may be numerous instances in which the buyer either clearly outwits the seller, or is obviously outwitted, and that accounting recognition should immediately be made of the implied gain or loss in the act of making the purchase. The vast majority of accountants rebel at this idea and prefer to let any "purchase gain" or "purchase loss" show up in the subsequent accounting for the asset.)

The determination of acquisition cost can be tricky sometimes. The easiest case, of course, is where we buy land, buildings, or equipment for cash (or by a down payment plus a mortgage or installment purchase contract). Two main points should be brought out in this connection: (1) Be sure to include *all* costs of acquisition, up to the point where the asset is *in place and ready for use;* and (2) do not "capitalize" (do not add to the cost of the asset) the interest that is paid or to be paid on any debt that is incurred in connection with the asset's purchase. Costs that should be capitalized include transportation, installation, and break-in, as well as basic construction costs where the company builds its own structures or equipment.

A more difficult determination of acquisition cost arises in the less common situation where we issue capital stock to someone in exchange for an asset or a "basket" of assets. In these days of intensive merger activity, it is not at all unusual for one company to acquire the "net assets" of another company by giving them an agreed-upon number of shares of capital stock. Two questions present themselves: (1) What actually is the *cost* to us of the assets that we acquire in this fashion (whether we get a basketful or a single asset); and (2) how do we allocate the total cost of the entire group of assets to the individual assets that make up the group? The usual (and apparently sound) accounting answers to these questions may be stated quite briefly. First, where capital stock is issued in the acquisition of assets, the assets should be recorded at their estimated *current market values* (with due allowance, of course, for their physical condition). If current market value is not ascertainable, an acceptable alternative is to determine the current market value of the capital stock that is being given and assign this same value to the assets that are acquired. The answer to the second question is that once the aggregate cost of a group (basket) of assets is known, this cost should be allocated to the component elements of the group in proportion to their respective market, or appraised, values.

The final acquisition deal for us to consider is the one in which we trade in an old asset on a new one—that is, a barter transaction in which, usually, we must give cash to boot. Here it is a great temptation to argue that the cost of the new asset is equal to the amount of cash (or future cash) we give plus the book value of the old asset traded in. Thus, if we trade an automobile that originally cost us $4,000, which we have depreciated down to a book value of $1,200, and if we give cash or notes payable to boot of $3,500, the cost of the new asset would be recorded at $4,700. This is appropriate for income tax purposes but it's poor accounting theory. Our real cost is the amount of cash paid ($3,500) plus the current market value (rather than our book value) of the asset traded in. If we assume the asset traded in had a current market value of $900, the correct cost of the new asset is $4,400. Many folks go astray in this same situation by being overly impressed by the list price of the new automobile. You and I know that list prices are not to be taken very seriously. Thus, if the new car had a list price of $5,000, another wrong recording of the trade-in would be the following:

Automobile (new—at list price)	5,000	
Allowance for Depreciation (old)	2,800	
Cash in Bank		3,500
Automobile (old)		4,000
Gain on Trade-in (balance)		300

This concludes our discussion of the initial valuation of fixed assets. In every transaction you are bound to encounter special circumstances that present difficulties; we have touched upon the major high points and we hope that you'll be able to resolve the unique problems of each situation as they arise.

SUBSEQUENT VALUATION OF FIXED ASSETS

There are so many conflicting opinions as to the proper accounting representation of fixed assets during their lifetime with an owner that we are about to take up their consideration one at a time.

Historical Cost Less Depreciation

The overwhelming majority of practicing accountants strongly favor carrying fixed assets in the books and on the financial statements at their historical dollar cost as adjusted for the amount of depreciation that has been recognized. In favor of this position is the accountant's ever-present affection for "objectivity." He likes to present figures that can be audited and confirmed; he likes to avoid estimates and appraisals as much as he can, because these tend to be "subjective" valuations, subject to bias and manipulation which may be detrimental to the interests of investors and creditors. Also, he favors historical cost because, he says, profit is earned only as we make use of our assets and write off (depreciate) their cost against the amounts (revenues) that we receive for their use. In other words, business profits are made through the current operations of the business—not by the purchase of assets at a bargain or by the subsequent (assumed) increases in the values of the assets (much of which increase is no more than a reflection of inflation). Some of the leading accountants who favor historical cost are gradually beginning to admit that cost should be restated in terms of the current value of the measuring unit—the dollar. We'll spend a whole chapter on this interesting subject later. Nothing has been so thoroughly neglected by accountants as the undeniable fact that our measuring unit has been changing in size by anywhere from 1 to 15 percent each year (always shrinking) and that it is simply ridiculous to add together dollars of different vintages and treat them as if they all had the same meaning.

Replacement Cost

Practicing accountants have never shown much enthusiasm for making formal recognition in the accounts and financial statements of appraised values for fixed assets. Admittedly, some knowledge of current values of the fixed assets of a business is important internally for purposes of getting adequate insurance coverage, and such information may be of considerable interest if property is the basis for rate regulation or is to be mortgaged in connection with a loan or bond issue. There are those who argue (for example, the theoretical economists) that the true income for any period is best defined as the difference between the amount of the net assets at the beginning and end of the period. (Net assets, to repeat, is the expression for the amount found by subtracting total liabilities from total assets—a difference frequently termed *net worth*.) The economists would, of course, require that the assets be recognized at their current values for their purposes in determining the net assets. Again we are faced with the question of recognizing holding gains if fixed assets (which we intend never to sell) fluctuate in value. The question of reporting fixed assets at replacement cost, or current value, has been the subject of many doctoral dissertations; undoubtedly, it will keep many a doctoral candidate occupied for years to come before it is finally laid to rest. For the present, at least, it would appear that in the case of nonregulated industries the historical cost folks still have the better of the argument. Let's see what some of their arguments are.

First, it would be quite costly to employ appraisers as often as once a year to supply us with their "educated" estimates of the current replacement costs of our properties.

Second, the basic definition of replacement is most elusive: What do we mean by replacement? Do we mean the literal reproduction of our existing buildings and machinery, using the same building materials, the same hand labor, the same building methods, etc? Or, do we mean the cost of buying, in the present market, closely similar assets that will provide the same amount of service as the assets we are now using, and with due allowance for the amount of depreciation that our assets have sustained to date? Needless to say, this question presents very major complexities.

Third, if we were to report the fixed assets in our balance sheet at their replacement values, would our investors have a significantly better basis for estimating *the value of their company?* Or does the value of the company depend very heavily upon the effectiveness and excellence of the management?

Fourth, if we were to make the necessary adjustments for recognition of the change in the value of our monetary unit (which we'll explore in Chapter 20), wouldn't this pretty well solve the problem? It can be argued quite successfully that reproducible fixed assets never, or at least rarely, increase in true value, though their cost, restated in dollars of current purchasing power, is very much subject to change. In other words, true holding gains, even if we wanted to recognize them, are likely to be quite immaterial.

Possibly a good compromise between historical and current costs would be to agree to recognize changed fixed asset values when and if it becomes perfectly obvious that some very substantial value changes have occurred—to the point where the company should be asking itself if it might be better to dispose of certain assets in order to realize the big gains, rather than continue to employ them in the business. It is quite probable that such value changes would almost never be called for, except in rare cases where the company's land had undergone dramatic value increase.

The Debit Balance School

We've just paid our respects to the replacement cost school. At the opposite pole is a surprisingly large school which I like to label the debit-balance school. In contrast with the replacement cost crowd, these folks couldn't care less about showing up-to-date values in the balance sheet. I'll never cease to be amazed by the fact that some of the leaders of the accounting profession are advocates of the debit balance position. They're ultraconservative. What they say is that what we reflect on the asset side of the balance sheet is merely a list of names and debit balances with no hint whatsoever that the dollar amounts have any meaning except that they are the debit balances that remain after we have recorded depreciation and other write-offs. Some of us feel that a balance sheet should to some degree reflect the amount of (current) dollars that remain invested in the assets and that our hired management bears responsibility for producing income that is commensurate with the amount of assets so displayed. The debit balance group, however, argue that once an asset has been written off it need no longer be reflected in the balance sheet, even though it is in good working order and has years of useful life remaining.

During World War II, American companies that had manufacturing plants in Paris, or thereabouts, wrote the plants entirely off when they fell into the hands of the enemy. Not too surprisingly, when the war was over and the Americans were able again to visit their French plants, they found them in far better condition than they were in before the Germans took charge. In my estimation, if such plants had been written off as "lost," they should have been restored in the financial statements when they became "found"—but you can't convince a debit balance believer of this! Somewhat the same was the case of the plant erected during the war under an emergency facilities certificate which permitted writing off the plant in 60 months, even though its physical life might extend to 20 or 30 years. When the war ended, much of our most modern manufacturing plant was of this sort, and most of it had been written down (amortized) to zero. The influential debit balance school insisted that none of these plants should have their costs restored even though it became absolutely evident that they would have great usefulness in postwar production of nonwar goods.

DEPRECIATION OF FIXED ASSETS

Any formula for the computation of depreciation must make use of at least four factors: asset cost, useful life, probable terminal salvage, and timing of service extraction. It's sad, but true, that every one of these factors presents difficulties (in many cases absolute impossibility) of accurate measurement. Nevertheless, we must recognize depreciation. Because of the vast amount of uncertainty, a lot of different methods of measuring depreciation have been proposed, and it would seem quite important for any executive to have a nodding acquaintance with the more common procedures and to be on guard against being misled by the numerous false impressions that so many people have with respect to the accounting for depreciation.

What Is Depreciation?

Depreciation is the exhaustion of the useful service potential of an asset through the combined effects of utilization, wear and tear, aging, and obsolescence. The first three of these factors tend to cause the asset to deteriorate physically, while obsolescence means the loss of usefulness from all other causes. For example, the asset is no longer large enough for our needs (our first computer); our competitors have acquired a more efficient machine and we must replace ours in order to match their reduced costs of production; or the output of our equipment has gone out of style. Depreciation does not include breakage or other casualty loss; these are losses rather than depreciation.

Accounting for depreciation consists in making accounting entries to recognize, with reasonable accuracy and in dollar amounts, the depreciation cost that should be borne by each accounting period. Every depreciable asset has its *depreciable cost,* which means original cost minus the amount we expect to get for the asset when we retire it—the so-called salvage. If an asset costs $100 and we predict that we will use it for 4 years and then sell it second-hand for $20, the depreciable cost is $80 so far as we are concerned. So, accounting depreciation boils down to this: For a given asset (or collection of assets) we must have a record of the cost, we must make an estimate (or assumption) as to the prospective terminal salvage (which, subtracted from the cost gives us the *depreciable cost*), we must make an estimate (or assumption) as to the useful life (that is, how long the asset will be useful *to us*), and we must then determine the most *appropriate pattern* to be followed in the allocation of the depreciable cost to the individual accounting periods making up the useful life of the asset or collection of assets.

Depreciation Patterns

Four general patterns are possible in the allocation of depreciable cost to the periods of useful life. One pattern assumes that each period realizes the same benefit from the asset and, accordingly, should bear the same depreciation charge. This pattern, logically enough, is termed *straight-line* depreciation. At the opposite extreme, one may predict that the utilization of the asset will vary in uneven fashion from year to year and that instead of a straight line we should contemplate use of a pattern of charges best depicted by a *wavy line*. This leaves only two other realistic choices. The best of all, in my opinion, assumes that most assets perform most effectively when new and that their effectiveness declines more or less continuously as they age, so that a *decreasing line* (to represent decreasing charges per period) may be appropriate. Lastly, in certain rare cases an *increasing line* may be chosen. From here on this chapter will be devoted to the respective merits and shortcomings of the various depreciation line assumptions.

Straight-line Depreciation

The periodic straight-line depreciation accrual is determined by dividing the depreciable cost of the asset by the number of accounting periods contained in the estimated useful life of the asset. Depreciable cost, as defined earlier, is the total cost of the asset minus the expected *net* salvage. Gross salvage is the total amount that we hope to recover from the asset at the time of its final retirement and disposition; net salvage is gross salvage less any costs that are incurred in the process of obtaining the gross salvage. For example, in the razing of a structure we might plan to recover used bricks worth a total of $500 (gross salvage), but if the probable labor cost of razing the structure is $400 then the net salvage, to be used in the straight-line depreciation calculation, is only $100. In making straight-line depreciation computations for assets with useful lives of 3 years or more, it is common to ignore the salvage factor if it is likely to amount to less than 10 percent of the cost of the asset itself.

Straight-line is by far the most popular depreciation method used by American industry; oddly enough, such popularity is not really warranted. It has only two arguments going for it, and neither is laudable. First, it's the simplest method, and this may be true. To work a problem in straight-line depreciation would perhaps require education in arithmetic through the second grade in school, whereas the other popular methods might demand the higher mathematics covered in the third or fourth grade. Second, straight-line depreciation constitutes a compromise in a sea of uncertainty. We don't really know the useful life of an asset at time of acquisition and we don't know the pattern in which the asset's services will be extracted, so we make the unwarranted assumption that over the uncertain life the same amount of service will be extracted in each period.

On the other side, there are some fairly potent arguments against straight-line depreciation. First, assets typically perform most efficiently and productively when they are new, and if a given period receives the benefit of superior service it should bear a correspondingly high depreciation charge. As the asset ages and performs less effectively, each period should receive a smaller depreciation charge. Certainly the straight-line pattern fails to match this performance picture. Compounding the inequity of straight-line depreciation charges is the typical pattern of repair and maintenance charges, which tend to increase perceptibly as the asset ages. So, with straight-line depreciation we end up with increasing charges for decreasing services as time passes! A final argument against straight-line depreciation is a relative one. It is a less conservative method than certain others. Not only does it delay the write-off of the asset somewhat, but also it fails to capitalize on tax benefits that may possibly be derived from use of the decreasing-line methods.

Wavy-line Depreciation

The method that results in a wavy line is commonly referred to as the *production units method*. The formula is similar to straight line except that the depreciable cost is not divided by the expected number of accounting periods in the asset's life but by the total number of units of output that the asset is expected to render. Thus, in the case of a taxicab the depreciable cost might be divided by, say, 200,000 miles to obtain the estimated depreciation cost per mile. Then the total depreciation charge for a given accounting period would be found by multiplying the miles driven by the depreciation cost per mile. The production units method has considerable theoretical appeal. It is based on the sound premise that when you buy a depreciable fixed asset you are acquiring a "bundle of services," and it follows logically that, if the services are identical, one unit of depreciation occurs as each unit of service is detached from the bundle. For a useful analogy, think of the purchase for $100,000 of a mine that contains 100,000 tons of coal. As each ton of coal is extracted, the cost of the mine content remaining would naturally be written down by $1. (The exhaustion of mines, oil and gas wells, etc., is called *depletion* rather than depreciation.) And so, we find strong support for the units of production, wavy-line, method of booking depreciation in those situations *where the units of service output are identical and the total, original service-unit content can be ascertained within reasonable limits of accuracy.* The unfortunate fact is that industry has found relatively few situations where these requirements can be met. It's virtually impossible to find a satisfactory definition of a service unit in the case of almost any structure, and it's even more difficult to make anything like a reliable estimate of the total number of service units that will be extracted from any piece of machinery. In short, the production units method has failed to gain widespread acceptance because of its apparent impracticability. In this respect it is similar to the identified cost method of valuing inventories where, as you will recall, accountants are prone to adopt flow assumptions which they believe satisfactorily *approximate* the realistic movement of goods. Something of the same thing is done in the realm of depreciation when accountants adopt a straight-line assumption, or the decreasing-line assumption which we are to examine next.

Decreasing-line Depreciation

As we've noted repeatedly, the tendency for most depreciable assets is to turn out less and less service as they grow older. Such service deterioration may manifest itself in several ways. Some machines simply run slower and slower; some have more breakdowns and more downtime; most require more attention as they age—more maintenance and repair; and some get out of adjustment and cause more defective products as time passes. Few depreciable assets escape what we might term *service deterioration* as they age, and such deterioration shows up in different ways for different assets. Buildings used for offices, apartments, and other purposes lose their attractiveness as they cease to be "modern." In many ways, assets perform less satisfactorily as they get older; they may produce a reduced flow of services, or they may render an undiminished amount of service but at a higher operating cost, or the same physical service may have lower and lower market value. The old apartment house or the old motel, for example, provides just as much space for occupancy as when new, but the revenue (and net income) to the owner suffers because customers can be attracted only in fewer numbers and at reduced rents. This tendency, then, for a depreciable asset to render considerably more than half of its total service during the first half of its life strongly encourages the conclusion that the depreciation line, or curve, should have a downward slant.

A final, very important reason for recognizing higher depreciation charges in the earlier years of an asset's life is that such a practice is permitted under income tax regulations. In general, it's good financial practice to delay the payment of income taxes (as well as any other indebtedness which bears no explicit interest) as long as possible; in this manner you can be "financed" at no cost by your creditors. One of the fine opportunities to perform this delay of payments is to deduct just as much depreciation as the law allows, as fast as you can. True, you'll have to make up for it later, but with no interest charge. For example, if it were legally possible for you to depreciate an asset by 70 percent during the first half of its life, the extra 20 percent would serve to delay your paying income tax at, say, 48 percent on the dollar amount represented by the 20 percent. Payment of that delayed tax would occur piecemeal over the last half of the asset's life. Such, then, is the tax effect of a decreasing-line depreciation plan. The plans are variously known as *accelerated depreciation, liberalized depreciation,* and *decreasing charges depreciation.*

There are two common plans for calculating the periodic depreciation charges under the liberalized concept. First is one which appears (and perhaps is) almost idiotic. It's called the *sum-of-years'-digits* method. If an asset has a 4-year life, you add the digits 1 through 4 (which equals 10) and your depreciation each year is found by applying a fraction, which consists of the numbers of years taken in reverse order over 10, to the depreciable cost of the asset. Assume that an asset costs $100 with an estimated life of 4 years and probable salvage of $10. Then the depreciation series for the 4 years would be: Year 1, $\frac{4}{10}$ of $90, or $36; Year 2, $\frac{3}{10}$ of $90, or $27; Year 3, $\frac{2}{10}$ of $90, or $18; Year 4, $\frac{1}{10}$ of $90, or $9, for a total of $90.

If you're unhappy with sum-of-years' digits, use the *declining-balance* method. This also has the blessing of the tax collectors and in many cases allows you more depreciation earlier than is allowed under sum-of-years' digits. Again the calculation is easy: If an asset has a 5-year life, the straight-line depreciation rate would be 20 percent each year, applied to the initial cost of the asset minus its salvage. The (double) declining-balance method permits you to use *double the straight-line rate,* but this double rate is applied each year to the amount remaining in the asset account, and no salvage value is fed into the calculation. If we apply the declining-balance method to the $100 asset used in the preceding paragraph, the succession of depreciation charges will be: Year 1, 40 percent of $100, or $40; Year 2, 40 percent of ($100 — $40), or $24; Year 3, 40 percent of ($60 — $24), or $14.40; Year 4, 40 percent of ($36 — $14.40), or $8.64, for a total of $87.04. Note that in this example there is a built-in salvage residual of $12.96 as compared with the $10 that was preselected in the sum-of-years' digits plan. The relative amounts recorded under the two plans are as follows: (SYD = sum-of-years' digits plan, and DB = declining-balance plan.)

Year	SYD	DB
1	$36	$40.00
2	27	24.00
3	18	14.40
4	9	8.64
	$90	$87.04

Income tax regulations allow the taxpayer to design his own decreasing-charges plan, with the proviso that he mustn't get ahead of the declining-balance plan at any time during the first two-thirds of the asset's life.

Composite and Group Depreciation

In spite of the availability of computerized depreciation accounting, common practice is to apply a single straight-line depreciation rate to all of a firm's assets, or to subdivide the assets into related collections and apply an appropriate rate to each collection. Such procedure is known as *composite depreciation,* and the rates are supposed to be determined for each collection of assets by an averaging process. Composite depreciation is usable for tax purposes; in fact, the government has supplied a set of acceptable composite rates for various classes of assets. Your accountant will refer to the government's recommendations as *guidelines* depreciation since the proposed rates are actually intended to serve as guidelines rather than mandatory rates.

Group depreciation is similar to composite depreciation except for the fact that under group depreciation the assets are classified into closely related groups in which, for example, each asset in a group has the same approximate useful life. The selected depreciation rate for the group then depends upon the probable mortality of the component units within the group. Thus, one might apply group depreciation to all of the utility poles owned by a public utility company and, though the useful lives might range from 8 to 20 years, the average life used to determine the group rate would depend upon the shape of the expected retirement curve for the poles.

One important characteristic of composite and group depreciation plans is the fact that *no loss or gain is recognized* when a given member of the collection is retired. The reason for this rule is that the depreciation rate employed rests on the assumption that some of the assets will be retired sooner than average and some later than average—all to come out even in the long run.

Typical Depreciation Entries

Some of the most common entries involving depreciation accounts are shown in the following illustrations:

(1)

Depreciation......	xxx	
Allowance for Depreciation......		xxx

To record periodic depreciation by any method.

(2)

Allowance for Depreciation......	900	
Cash......	200	
Retirement Loss......	400	
Machinery......		1,500

To record sale of machinery in secondhand market for $200 when book value is $1,500 − $900, or $600, for a loss of $400.

(3)

Allowance for Depreciation......	900	
Cash......	800	
Machinery......		1,500
Retirement Gain......		200

To record sale of machinery in secondhand market for $800 when book value is $600, for a gain of $200.

(4)

Allowance for Depreciation...............................	1,300	
Cash..	200	
Machinery.......................................		1,500

To record sale of machinery in secondhand market for $200 with no gain or loss recognized since the machinery is being depreciated by composite plan.

(5)

Allowance for Depreciation...............................	700	
Cash..	800	
Machinery.......................................		1,500

To record sale of machinery in secondhand market for $800 with no gain or loss recognized since the machinery is being depreciated by composite plan.

Depreciation Fallacies

Some companies still use the term *reserve* for depreciation in their financial statements; others are now using *accumulated depreciation*. The former title is fast disappearing because of its misleading nature. When it is used it leads many people to assume that the company always has reserved an amount of cash equal to the amount shown as the reserve for depreciation. This is totally foolish, but too common to be ignored. Should there be any misgivings in your own mind, just assume that in your balance sheet you show an allowance, or reserve, for depreciation in the amount of $100,000 and that you actually do have exactly $100,000 in the cash accounts—so they do match. What, now, is the entry to record the purchase of $100,000 worth of merchandise for cash? Obviously, it's a debit to Merchandise and a credit to Cash in Bank—with the allowance for depreciation completely undisturbed even though your cash has gone down to zero.

One of the more hideous fallacies related to depreciation is that depreciation in some way is capable of generating cash, or funds. Probably most nonaccountants (who give the matter any thought) have this misunderstanding. Cash flows in from the sale of merchandise and the collections from customers, whether you show $1 of depreciation or $100,000. The amount of depreciation recorded has absolutely no effect on the amount of cash inflow. True, depreciation is deductible for tax purposes with the result that fewer tax dollars are paid out as more depreciation is deducted, but this is not what the mistaken people have in mind. If depreciation produces funds, one should find at least a few dimes lying under his car at the end of each day at the office! Certainly, if a firm has an oversupply of cash, and poor management, it may hoard an amount of cash each year equal to the recorded depreciation, but the depreciation does not create the cash in any way.

A third fallacy, which actually stems from the one just mentioned, is that depreciation does, or must, provide for the *replacement of an asset*. This is simply impossible. Depreciation is nothing more or less than the spreading, or allocation, of *the cost* of an asset over its useful life. If you want to "provide" for the replacement of an asset you must set aside in a sinking fund, or in a portfolio of investments, cash that you collect from your customers. This has nothing to do with depreciation. To illustrate the point, if you record depreciation of a given asset as $10,000 per year and at the same time want to dedicate some cash to the future replacement of that asset, you would need to make two separate and unrelated entries each year as follows:

(1)

Depreciation..	10,000	
Allowance for Depreciation.............................		10,000
To record depreciation.		

(2)

Asset Replacement Fund (bank account)....................	10,000	
Cash in Bank...		10,000

TEST PROBLEM

At the beginning of a year Our Company buys a machine for $10,000 cash. The estimated useful life is 5 years and probable salvage is $1,500. At the beginning of the fourth year the machine is sold for $3,000.

Required:

In simple journal form record the depreciation for each of the 3 years and record the sale, using straight-line procedure. Repeat, using the sum-of-years'-digits method.

TEST PROBLEM Solution Space

Straight-line procedure: *Debit*   *Credit*

YEAR 1

YEAR 2

YEAR 3

YEAR 4

Sum-of-years' digits procedure:

YEAR 1

YEAR 2

YEAR 3

YEAR 4

{ Chapter Nine }

Corporation Accounts

What Is Unique about Corporation Accounting?

The unique aspects of corporation accounting focus entirely upon one characteristic—the manner in which the enterprise raises its capital. Neither the sole proprietorship nor the partnership issues capital stock, but the corporation does. Neither the sole proprietorship nor the partnership employs a surplus (retained earnings) account, but the corporation does. The unincorporated enterprises do not issue bonds, as the corporation does if necessary. The financial statements of a partnership or proprietorship are usually not made available to the general public, whereas a corporation which is listed on one of the stock exchanges, or which otherwise has the requisite characteristics, must publish its balance sheets and income statements regularly and may be required to submit to annual audit by independent public accountants.

In spite of the fact that the corporate form of organization has certain drawbacks, such as being subject to income taxation, lawsuits, etc., it dominates the American financial scene, which includes well over 1½ million corporations, ranging from corner grocery stores to large farms, to giant conglomerates, to even larger nonconglomerates such as General Motors, Standard Oil, and American Telephone and Telegraph. The principal reasons for popularity of the corporate form include the facts that the owner's liability is limited to the amount of his investment, ownership interests are readily transferable, and the value of one's investment (in the case of "listed" securities) is readily determinable on a day-by-day basis.

In recent years the managers of corporations have surely taken full advantage of the powers to issue securities of all shapes and sizes. Indeed, the tendency to invent special classes of securities has created some tough problems for the accountants and the financial analysts. In this chapter we'll look at the major types but by no means can we exhaust the arsenal.

The Issue of Capital Stock with Par Value

Much of the power of the corporation rests on the provisions of its charter and bylaws. The charter may provide for the issuance of shares of stock that do, or do not, have a par value. As a matter of fact, par value means very little aside from the fact that it sets a minimum issuing price for the shares. State corporation laws, almost without exception, stipulate that shares with a par value may not be issued at a discount; that is, they may not be issued for consideration that has a value less than the par value of the stock. Many companies establish what amounts to a nominal par value for their stock, which may be issued for many times the par value; in other cases the par value of the capital stock may start out at, say, $10 or $100 and then, as the result of several stock "splits," the par is repeatedly reduced until it becomes an almost inconsequential part of the overall stockholders' equity of the company.

When capital stock is issued at a price higher than its par value, the excess over par is typically recorded and reported as Capital Stock—Premium, or as Capital Paid In in Excess of Par, or simply as Capital Surplus. Use of the last title, because it contains the word "surplus," has been strongly discouraged. For example, the Committee on Terminology of the American Institute of Certified Public Accountants, in its discussion of the undesirability of "surplus" as an accounting term, simply says, "The use of the term *capital surplus* (or, as it is sometimes called, *paid-in surplus*) gives rise to confusion."[1] The committee goes on to point out the obvious fact that the word "surplus" (like surplus fat) implies too much of something—something that the corporation plans, or should plan, to eliminate as soon as possible.

For an example of low-par stock as well as use of the term "capital surplus," the December 31, 1969, consolidated balance sheet of Ling-Temco-Vought, Inc., shows common stock with par value of $.50, totaling $1,212,000, and on the next line shows capital surplus of $234,150,000—more than two hundred times the amount of the capital stock par. In these days when so much emphasis is being placed on the market value and trading volume, and with $20 to $30 per share being considered the most popular price range, it is doubtful that many new corporate stock issues will carry the once-familiar $100 par value designation.

Common stock is known as the *residual equity* of the corporation. This means that in the event that the corporation is dissolved, either voluntarily or involuntarily, the common stockholders get "what's left" (if anything) after the claims of all creditors and preferred stockholders (in that order) have been met as fully as possible. Preferred stock ranks senior to common stock with respect to dividend payments as well as in dissolution, and the dividends on certain forms of preferred stock may "accumulate" from year to year if they remain unpaid.

Entries to record the issue of common and preferred stock are the same. Assume, for example, that 100 shares of $10 par common stock are issued for $12 each, in cash. The entries are:

Cash in Bank...............................	12,000	
Capital Stock—Par......................		10,000
Capital Paid In in Excess of Par...........		2,000

The Issue of Capital Stock with No Par Value

No-par stock was invented in the hope of eliminating the confusion and opportunities for fraud that par-value stock appeared to create. It was thought that avoiding the expression "par value" would cause shareholders to view their shares as nothing more than evidence of fractional interests in the total common stock ownership of the corporation. Soon, however, it became common practice to establish a "stated value

[1] *Accounting Terminology Bulletin No. 1,* August, 1953.

per share" for no-par shares and, as in the case of par value stocks, amounts received in excess of the stated value were credited to Capital Surplus or to paid-in surplus. This practice is commonplace today although the word "surplus" tends to be disappearing.

When no-par stock is issued for cash, the most logical entry is to debit Cash for the amount received and to credit Capital Stock—No Par *for the same amount*. If, however, there is an established stated value per share, it is almost unavoidable that only the stated-value portion of the proceeds of issue will be credited to the Capital Stock account and the excess will be credited to Capital Paid In in Excess of Stated Value or a similar account.

The Issue of Capital Stock for Property

When capital stock is issued for cash, there is no question as to the dollar amounts involved, even though there may be some choice as to the accounts to be credited. However, when stock is issued to someone in exchange for land, buildings, machinery, securities, or other forms of property, uncertainties can arise. One thing ought to be certain: When we issue stock for cash, we record the transaction for the amount of dollars that actually change hands, and few people would have the courage to argue that any different figure should be used; then, when we issue stock for something other than cash, we should surely record the transaction, as accurately as we can, *at the cash value* of the thing received. Unfortunately, there is a school of thought that believes the absence of cash in the case of a stock issue gives license to pick a valuation of the thing received that may bear not even a remote relationship to its current value. We'll take a closer look at this phenomenon in Chapter 19 when dealing with mergers and acquisitions.

For the time being, let's be purists and at least attempt to record the noncash assets received in exchange for stock at their current cash values. If, for example, we issue 10,000 shares of common stock with a par value of $.50 per share for a tract of land worth $25,000, our entry should be:

Land..	25,000	
Capital Stock Common—Par.............		5,000
Capital Paid In in Excess of Par..........		20,000

Or, if we issue 100,000 shares of no-par stock to the stockholders of another corporation in exchange for all the stock of that corporation that they hold, and if their stock has as aggregate market value of $2,500,000, our entry should be (ignoring pooling-of-interests rules) :

Investment in Common Stock of X Co................. 2,500,000
   Capital Stock—No Par (and no stated value)........   2,500,000

Sometimes the current market value of the property received may not be readily ascertainable, while the current market value of the stock that we issue in exchange is known. Then there should be no objection to using the latter value in recording the acquisition of property.

Treasury Stock—What, Why, and How?

In its July 29, 1969, issue the *Wall Street Journal* devoted one of its splendid feature articles to the subject of "buying yourself," with the headline, "More Companies Find Their Shares Are Rewarding Investment." The first sentence of the article reads: "Keebler Co., a Chicago-based cookie and cracker maker, has found what it considers a hot investment for some extra cash it has on hand. The investment is called Keebler Co."

To "buy itself" a corporation merely places an order for some of its own outstanding shares in the stock market, much as you or I might purchase shares through our broker. When the corporation does acquire its own shares they may be canceled and retired, or they may be held in an inactive state in the corporate treasury (wherever that may be). Shares held in the treasury are aptly termed *treasury shares* or *treasury stock.*

Treasury shares have no voting rights and dividends cannot be paid on them since such an act would constitute the farce of taking money out of your pocket, putting it right back in that same pocket, and claiming you had both paid a dividend and received some dividend revenue. Before Securities and Exchange Commission rules put an end to this charade, some companies were actually siphoning book dollars out of their "surplus" accounts to symbolize a dividend and were reflecting the very same dollars as "dividend income" in their income statements! In the absence of the prohibition, a company with $1,000,000 in its Retained Earnings account could show net earnings of nearly $1,000,000 per year and not do a tap of work. It would merely declare a dividend, mostly payable to itself, recorded as follows:

(1)

Retained Earnings....................................	1,000,000	
Dividends Payable...............................		1,000,000
To record declaration of dividend.		

(2)

Dividend Payable.................................	1,000,000	
Cash..		100,000
Dividend Revenue..............................		900,000
To record "payment" of dividend of which 10% is paid on		
stock held by outsiders and 90% on stock held in our treasury.		

In describing what treasury stock *is* we should also understand what treasury stock *is not*. The investments that your company makes and holds in the form of securities issued by other companies are, without a doubt, *assets* (either current or noncurrent); the "investments" your company makes in its own stock, contrary to the implications of the *Wall Street Journal* headline quoted earlier, are not investments; shares of treasury stock are *not* an asset. Certain companies, such as General Electric, General Motors, and Eastman Kodak (and that is pretty good company!) apparently aren't hep to this truth, and they doggedly persist in displaying their treasury stock on the asset side of their balance sheets. But this is ridiculous (even though it appears that the shares are held primarily for distribution under executive bonus plans). How can a company own all its assets and also own, and treat as an asset, *shares of stock that represent those same assets?* Beginning students of accounting often protest that the shares of treasury stock may be readily salable and, thus, a ready source of cash. The answer to this, of course, is that the *possibility* of obtaining cash is not in itself an asset; if it were, we should then also list as an asset any capital stock which is authorized by our charter but which we have not yet issued (unissued stock), and we should list the notes payable that we have paid off, because we could, no doubt, reissue them for cash on a moment's notice.

Why corporations acquire treasury stock has not always been clear, but the leading reason cited in the WSJ article makes good sense. The article goes on to point out that the cookie business hadn't been so good for Keebler lately; as a result, both the market price and the earnings per share of the company's outstanding common stock had dropped sharply while, in the meantime, the company's cash balances had risen in response to declines in inventories and receivables. If business is bad and you have a pile of idle cash, why not pull in your horns by retiring some of your outstanding stock at bargain prices? Of course, one important hoped-for effect will be a resulting rise in the amount of earnings per share of the stock that remains outstanding. Such rise in earnings per share, coupled with the impact of your purchases of the stock, may cause a slackening of the decline, or an upturn, in the price of your stock in the market.

It is argued that it's fine to have some treasury stock around not only for management bonuses but for possible use in accomplishing a merger with another company. An important amount of stock may be involved in a merger transaction and in such case use of treasury stock, rather than unissued stock, limits the total number of shares outstanding and tends to ward off the dilution of the amount of earnings per share of stock.

It goes without saying that some companies acquire treasury stock at bargain prices when they are confident that the market price at which they can be reissued is going to rise. The gain in cash resulting from successful accomplishment of this aim is not classed as taxable income.

The accounting entries to record the acquisition and reissue of treasury shares are simple. The most widely used procedure consists in recording the acquired stock at cost. To illustrate, assume that our company buys 1,000 shares of its own $10 par common stock in the market for $25 per share. The entry is:

(1)

Treasury Stock..	25,000	
Cash in Bank..		25,000

To record purchase of 1,000 shares of our own stock at $25 per share, to be held in treasury as treasury stock.

To illustrate reissue of these shares, let's make three different assumptions, as follows: The shares are (*a*) reissued for cash at their purchase price of $25 per share, (*b*) reissued at $35, and (*c*) reissued at $15. The respective entries are:

(2a)

Cash in Bank..	25,000	
Treasury Stock—Cost.................................		25,000

(2b)

Cash in Bank..	35,000	
Treasury Stock—Cost.................................		25,000
Capital Arising from Treasury Stock Transactions..........		10,000

(2c)

Cash in Bank...	15,000	
Retained Earnings.......................................	10,000	
Treasury Stock—Cost..................................		25,000

Note that no operating gain is recognized when treasury shares are re-issued above cost; however, when reissued at less than cost, it is apparent that a loss of some sort has been incurred. If at the time of reissue there is a balance in the account shown in (2b) as Capital Arising from Treasury Stock Transactions, that account should be used rather than Retained Earnings. Lacking such a balance, Retained Earnings would appear to be the inevitable recipient of the reissue loss.

On the balance sheet, any treasury stock should be displayed as a subtraction (negative item) in the owner's equity section. There is general agreement that the subtraction should be made from the total of the capital stock and retained earnings as follows:

Stockholders' equity (section of balance sheet):

Capital stock (with details shown).................	$1,000,000	
Retained earnings...............................	375,000	
	$1,375,000	
Treasury shares (1,000 at cost, $25)...............	25,000	$1,350,000

Stock Splits—What, Why, and How?

Stock-splitting surgery is usually performed when the management believes that the stock would be more popular and have wider ownership if the market price were brought to a lower level. To accomplish this, the company may put in the hands of each existing stockholder two shares for each one now held, or five shares for each four, or some other modification which increases the number of shares held, *without any additional investment* by the stockholders and *without any reduction of the retained earnings* of the corporation. Thus, if the current market price of the outstanding stock is $100, a two-for-one split should cause the market price to decline approximately to $50. The stockholder now owns twice as many shares but realizes no income and is not liable for any income tax directly as the result of the split.

A stock split has much in common with a stock dividend (which will be examined in the next chapter) since each is likely to have the same effect on the market price and neither is taxable. The only real difference is that in the case of a stock dividend a certain amount of retained earnings disappears from the balance sheet and becomes embedded in the Capital Stock account.

To demonstrate the entry made for a stock split, assume that our company has 100,000 shares of $5 par common stock outstanding; because it is selling for $120 per share, it decides upon a four-for-one split. Entries to reflect the action are made as follows:

Capital Stock Common—par $5   500,000
    Capital Stock Common—par $1.25   500,000
To record issue of 400,000 shares of $1.25 par common in exchange, for 100,000 shares of $5 par common, in the form of a stock split.

Stock Rights

The terms *rights, options,* and *warrants* tend to be used without distinction by persons speaking about securities. Although there may be no established legal basis for drawing precise distinction, for our purposes it seems best to make the attempt and to take them up one at a time.

In many jurisdictions, when a corporation undertakes to offer additional shares of a class of stock that is already outstanding, the existing holders of shares of that class must be given the opportunity to "preempt" the issue on a pro rata basis. That is, the existing holders have automatic, preemptive rights to buy the same fraction of the supplementary issue as they hold of the shares now outstanding. Apparently some states require that preemptive rights go with any issue of stock; other states do not have such a requirement; and still others provide for waiver of the rights by a vote of the stockholders or by other appropriate action.

To illustrate, if a corporation has outstanding 100,000 shares of $10 par common with a current market value of $45 per share and it wishes to issue an additional 50,000 shares, the corporation might offer the new shares to the holders of preemptive rights at a bargain price of any amount under $45, say, $39 per share. This offer would make the preemptive right attached to each old share worth $2, and the corporation would make provision for the rights to be separately traded on the market. In other words, the $45 *includes the value of one right;* because two rights must be turned in with $39 to buy one new share, each right is worth $45 — $39 divided by 3, or $2. Stated differently, an old share, after its right is detached, differs from a new share by the amount assigned to two rights, but before the right is detached the difference is equated with three rights (counting the one included in the $45).

Because preemptive rights are embodied in the stock issue from its inception, the corporation makes no entry on its books when certificates evidencing ownership of rights are issued to present holders. After a month or so the rights expire and the issue price of any leftover stock may be reset. In the meantime shares that are issued at $39 plus two rights are recorded exactly as are straight cash issues. Assume that all the 50,000 shares are issued; the entry is:

```
Cash............................................  1,950,000
    Capital Stock Common—Par $10...................              500,000
    Capital Paid In in Excess of Par...................            1,450,000
```

Stock Options

An option is also a form of right, but commonly an option is acquired by some specific act or payment. Stock brokers sell options which are known as *puts, calls,* and *straddles* which, respectively, mean rights to sell, to buy, or to do either, within a given period of time. These have no effect on the corporation's financial accounts since they involve only deals among outsiders. On the other hand, during recent years, with sky-high rates of personal income taxation, corporations have made extensive use of stock option offers to present and potential executives of the corporation. In order to qualify for favorable tax treatment, a number of technical restrictions must be observed but basically an executive stock option plan grants the executive the right (option) to purchase a specified number of shares of the company's common stock, at a set price, after specified intervals of continuous employment with the company. The expectation, of course, is that the market price of the stock will rise to a level which will make the purchase at the set price something of a bonanza for the officer. As history has shown, the bonanza is by no means guaranteed, and many option recipients have attached themselves to a company with exciting option grants only to see the stock tumble to a fraction of the initial value so that the options are worthless. On the other hand, many corporate executives have realized spectacular gains through option programs—gains which far exceeded their basic salaries.

There is virtually no accounting for options of the type we are considering except to record receipt of cash and the issue of stock when an officer exercises his options. One might well theorize that the options are granted in lieu of a certain amount of cash salary (for the tax advantages), but most accountants have concluded that there is insufficient basis usually for determining a value for the options that are granted and that accordingly no entry is to be made on the corporate books until the shares of stock are actually sold to the executive.

Stock Warrants

Warrants commonly are detachable rights that are originally attached to bonds or to preferred stock when issued. The warrants are exercised (or detached and sold) by detaching and turning them in for shares of common stock along with a specified amount of cash. In other words, when a share of preferred stock, or a bond, is issued with a warrant attached, the investor is actually buying two things—the preferred stock or bond *and* a warrant which entitles him, at specified dates in the future, to buy a share of common stock at a fixed price, or a schedule of prices varying with time in the future.

Because the warrants are separable, the Accounting Principles Board of the American Institute of Certified Public Accountants has ruled that, when the preferred stock or bond is issued, recognition must be given to the amount of the purchase price allocable to the attached warrant. Assume, thus, that our corporation issues 10,000 shares of $50 par preferred stock at $56 per share, and to each share is attached a warrant to buy one share of common at some future date at a specified price. Assume further that the market assigns a value of $3.50 to a warrant. In such case the entry for issue of the preferred stock and warrants is:

Cash in Bank	560,000	
Capital Paid In—Common Stock Warrants		35,000
Capital Stock Preferred—$50 Par		500,000
Capital Stock Preferred—Premium		25,000

In the future as each warrant is exercised a debit of $3.50 is made to the warrant account, a debit is made to Cash for the contractual price, and a credit is made to the common stock accounts for the total.

In this day of exotic types of securities, we find some companies issuing warrants that are not attached to anything. They are simply rights to purchase (options) a share of stock, sometimes in the future, at a price which, we hope, will turn out to be a bargain. Warrants bear no interest and no dividend is paid on them. If a corporation can issue them in exchange for income-producing assets, it would seem that the deal may be quite favorable from the corporation's point of view, unless the exercise price turns out to lead to excessive dilution of the value of the shares held by existing stockholders.

Convertible Preferred Stock

Somewhat akin to the various kinds of rights is the conversion privilege that attaches to convertible preferred stock. The essence can readily be explained by an example. Our corporation may issue shares of $100 par preferred stock with the understanding that for each $20 of par the investor can convert his preferred stock into one share of common stock which now is selling for $16 per share. This at first glance doesn't look like much of a bargain, but if the conversion privilege extends over a period of many months or years, the chances may be excellent that the common will rise in value above $20 and make conversion profitable for the investor. Quite commonly this preferred stock is also *callable,* which means that the corporation can demand that it be turned in for cash (usually at a significant premium over par) or be converted into common stock under existing market conditions.

Although, clearly, the conversion right that is embodied in the convertible preferred stock makes it relatively more attractive, accountants have agreed that no attempt need be made to account for it separately, as is done with the detachable warrants described in the preceding section. In other words, when the convertible preferred stock is issued, the entries are the same as if no conversion privilege were present.

Common Stock Equivalents

In the preceding four sections, we have been surveying not common stock itself but some kinds of securities that have certain of the qualities of common stock as well as the potential for being exchanged for common stock. Stock rights, stock options, stock warrants, and convertible securities all benefit when the common stock for which they may be exchanged goes up in value; that is, these securities, or instruments, have the capacity to share in the speculative gyrations of the stock market. Rights, options, and warrants can be exchanged for common stock upon the payment of the required amounts of cash; convertibles can be exchanged for stock with no further cash payment. Each of these, then, represents a potential addition to the number of shares of common stock that a corporation already has outstanding. For purposes of determining EPS (earnings per share), these potential additions to the number of common shares outstanding may have to be treated as if they were the actual equivalent of shares of common stock.

Earnings per Share

Opinion No. 15 of the Accounting Principles Board, issued in May of 1969, struggles with what turns out to be the difficult problem of setting equitable rules for computing, and reporting to investors, the amount which a corporation has earned per share (of common stock and equivalent) during the reporting period. Scant trouble exists in the case of the corporation with an elementary capital structure, that is, one with nothing but common stock and perhaps some old-fashioned bonds and preferred stock. But, if the company also has one or more of the so-called *common stock equivalents* in its bag, these may have to be translated into their equivalent number of common shares and added to the pure common total, which is then to be divided into the earnings available to common, with the resulting amount labeled earnings per share.

Even the elementary structure may call for some second-grade arithmetic. The earnings for the year should be divided by the weighted average number of shares outstanding during the year rather than by the simple number outstanding at the end of the year. If there has been a stock split or a stock dividend during the year, the average number of shares outstanding last year must be adjusted as if they had been split if a comparison is to be made between this year's EPS and last year's.

When the structure becomes more complex, we must be on the lookout for the potentially "dilutive" effects of stock options, rights, etc. Opinion No. 15 is nearly 30 pages long and makes tough reading. We cannot possibly present its content here faithfully; however, one paragraph from the summary opinion may serve to indicate the objective. Paragraph 15 is as follows:

> Corporations with capital structure other than those described in the preceding paragraph should present two types of earnings per share data (dual presentation) with equal prominence on the face of the income statement. The first presentation is based on the outstanding common shares and those securities that are in substance equivalent to common shares and have a dilutive effect. The second is a pro-forma presentation which reflects the dilution of earnings per share that would have occurred if *all* contingent issuances of common stock that would individually reduce earnings per share had taken place at the beginning of the period (or time of issuance of the convertible security, etc., if later). For convenience in this Opinion, these two presentations are referred to as "primary earnings per share" and "fully diluted earnings per share," respectively, and would in certain circumstances discussed elsewhere in this Opinion be supplemented by other disclosures and other earnings per share data.

Organization Costs

Organization costs, commonly called *organization expense* by accountants, include the general costs of launching a business concern. This category consists of fees paid for legal services (such as the drafting of the corporate charter and bylaws), fees paid for accounting services, costs of issuing securities, printing costs, etc.

Possibly because organization services are in the main invisible and do not clearly attach to any tangible asset, businessmen and their accountants seem to be anxious to get such costs written off as soon as possible. Actually, the cost of launching an enterprise may well deserve to be maintained as a significant asset for so long as the organization exists.

Tax rules allow the amortization of some of the organization cost items over a period of 60 months or more, but this permission does not apply to the costs of issuing securities, costs of transfer of assets to the corporation, or costs of reorganization.

No one can seriously object to the accumulation of all the productive costs incurred to get an enterprise started in an account labeled Organization Costs. This account is then properly listed permanently in the balance sheet of the corporation. It may be shown as an intangible or it may be shown separately at the bottom of the noncurrent asset section.

TEST PROBLEM

The position statement of our corporation, at the end of a year, contains the following stock equity section:

Stockholders' equity:

Capital stock, 5 percent, $100 par preferred........................			$ 1,000,000
Capital stock common, no par, stated value $2, authorized			
2,000,000 shares, issued 750,000 shares................	$ 1,500,000		
Capital paid in in excess of stated value................	8,500,000		
	$10,000,000		
Retained earnings..................................	6,800,000	16,800,000	
		$17,800,000	

During the next year the following transactions occur:

(1) 250,000 shares of the unissued common stock are issued for cash at $45 per share.

(2) A two-for-one common stock split is performed. This is accomplished by reducing the stated value to $1 per share and by distributing 1,000,000 unissued shares to the present shareholders.

(3) A charter amendment is accomplished which authorizes an additional 1,000,000 shares of no-par common (no entry required).

(4) We acquire 100,000 shares of common stock for cash at $30 per share, to be held as treasury stock.

(5) We sell 50,000 shares of treasury stock for cash at $35 per share.

(6) We call in the preferred stock, in accordance with the written provisions of the issue, at a cash call price of $110.

(7) We issue 10,000 shares of $100 par, 6 percent preferred stock. To each share is attached a warrant to purchase one share of no-par common for $42. The warrants will expire in 5 years. The market value of a warrant is estimated to be $4. The shares, with warrants attached, are issued for cash at $105.

(8) Earnings retained during the year total $300,000 (no entry called for).

Required:

Prepare journal entries to record the numbered transactions and, in the form provided, present the stockholders' equity section as it stands at the end of the year.

TEST PROBLEM Solution Space

	Debit	*Credit*
(1)		
(2)		
(3)		
(4)		
(5)		
(6)		
(7)		
(8)		

Stockholders' equity:

Capital stock preferred—6 percent, $100 par........................ $

Capital paid in in excess of par....................................

Capital stock common, no par, stated value $1, authorized
3,000,000 shares issued 2,000,000 shares.............. $

Capital paid in in excess of stated value...............

Capital stock common—warrants....................

Retained earnings....................................

$

Less: Capital stock common in treasury at cost (50,000
shares)...

$

{ Chapter Ten }

Dividends and Reserves

What Is a True Dividend?

If we were to prepare a catalog of business transactions and financial terms that are thoroughly misunderstood by laymen, "dividend" should appear high on the list.

While a sole proprietorship and a partnership are made up of the individuals who contribute the capital, that is, the owners, this is emphatically not so in the case of a corporation. The corporation has legally constituted existence as an entity in its own right, quite separate from its owner-investors. The earnings of the sole proprietorship and of the partnership are legally earnings of the proprietors (sole proprietor or the partners), but the earnings of a corporation are legally earnings *of the corporation;* they do not become earnings of the investor-owners *until a true dividend is rendered.* A true dividend is rendered only when something is detached from the corporation and presented to the stockholders, and this transaction does not qualify as a true dividend to the extent that it reduces the stockholders' paid-in capital accounts.

In short, a true dividend (in double-entry style) has two facets: (1) The *stockholders are given something* (usually cash, but it can be in the form of other valuable assets such as merchandise or even a "promise to pay" cash sometime in the future); and (2) the *Retained Earnings* (or Income Summary) account is correspondingly *reduced*.

Thanks to the accounting method of depicting transactions, the series of accounting entries to record the declaration and payment of the classical cash dividend are as follows:

DECEMBER 15

Retained Earnings (or Income Summary, or Dividend Charges) 100,000
    Dividends Payable.   100,000
On December 15 the directors of our corporation meet and declare the regular quarterly cash dividend of $.25 per share on the 400,000 shares of $10 par common then outstanding; the dividend is payable on January 15 next, to those who are listed holders of shares (holders of record) on January 5.

JANUARY 15

Dividends Payable. 100,000
    Cash in Bank.   100,000
To record payment of cash dividend declared on December 15.

Note the two effects of the dividend in this example. First, an asset, cash in bank, is reduced (and given to the stockholders); second, retained earnings is reduced by the same amount. Also, take particular note of the fact that at the moment the directors declare the $100,000 dividend they create a current liability.

In some cases a corporation may own shares of stock in another corporation and, for a variety of reasons, the directors elect to distribute these shares to the company's stockholders instead of giving them cash. The entries are the same except that instead of Cash in Bank being credited on January 15, the credit is made to Investments or to Marketable Securities. This is a *true* property dividend.

On rare occasions, when a corporation is short of cash but wishes to make a dividend distribution which the stockholders will be able to convert into cash, the corporation mails promissory notes (scrip) to the stockholders for an amount of cash that is to be paid sometime later. Such a distribution qualifies as a true dividend since the corporation establishes a legal liability to pay the stockholders. Entries for such a declaration and ultimate payment are:

DECEMBER 15

Retained Earnings..	100,000	
Dividends Payable.......................................		100,000

To record declaration of dividend for which we will issue, on January 15, in the form of promises to pay the cash sum of $.25 per share.

JANUARY 15

Dividends Payable...	100,000	
Dividend Scrip Payable.................................		100,000

To record distribution of interest-bearing (or noninterest-bearing) scrip (notes payable) to stockholders (scrip to bear interest at 6% and to become due in 30 days).

FEBRUARY 14

Dividend Scrip Payable......................................	100,000	
Interest Expense..	500	
Cash in Bank...		100,000

Cash payment of maturing scrip plus 6% interest for 30 days.

Corporate Investment in Affiliated Company

Although in the preceding section the corporation was characterized as being a distinctly separate entity and, as a corollary, it was pointed out that earnings of a corporation are not concurrently or automatically earnings of the owners, this principle is routinely violated in modern accounting practice in one situation. This is where one corporation holds a majority interest (more than 50 percent) of the common stock of another corporation where the resources of these two affiliated corporations are not reported in combined form in a "consolidated" balance sheet. We'll look at the techniques of preparing consolidated statements later, but for the present let's assume that our dominant or "parent" corporation elects *not* to prepare fully consolidated statements. When such a choice is acceptable, the parent will merely publish its "legal" balance sheet and will show, as a noncurrent asset, its investment in the affiliate (known as a *subsidiary*).

To report the investment at its cost, however, is held to be inappropriate under the circumstances mentioned. Rather, it is preferred practice to accrue, as an increase (or decrease) in the investment account, the parent company's share of the earnings of the subsidiary, even though the subsidiary has not paid them to us in the form of dividends. When the earnings are then received from the subsidiary in the form of true dividends, the investment account is literally converted into cash to the extent of the dividend received. Assume, for example, that our corporation does the following:

(1) It buys 70 percent of the outstanding common stock of Subsidiary Corporation for $95,000; (2) at the end of the year Subsidiary reports earnings of $20,000 since the date of our company's investment; (3) lastly, next year Subsidiary pays a cash dividend of $15,000 and our corporation recognizes receipt of its 70 percent share. The entries on our corporation's books under the method that we have been considering are:

(1)

Investment in Subsidiary Corp.	95,000	
Cash in Bank.		95,000

Purchase of a 70% interest in the common stock of Subsidiary Corp. for cash.

(2)

Investment in Subsidiary Corp.	14,000	
Earnings of Subsidiary Corp.		14,000

To accrue as income our 70% share of the $20,000 of earnings recorded by Subsidiary Corp. this year since the date of our acquisition of Subsidiary Corp. common stock.

(3)

Cash in Bank.	10,500	
Investment in Subsidiary Corp.		10,500

To record receipt of cash dividend from Subsidiary Corp. and to treat this as conversion of part of our investment into cash since our share of Subsidiary Corp. earnings has already been accrued in entry (2).

The reasoning in support of this violation of the entity convention is that (1) Subsidiary Corp. is in a field of activity so foreign to that which we are in that to consolidate the statements of the two companies might produce misleading results; and (2) at the same time, the earnings strength of the affiliated companies may not be adequately disclosed unless the parent company's share of Subsidiary Corp. earnings is accrued on a current basis. More recently the Accounting Principles Board has prescribed this so-called *equity* procedure even where ownership is less than 50 percent if the "investor" is able to exercise significant influence over affairs of the "investee."

Liquidating "Dividends"

The term *dividend* is commonly applied to two classes of transactions to which it is not fully applicable. The first is the return of capital to the owners; the second, considered in the next section, is the stock dividend.

If we are to make good use of terms in accounting, we should be able to rely on the meaning intended by the user. Certainly most people who give it any thought at all think that when someone receives a dividend he earns some revenue or income. Clearly, though, there is no income where the corporation is undergoing partial or total dissolution and the stockholder is merely having his investment returned to him.

Entries on the books of the corporation when a liquidating dividend is paid fall in the following pattern:

(1)

Capital Paid In in Excess of Par.........................	25,000	
Capital Stock—Par......................................	75,000	
Cash in Bank.......................................		100,000

To record return of capital to stockholders, first by a reduction of "Excess of Par" to zero, then by a debit to Capital Stock—Par for the balance of the payout.

Payments in liquidation, improperly termed *liquidating dividends,* occur when the affairs of a corporation are being wound up and also in extractive industries that make an investment in a single venture with no intention of continuing actively when that venture (e.g., a mine of limited extent) is terminated.

Pseudo (Stock) Dividends

To illustrate what are known, misleadingly, as stock "dividends," let's start with an assumed stock equity section for our corporation as follows:

Capital stock, par $10, authorized 100,000 shares, issued 60,000......	$ 600,000
Capital paid in in excess of par................................	120,000
Retained earnings..	1,000,000
	$1,720,000

Now assume that our directors vote to "distribute" (what a poor word choice) a 50 percent stock dividend. First, understand clearly that 50 percent means that we shall issue new shares in quantity equal to 50 percent of the number of shares now outstanding. (Many people think the 50 percent means we'll use up 50 percent of the retained earnings.) Second, with an issue in excess of 20 to 25 percent, the *amount* can be any amount that the directors choose to record so long as it is no less than the par value (in this case $10 per share). If the issue is less than 20 to 25 percent, as we'll note next, we encounter certain restrictions.

If we now assume that the directors vote to capitalize for each new share issued $10 representing par, plus $2 per share to match the present "excess" account, or a total of $12 per share, the entry is:

```
Retained Earnings......................................  360,000
    Capital Stock—Par....................................           300,000
    Capital Paid In in Excess of Par.....................            60,000
To record issuance of a 50% stock dividend, or 30,000 shares,
capitalized at $12 per share to match the $10 par plus average $2
of excess over par from earlier issues.
```

If you analyze the above entry, you will recognize clearly that a stock dividend is in no sense of the word a true dividend. The corporation gives up absolutely nothing; the stockholders, individually and as a group, receive absolutely nothing but an additional piece of paper to represent exactly the same fractional ownership that they each held before the event. There are, however, two effects of stock dividends that may in some cases be quite significant. First, some retained earnings is wiped out as such and is established in a frozen state in the legal capital accounts. Since this eliminates the retained earnings (in our case $360,000) as a possible future source of dividend appropriation, perhaps some of the stockholders may be worse off as the result of the so-called dividend. Second, the market value of the stock should drop since we now have 90,000 rather than 60,000 shares representing exactly the same net assets. This second effect could improve the marketability of the stock because the price per share should drop about one-third.

In recent years it has become quite popular for certain "growth" companies to issue stock dividends of less than 10 percent; in fact, some companies started the practice of declaring "regular" stock dividends, even on a quarterly basis, of 2 percent or some similar amount. Undoubtedly the stockholders have believed that they are actually getting *paid* dividends of 2 percent per quarter while the corporation, at the same time, is enabled to retain its cash resources for expansion! These companies typically pay no cash dividend until they have attained their desired size (if ever). In some other companies, minor stock dividends are issued in order to accomplish a minor increase in cash dividend payout without having to change the traditional cash dividend per share. Thus, instead of increasing the cash dividend from $1 to $1.02 per share, the company presents each holder with two new shares of stock for each 100 held and continues to pay $1 per share.

It appears that the use of minor stock dividends may have been subject to abuse in view of the average stockholder's total ignorance of its significance. The trouble is that the market price of stock upon distribution of a 2 percent stock dividend should go down proportionately, but investor psychology (or ignorance) is such that the price is just about as likely to remain unchanged or even to rise. So, in order to put a damper on the excessive use of such "distributions" (and, believe it or not, brokers, financial writers, and other experts even use the word "payout" for a stock dividend), the Accounting Principles Board and the New York Stock Exchange, among others, have established the requirement (for the companies subject to their influence) that, when a stock dividend is under 20 to 25 percent, the corporation must capitalize an amount equal to the current market value per share. This, of course, can make a great difference in the amount of retained earnings that is frozen by the stock dividend action. Consider, for example, a corporation with a common stock par of $1.50 per share and a current market value of $75 per share.

A final word on stock dividends. Truly a stock dividend (particularly if it ranges above 25 percent in size) amounts to nothing more than a stock split with one added feature—the capitalization of retained earnings.

What Do Accountants Mean by "Reserves"?

My dictionary lists seven meanings for "reserve" used as a noun; of these, the one that addresses itself to financial matters says a reserve is "money or its equivalent kept in hand or set apart usually to meet liabilities." The first of the seven definitions leans in a similar direction, stating that a reserve is "something stored for future use." This is not what accountants have in mind.

For many decades accountants have made liberal use of "reserve" and for a comparable period of time the uninitiated reader has been totally confused. The upshot of all this is that now accountants, spurred by the American Institute's Committee on Terminology, have all but eliminated the confusing word from their vocabulary. In the next three sections we'll become acquainted with three different ways in which "reserve" formerly was used and will see what obedient accountants are now using in its place.

Contra Accounts Used to Be Called Reserves

As the annual reports from the companies whose stock you hold come rolling in, examine their balance sheets (we should now say statements of financial condition or position statements) to see if any show a reserve for depreciation or a reserve for uncollectibles. If so, the guilty company is probably a good, old-fashioned, conservative blue chip on which you suffered much less during the 1969–1970 bear market than you did with those that used modern terminology! Nevertheless, the obsolete term didn't contribute to the company's success, and the accountants should update their language. A reserve for depreciation is an expression, a measure, of the amount by which depreciation has been recognized in the accounts with respect to the related assets. In other words, a reserve for depreciation is a *subtraction* from depreciable assets; it's a representation of services that have been removed from the asset's original bundle. Far from being anything that has been set aside, a reserve for depreciation is, figuratively, a hole in an asset.

Numerous times in this book we have mentioned contra accounts—accounts that are used as negatives or as offsets to other accounts. This is precisely what every reserve for depreciation is—a contra account. So, also, is the reserve for uncollectibles or bad debts.

It's not exactly easy to find a satisfactory substitute for "reserve" where a contra account is involved, but perhaps "allowance" is the best one of the present candidates. Some companies show depreciable assets on the position statement followed by a subtraction simply labeled Accumulated Depreciation. This is not too bad, though some readers are bound to infer that the company has actually accumulated something. Can you "accumulate" a hole in the ground? In any case, I'm planning to use, and continue to use, Allowance for Depreciation and Allowance for Bad Debts whenever I mean to disclose the amounts that, in my accounting system, have been set up as offsets to my depreciable assets or to my accounts receivable.

Some Liabilities Used to Be
Called Reserves

One still occasionally sees such titles as Reserve for Federal Income Taxes, or Reserve for Product Warranties, in present-day position statements. Why? What do they mean?

In these cases the word "reserve" is probably used solely because the dollar amount involved is an estimate, an approximation. The accounts are, clearly, liabilities. The first signifies that we owe "some" income taxes, but the final definite amount due for this year has not yet been established. Also, we undoubtedly have some outstanding customer claims under our warranty agreements, but the sum of these claims is, at best, an educated guess. Does the fact that the amount of a liability is uncertain justify dodging a true liability title? Obviously not. Let's be candid. Correctly, these two titles should be changed to Estimated Liability for Federal Income Taxes and Estimated Liability under Warranty Agreements.

Another situation in which the confusing terminology has been used is in the case of accrued pension obligations. Here we have a tangled skein of accounting preferences and theories and a variety of uncertain actuarial calculations, sufficient to render the result quite speculative; but there is no justification for dodging the estimated liability label through use of a reserve.

In short, when you're tempted, because of the uncertainties of the situation, to call a liability a reserve, don't.

Retained Earnings May Be Reserved

Before becoming simon-pure, many of us chose to use the word "reserve" to designate reservations of retained earnings. It's a bit hard to determine just what is accomplished by such reservations but, in order to attain the ultimate in shunning a misleading term, let's even restrict it here.

A couple of examples of retained earnings reservations may be worth mentioning. First, the corporation laws of many of our states specify that, if a corporation holds any treasury stock, the retained earnings of that corporation, in an amount equal to the cost of the treasury stock, must be reserved; that is, this amount of retained earnings stands unavailable for dividend charges so long as the treasury stock remains on hand. Some companies make no entries in the Retained Earnings account and merely state, parenthetically in their positions statement, that so many dollars of retained earnings are restricted because of treasury stock holdings; other companies make explicit entries, somewhat as follows:

Retained Earnings.   xxx
    Retained Earnings Reserved for Treasury Stock.   xxx
To record reservation of retained earnings in amount equal to the cost of
stock now held in treasury.

Note that such an entry reserves retained earnings but it still avoids the outright use of a reserve; there is no Reserve for Treasury Stock.

In summary, with respect to reserves in general, we may conclude that the title is a dead one. Don't use it at all under any conditions. If you have an account which nobody can explain, don't resort to the old dodge of calling it a reserve; get rid of it some way and stick to accounts that are clearly understood.

Deferred Credits When in Doubt

Accountants need a convenient receptacle or two into which they can deposit (dump or hide?) certain debits and credits which they don't clearly understand. One of the modern favorite dumping sites is under the caption, Deferred Credits. But, let's back up a minute.

When you were introduced to the statement of financial condition, the position statement, you were quite willing to accept the proposition that the formal financial structure of any business enterprise consists of two coequal quantums—the aggregate of assets expressed as a dollar total and the aggregate of equities expressed as a dollar total, with the latter in turn made up of amounts due to creditors and the residual, or amount assigned to the owners. To cut through the verbiage, let's just say that one side of the financial coin consists of all the assets of the enterprise while the opposite side shows the allocation of the very same total as between amounts owed to outsiders and the amount left over, known as the *owner's equity*. "Assets" equal "equities."

Then, what in the devil is a deferred credit? They always appear on the equities side of the balance sheet, but do they then represent claims other than those of outsiders and insiders? Perhaps there's life on Mars after all!

Here are some typical deferred credits. The *Friday Monthly Post* collects subscriptions, running from 1 to 3 years in advance, totaling $100,000. Their accountant makes the following entry:

(1)

Cash in Bank   100,000
    Deferred Subscription Income   100,000
To record collections from subscriptions during month of June.

How do you like that entry?

Well, the debit title is OK and we must assume the dollar amounts are correct (though most of us are suspicious of "round" numbers), but in his excitement the accountant stumbles all over himself in coining the credit title. He realizes that, in exchange for the $100,000 cash received, his company is obligated to deliver 12 monthly copies per year to each subscriber. As each monthly batch of magazines is sent out, the company "earns" one-twelfth of the amount it has collected on each annual subscription. So, as deliveries are made the accountant will make the following entry:

(2)

Deferred Subscription Income   xxx
    Subscription Revenue   xxx
To recognize revenue earned by delivery of magazines against subscriptions collected in advance.

Quite obviously the $100,000 collected and recorded in entry 1 is not yet revenue, but *it becomes revenue* as deliveries are made. Thus, the accountant reasons, the $100,000 initially is "deferred" revenue (surely not "income"). But, he then flunks the course by failing to recognize that, when trusting people have put a wad of money in your hands in the expectation of receiving future services, you have a simple, old-fashioned *liability*.

Most so-called *deferred credits* will turn out to be liabilities if properly analyzed. Think, for example, of advance collections of insurance premiums, club dues, telephone service charges, and a host of similar transactions

A few deferred credits, on the other hand, are actually asset contras. One large factoring company, in buying notes receivable from automobile dealers, recorded the purchase transaction essentially as follows: (The inserted percentage figures merely signify amounts).

        Notes Receivable—Face 100%
            Cash in Bank 92%
            Deferred Discount Revenue 8%

In this situation the finance company will collect 100 percent (plus interest) from the customer at maturity and, since the company paid only 92 percent face for the notes taken over, the balancing 8 percent becomes a gain, or revenue, from the factoring operation. But, is there no better place than a Deferred Credits section of the balance sheet in which to report the unearned discount? Of course there is. The company paid 92 percent for this batch of notes because at this time the notes have a value of 92 percent of face. The proper conclusion, then, is to show the discount of 8 percent as a contra (subtraction) from the notes receivable on the balance sheet.

TEST PROBLEM

At its meeting on March 15, the directors of Our Company declare a 10 percent stock dividend which is distributed on April 15. Also at the meeting the directors ask the accountant to establish two retained earnings reserves of $100,000 each: a reserve for possible fire losses and a reserve for general contingencies. At the date of the director's meeting, the stockholders' equity section of the position statement stands as shown below. At the time of the stock distribution, the current market value is $25 per share.

        Stockholder's equity:
            Capital stock common, par $5 . . . . $1,000,000
            Capital in excess of par 500 000
            Retained earnings   750,000
                                                                               $2,250,000

Required:

Give journal entries to record the reservations of retained earnings and the issuance of the dividend shares.

TEST PROBLEM Solution Space

Debit   *Credit*

MARCH 15

APRIL 15

Chapter Eleven

Long-term Debt

Why Go in Debt?

As individuals most of us shun debt. We worry about the size of the national debt and fret over the charge accounts our wives propagate. But, actually, if one really makes a science of it, isn't it possible for debt to be a thoroughly useful, profitable instrument of financial management?

One can readily think of at least four solid reasons for going into debt.

First, it is unbelievable that an enterprise of any size would pay cash on the spot for everything it buys; in fact, it would be virtually impossible to avoid getting in debt to the employees of the company. Debt, particularly the short-term variety, is a great *convenience*.

Wages are paid at weekly intervals, vendors' invoices are accumulated and paid monthly, etc. But this is true primarily of interest-free short-term debt. Why does a company incur long-term debt?

Very often long-term debt is incurred to provide the company with more working capital. So often we find that when the business is growing—just as everything seems to be going well—we're short of cash.

What has happened is that we've increased our sales and, at the same time, we've gone into the lending business ourselves by allowing our customers to open charge accounts (which earn no interest!); and with the growth of business we must carry more inventories (which earn no interest!). If we're running a family-owned corporation, we refuse to raise money by selling stock to outsiders; so we must either get long-term bank loans or issue bonds. In other words, long-term debt becomes a *necessity*. Even if our company is not closely held, we may not wish to increase the amount of common stock outstanding because market conditions are unfavorable.

Perhaps the most popular reason for long-term debt financing is covered by the word "leverage." This is the more modern term for what used to be called *trading on the equity,* and all it means is that you borrow somebody's money at an interest rate which is lower than the rate which you can earn on that money. If, for example, you can borrow a million dollars for a year at 8 percent and can employ the million dollars so that it produces a return of 10 percent, you should be a net gainer (before taxes) of 2 percent. This is the strategy used by so many corporations to enhance the earnings rate on the common stock equity. Thus, if our company has assets of $2,000,000 which earn 10 percent and if half of our funds have come from an 8 percent bond issue, the earnings of our stockholders will amount to 10 percent on the $1,000,000 that they invested plus 2 percent leverage gain on the bonds, for a total of 12 percent. One should not overdo a good thing, however. If, for instance, the financial structure of this company were made up of 10 percent equity ($200,000 of capital stock) and 90 percent debt ($1,800,000 of 8 percent bonds), the return on common stock would skyrocket to 10 percent of $200,000 (or $20,000) plus 2 percent of $1,800,000 (or $36,000) for a total of $56,000 divided by $200,000, or 28 percent. This would be known as a "thin" equity position. The net income before interest charges would be 10 percent of $2,000,000, or $200,000, which covers the $144,000 interest requirement, but the margin of coverage is not sufficient to assure the bondholders of being paid during hard times. In other words, the thinner the equity, the more risky the situation; and the determination of how far to go with leverage requires exercise of managerial intelligence.

The final reason for the popularity of long-term debt is that your interest charges are legitimate deductions on your tax return. Thus, with a corporate tax rate of approximately 50 percent, the net cost of the interest payments is only half of the gross cost. That is, for every $1 of interest that you pay out you save $.50 of income taxes (providing, of course, that you are operating at a profit). This fact alone accounts for a great deal of the long-term debt. Some banks, for example, (though they might deny it) issue bonds (debentures) on which they must pay 8 percent interest and invest the funds in tax-exempt municipal bonds on which they earn only 5 percent. Since the 8 percent interest has a net cost of about half that much and the 5 percent is nontaxable, the bank earns a net of approximately 1 percent on the borrowed funds. It should be added that the tax collectors are keeping an eye on such operations.

Long-term debt takes many different forms though, basically, the principles are the same. Since this is a book on accounting rather than corporation finance, let's take a look at some of the debt forms and examine them by the method of *accounting analysis,* that is, by reducing them to journal entry form.

Installment Purchases

It seems quite unlikely that there is anybody old enough to read this material who hasn't at some time participated in an installment purchase. Because of the risk of running afoul of legal technicalities, let's not attempt to define our terms too precisely. As I understand it, when you buy something under an installment contract you make periodic (monthly) payments of equal amount that apply first to accumulated interest and then to the principal of your debt, and you don't obtain legal title to the thing until you've made your final payment.

We can't afford much space on any of these forms of debt, so let's go directly to an example and journalize enough of it to be sure we fully understand it.

Our company buys a machine at a list price of $12,000, under an installment contract which calls for a down payment of $2,000 and quarterly payments of $500 including interest at 10 percent per annum. The machine is delivered and the contract signed on September 1. The entries through the first three payments are as follows:

SEPTEMBER 1, 19X1

Machinery...	10,000	
Cash in Bank...		2,000
Installment Contract Payable...........................		8,000
(Explanation of terms)		

DECEMBER 1, 19X1

Interest Expense..	200	
Installment Contract Payable.............................	300	
Cash in Bank.......................................		500

Payment of first quarterly installment of $500, of which $200 pays the interest up to date, leaving $300 applicable to the debt itself.

DECEMBER 31, 19X1

Interest Expense..	64	
Interest Accrued Payable.............................		64

To accrue unpaid interest, for purposes of end-of-year financial statements, at 10% on balance of debt ($7,700) for one month (rounded to nearest dollar).

MARCH 1, 19X2

Interest Accrued Payable..................................	64	
Interest Expense..	128	
Installment Contract Payable.............................	308	
Cash in Bank.......................................		500

Payment of interest accrued on December 31, and interest for January and February, and balance of $308 on debt.

JUNE 1, 19X2

Interest Expense..	185	
Installment Contract Payable.............................	315	
Cash in Bank.......................................		500

Payment of interest for 3 months on contract balance of $7,392, and payment of $315 on debt.

There's no point in continuing the journal entries through final payment. Needless to say, the debt would finally be paid off through the installments that include a bit less interest expense each quarter as the principal of the debt diminishes. The final payment would undoubtedly be some odd figure necessary to pay a very small amount of interest and the balance of the debt. Incidentally, you will occasionally hear someone say that when you are paying off a debt in installments you are "amortizing" it.

Leases and Sale-and-leaseback Transactions

We all know that to lease something is the equivalent of renting something—except that a lease implies the signing of a contract to pay the agreed-upon periodic rental for a minimum number of periods, usually a year or more. From the accounting standpoint the recording of the performance of such contracts would be easy if it were not for the fact that the lawyers and others have figured out ways to complicate matters. In the absence of complications, our periodic entry is merely to debit Rent Expense and credit Cash in Bank for the contractual amount.

Actually, there are only two complications of importance. First, if the lease is noncancelable, it has some of the earmarks of a long-term debt; in fact, if we add certain other features, it becomes almost impossible to determine whether you are dealing with a lease or whether the transaction is in actuality an installment purchase.

Some accountants (a minority) argue that any noncancelable lease, because it is a promise to pay a periodic series of fixed amounts, is nothing less than a debt from the start. They want you to show the sum of the payments to be made in the future as a long-term liability and to show the same amount on the other side of the position statement as an asset. Note one important qualification: We aren't merely to use the sum of the future payments; rather, we find the *discounted, present value* of those payments and show it on both sides of the position statement. These accountants argue that you have a fixed obligation (and a valuable right of occupancy) and that they can only be disclosed effectively if they are entered in the position statement. At the risk of oversimplification, I'm going to "destroy" this position by asserting that, although you have an obligation to pay the series of rents, you have no true liability for any one of them until you have received the service (the occupancy for one month, etc.). You are dealing with an "executory" contract, which essentially means you have agreed to buy a series of services one at a time; in spite of your inflexible agreement, you don't actually owe for any one of the services until it is delivered to you. Conclusion: Don't do what these folks recommend. Treat the lease exactly as you would a common rental, but be sure to *disclose* any significant terms of the lease in a footnote to your statements.

Now, there are certain features that may be written into a lease which can make us believe it is actually an installment purchase. For instance, if the agreement includes an option to buy the item at much less than its fair value at the end of the lease, doesn't this imply pretty clearly that you will effectively purchase the asset during the initial term of the lease? Or, if the agreement includes an option to extend or renew the lease after it first runs out, and if the extended period covers the remaining useful life of the asset at a rental that is substantially less than the fair rental value, doesn't this also imply that you actually are *paying for the asset* during the initial term on the lease? The guiding rule nowadays is that we must interpret an agreement as an installment purchase, rather than as a lease, if either of these conditions is present.

An interesting complication appears where a company, by prior agreement, (1) buys or constructs a building or other asset, (2) sells the asset to another company (a subsidiary?), and (3) immediately leases the asset back. This is a *sale and leaseback*. The point of the whole thing is that whether the sale was made at a profit or at a loss, it is generally assumed that such gain or loss is all part of the sale-and-leaseback plan and is really just a fiction because the parties to the contract are not likely to have an arm's-length relationship. This brings the Accounting Principles Board of the American Institute of Certified Public Accountants to the conclusion that the gain or loss should not be recognized as such in the year of the sale but should be prorated over the life of the lease. Thus, if a lease calls for rental payments of $12,000 per year for 20 years and if the lessee (occupant) built the asset for $100,000 and sold it to the lessor for $120,000, then the $20,000 of gain would be recognized at the rate of $1,000 per year which, in effect, produces a net rental cost of $11,000 per year. In journal form the entries to depict this deal are:

(1)

Building..	100,000	
Cash, etc.......................................		100,000
To record cost of constructing (or buying) a building.		

(2)

Cash..	120,000	
Building.......................................		100,000
Deferred Gain on Sale of Building....................		20,000
To record sale of building to subsidiary.		

(3)

Rent Expense..	12,000	
Cash..		12,000
Rent payment for first year.		

(4)

Deferred Gain on Sale of Building.......................	1,000	
Rent Expense...................................		1,000
Portion of gain recognized in first year.		

As we leave this subject, I hope you won't ask me what kind of an account is Deferred Gain on Sale of Building. Frankly, I don't know.

For a final subtopic on leases, note that some companies practice what has come to be known as *off-balance-sheet financing*. The major (parent) company establishes a satellite corporation (a subsidiary) and owns all its stock in exchange for cash or other assets. The subsidiary issues bonds or other debt and constructs or buys an asset which, by prearrangement, it will lease to the parent corporation. The subsidiary pledges the lease proceeds as security for the bonds or other form of debt so that, in a sense, the parent company is really the guarantor of the subsidiary's debt. By following this procedure the parent has use of the asset but the debt incurred to buy the asset does not show on the parent's position statement—*unless it prepares a consolidated position statement.* The fact is that the Accounting Principles Board calls for the preparation of a consolidated statement under these circumstances. (We'll look at the subject of consolidations in Chapter 17, but for the present will merely assume that a consolidated statement is essentially one that combines the statements of two or more affiliated companies.)

Long-term Notes

Possibly the most common form of long-term (more than one year) debt consists of borrowing from banks, insurance companies, pension funds, and other institutional sources on the basis of a promissory note, with a specified maturity date. A well-known variation of this is the so-called *line of credit* with a bank, whereby the borrower is extended the right to draw funds at will, up to an agreed-upon maximum, and to repay them at will. Under the line-of-credit plan the borrower will be charged a modest rate of interest on the unused portion of the available funds.

One cost-producing feature of borrowing from banks is the common requirement that if a company borrows, say, $100,000 at a stipulated interest rate, no more than $80,000 will actually be withdrawn; in other words, a "compensating balance" equal to a stated fraction of the loan must be left unused even though interest is paid on it. A typical fraction is 20 percent.

Accounting for long-term borrowing via promissory note presents no special problems. The interest costs of the loan should, of course, be recognized on an accrual basis.

Mortgage Loans

A mortgage loan, commonly referred to as a *mortgage payable,* consists simply of a long-term note which is backed by a mortgage on real or personal property. Where the security is personal property, the mortgage is called a *chattel mortgage*. Essentially, the mortgage itself is a document that lists the provisions of the loan and what will happen in the event of default. If the borrower does fail to comply with the mortgage provisions, title to the property is transferred to the lender, though the defaulting party may be entitled to recover the property (his so-called *equity in redemption*) if he makes good within a year. (See your lawyer for further information on this subject.) Mortgage notes are customarily paid off in regular monthly installments including interest.

Mortgage and Debenture Bonds

A bond is, again, a form of note payable with a definite maturity date except where callable "by lot." A debenture bond provides no collateral security; that is, the general credit of the company constitutes the security. A mortgage bond is backed by a mortgage on some or all of the real estate of the company.

Bonds commonly are issued in $1,000 denominations and are quoted in the bond market at prices which fluctuate with changes in the financial condition of the company and with changes in the bond market. The bond market responds continuously to fluctuations in market rates of interest. For example, if we issue a series of 6 percent, 20-year bonds at par (that is, in a 6 percent market) and later the prime interest rate (a somewhat mythical interest rate which big New York banks charge their "prime" customers for loans) rises to 7 percent, then our 6 percent bonds will be attractive only if they can be bought at a discount. To explain further, a 6 percent bond is a $1,000 bond which pays $30 of cash interest each 6 months, for a total of $60, or 6 percent per year. Because the amount of cash interest cannot conveniently be varied from year to year as the market rate of interest fluctuates, the value of the bond itself fluctuates, with the result that a buyer will pay for the bond an amount above par (premium) or below par (discount) which will result in his earning whatever rate is necessary, provided he holds the bond until it matures.

Let's issue some bonds at par, some at a premium, and some at a discount. For an example, assume that our company issues $100,000 in 7 percent, 20-year, first-mortgage bonds (1) at par, (2) at a premium which will produce a true yield rate of 6 percent, and (3) at a discount which will produce a true yield rate of 8 percent. For each alternative the entries on our books through the first two years are shown below. Assume in each case that we issue the bonds on January 1 and that interest is paid through the use of coupons.

(1) ISSUE AT PAR
JANUARY 1, 19X1

Cash...	100,000	
Bonds Payable......................................		100,000
To record issue at par.		

JULY 1, 19X1

Bond Interest Expense.................................	3,500	
Cash..		3,500
To record payment of first interest coupons.		

DECEMBER 31, 19X1

Bond Interest Expense.................................	3,500	
Bond Interest Payable..............................		3,500
To accrue interest from date of last payment to end of year.		

JANUARY 1, 19X2

Bond Interest Payable.................................	3,500	
Cash in Bank..		3,500
Payment of second interest coupons.		

JULY 1, 19X2

Bond Interest Expense.................................	3,500	
Cash in Bank..		3,500
Payment of third interest coupons.		

DECEMBER 31, 19X2

Bond Interest Expense.................................	3,500	
Bond Interest Payable..............................		3,500
Accrual of interest for fourth 6-month period.		

At maturity, we merely debit Bonds Payable and credit Cash in Bank for repayment of the $100,000 borrowed initially.

(2) ISSUE AT A PREMIUM
JANUARY 1, 19X1

Cash...	111,557	
Bonds Payable......................................		100,000
Bonds Payable—Premium..........................		11,557
To record issue of 7 percent, 20-year bonds at a price (premium) which will provide a true earning rate of 6 percent to holder to maturity.		

JULY 1, 19X1

Bond Interest Expense...................................	3,500	
Cash in Bank......................................		3,500

Payment of first interest coupons

Bonds Payable—Premium..............................	289	
Bond Interest Expense.............................		289

To amortize one-fortieth of the initial bond premium as a reduction, or offset to our interest expense, since we will repay only par to the lender at maturity.

DECEMBER 31, 19X1

Bond Interest Expense...................................	3,500	
Bond Interest Payable.............................		3,500

Accrual of interest to year-end.

Bonds Payable—Premium..............................	289	
Bond Interest Expense.............................		289

Same as entry on July 1.

JANUARY 1, 19X2

Bond Interest Payable..................................	3,500	
Cash in Bank......................................		3,500

Payment of second coupons.

JULY 1, 19X2

Bond Interest Expense...................................	3,500	
Cash in Bank......................................		3,500

Payment of coupon 3.

Bonds Payable—Premium..............................	289	
Bond Interest Expense.............................		289

Amortization of one-fortieth of initial premium.

DECEMBER 31, 19X2

Bonds Payable—Premium..............................	289	
Bond Interest Expense..................................	3,211	
Bond Interest Payable.............................		3,500

Same as December 31, 19X1, with entries combined.

The logic of the entries for the bond issued at a premium should be clear to you. Because the bonds pay an excessively high *cash* interest, the lenders are willing to pay us a premium of $11,557 which they will never get back, and the result is that they effectively earn only 6 percent rather than the "nominal" 7 percent. We, in turn, spread the $11,557 evenly over the life of the bond as a sort of gain but, more accurately, as an offset to our cash interest cost.

(3) ISSUE AT A DISCOUNT
JANUARY 1, 19X1

Cash...	90,104	
Bonds Payable—Discount...............................	9,896	
Bonds Payable.......................................		100,000

To record issue of 7 percent bonds at discount of $9,896, which will provide lender with a true earning rate of 8 percent if held to maturity when he is repaid the full $100,000.

JULY 1, 19X1

Bond Interest Expense...................................	3,500	
Cash in Bank.......................................		3,500

Payment of coupon 1.

Bond Interest Expense...................................	247	
Bonds Payable—Discount.............................		247

To accumulate one-fortieth of the original discount as an addition to interest expense, because at maturity lender must be paid amount borrowed ($90,104) plus the discount ($9,896) for a total of $100,000.

DECEMBER 31, 19X1

Bond Interest Expense...................................	3,500	
Bond Interest Accrued Payable.......................		3,500

To accrue coupon 2.

Bond Interest Expense...................................	247	
Bonds Payable—Discount.............................		247

To accumulate one-fortieth of the discount to be paid at maturity.

JANUARY 1, 19X2

Bond Interest Accrued Payable...........................	3,500	
Cash in Bank.......................................		3,500

Payment of coupon 2.

JULY 31, 19X2

Bond Interest Expense...................................	3,500	
Cash in Bank.......................................		3,500

Payment of coupon 3.

Bond Interest Expense...................................	247	
Bonds Payable—Discount.............................		247

To accumulate one-fortieth of the discount.

DECEMBER 31, 19X2

Bond Interest Expense...................................	3,747	
Bond Interest Accrued Payable.......................		3,500
Bonds Payable—Discount.............................		247

To accrue coupon 4 and accumulate one-fortieth of the discount. (This again illustrates use of a combined journal entry).

At the end of the second year, as we have recorded the bond issue and interest expense under three different assumptions, the bonds would be displayed in the position statement as follows:

(1) Par:		(2) Premium:		(3) Discount:	
Bonds		Bonds		Bonds	
payable—par	$100,000	payable—par	$100,000	payable—par	$100,000
		Bonds		Bonds	
		payable—		payable—	
		premium....	10,401	discount.....	8,908
			$110,401		$ 91,092

A couple more comments should be made concerning bonds issued at odd prices. First, bond discount is a contra account. It measures the difference between the maturity value of the bonds (par) and their present book value (initially, the amount borrowed). Some old-time accountants still believe bond discount is prepaid interest, a logical impossibility, and they insist on showing it as an asset. Second, bond premium is an "adjunct" to bonds payable—to show the effective amount of debt at any given time, it must be added to the face amount of the bonds. Some old-fashioned accountants classify bond premium as a *deferred credit*—a monstrosity.

Finally, we could use the true interest rate (also known as the *yield rate* or the *effective rate*) in recording the interest expense each period and our results would be more accurate. Instead, we have used the simpler straight-line procedure. The Accounting Principles Board currently is displaying increased interest in the effective-rate procedure.

Convertible Bonds

When the market rate of interest for debenture bonds issued by a company with our credit standing is around 8½ percent and our common stock is being traded in the market at around 35, we elect to issue 20-year *convertible* bonds with a 6 percent coupon and with the proviso that the buyers can trade the bonds in for common stock at the exchange ratio of one share of common for each $40 of bond principal. The bonds can be "called" by us after 5 years, at 105 per 100. (Bonds are always quoted at so much per 100 of par.)

Needless to say, nobody will pay us par for a 6 percent bond if the market says we must pay 8½ percent, but they might pay us par for a 6 percent bond if the bond also carries the privilege of being converted into our common stock whenever the bondholder wants to. In other words, we can get by with a significantly lower interest payment until the price of our stock rises to a point where the bondholder would gain by exercising his option to convert; all of this assumes, of course, that the market has real hope of a surge in the market value of our common stock.

From the investor's point of view, a convertible bond has a certain attraction. The investor stands able to "get a piece of the action" if the value of our stock rises above 40; on the other hand, should the value of our stock tumble, he will not lose heavily because the market value of his bond will fall only to the point where its effective yield is approximately 8½ percent. The convertible bond, thus, has an unlimited ceiling in value and, at the same time, a floor which limits the size of the possible loss.

Entries to record the issue of convertible bonds are made exactly like those to issue regular bonds. If and when some or all of the bonds are converted into common stock, the form of the entry is as follows:

```
Bonds Payable—Par..........................................    1,000
     Capital Stock—Common—Par $10.........................         250
     Capital Paid In in Excess of Par.........................         750
To record conversion of bond into 25 shares of common stock on the
basis of 1 share for each $40 of bond.
```

It has been estimated that about one-third of the bond issues in recent years have been convertibles.

Bonds with Warrants Attached

In some cases a company issue bonds which carry warrants that can be detached and turned in for common stock at a specified price. To illustrate, assume that we issue a series of 6 percent bonds, each with a warrant to buy one share of our stock at $40, and that our stock is currently trading at around $35. The Accounting Principles Board has held, wisely, that we are really issuing two securities rather than one; we're issuing a bond plus a warrant. If we issue the package at par, since part of the proceeds is attributable to the warrant, the bond itself is actually being issued at a discount. The question then is: How do we allocate the proceeds as between the two securities? Common sense suggests that we should attribute to the bond an amount which would give it a true yield commensurate with our credit standing, say,

8 percent and attribute the remainder to the warrant. To illustrate, assume that the bond provisions are as just described and that the common stock is trading at $35. The entry to record this bond-and-warrant issue for $1,000 would then be:

```
Cash...............................................  1,000
Bonds Payable—Discount................................    20
     Bond Payable—Par......................................       1,000
     Common Stock Warrant Outstanding......................          20
```
To record 20-year bond issued at discount to provide 8% yield and to attribute remainder of $1,000 to the warrant. A 6% bond priced to yield 8% in 20 years is $980, or at a discount of $20 which we attribute to the warrant. (Were the package issued at more or less than $1,000, the procedure would be the same; assign a fair value to the bond and the balance to the warrant.)

In the position statement the common stock warrants should be shown in the stockholders' equity section.

TEST PROBLEM

Our Company issues $100,000 in 20-year, 7 percent debenture bonds with warrants attached that provide for purchase of one share of our $10 par common stock at $20 per share. Each bond carries one warrant. Without warrants, our bonds would have to carry 9 percent interest coupons to be salable at par, so the bond portion of the package is determined to amount to $81,598. The bonds and warrants are sold to a bank for $97,000.

Required:

Journal entries (1) to issue the package; (2) to pay interest at the end of the first 6 months: (3) to record exercise of all the warrants.

TEST PROBLEM Solution Space

Debit   *Credit*

(1)

To record issue of 100 par $1,000 bonds, each with one warrant to buy one share of $10 par common stock for $20.

(2)

To record payment of coupon 1.

(3)

To record issue of 100 shares of common stock at $20 cash plus one warrant per share.

{ Chapter Twelve }

Basic Cost Accounting

What Is Cost Accounting?

Actually cost accounting is not a separate area of accounting, but because it employs a few technical words and procedures of its own we often think of cost accountants as somewhat separate from the so-called *financial accountants*.

The cost accountants specialize in finding the "cost of" products that we make, or the cost of operating a department within the manufacturing area of the company. In more recent years the talents of the cost accountants have been applied more and more to finding the costs of nonmanufacturing departments as well. For example, cost accountants now do a lot more cost accounting in banks and insurance companies, where there is no product output in the physical sense, and also work in the areas of selling and administrative expenses as well as in the manufacturing area.

What Are the Purposes of Cost Accounting?

There are three well-recognized purposes of cost accounting. The first, which is routine, is to help in the process of *determining the income* of any given accounting period. This consists primarily of determining the manufacturing costs and the amounts assignable to end-of-period inventories, so that we can compute the cost of goods sold. When the company makes a variety of products, the determination of the manufacturing costs of each kind of product and the cost of goods sold for each class of product is no simple task.

A second and tremendously important responsibility of cost accounting (and, again a routine one) is to assist in *cost minimization*. By this we of course mean minimizing cost while still accomplishing the production and sales objectives of the company each period. The cost accounting devices that are specifically aimed at cost minimization are such things as standard costs, flexible budgets, and responsibility accounting. We'll look into these later.

The third major contribution of cost accounting is to assist management in *making decisions* where costs are a factor (aren't they always?). Most of these are ad hoc decisions—decisions which call for special studies and intelligent selection of cost factors relevant to the decision.

In the present chapter we'll concentrate mostly on the first purpose— the routine job of income determination. We're concerned here about assigning costs to departments, reassigning the costs of service departments to producing departments, and then applying those costs to the product output, so that we can determine the cost of goods sold and its complement, the cost of goods remaining in inventory. This whole chapter will be devoted to what is usually called "historical" or "actual" cost accounting—in contrast with "standard" cost accounting which we'll investigate later.

Job Order versus Process Cost Accounting

Although the distinction is not always clearly defined, it is customary to recognize two general kinds of actual cost accounting. One is known universally as *job order* and the other is *process*. Job order means that the company makes things that are, usually, designed specially to a customer's order. A good example would be the construction of houses, where each is designed by an architect to comply with the wishes of the buyer. Here each job is a separate project and one would, of course, keep a separate cost account for each. There are many examples of job-order manufacture though, obviously, they are not mass-production industries. On the other hand, an individual "job" may call for production of any number of identical products. The key feature of job-order cost accounting, then, is that we must keep a cost sheet for each job and be sure to record on each cost sheet all the costs we incur that are chargeable to that job.

Process-cost accounting is applied in situations where one or more products are being manufactured on a more or less continuous schedule. Here, rather than find the cost of each unit separately, we accumulate our costs for a period of time (often for a month) and then divide the total cost for the period by the number of product units to get an average unit cost. In job-order situations the product is usually made to order and is not held in storage for future sale; in process situations commonly we manufacture finished goods that are stored for future sale.

Needless to say, many manufacturing situations represent a mixture of job-order and process activity; and hybrid accounting techniques are then applied to determine costs of manufacture, inventories, and costs of goods sold. In general, where there is room for choice, the simpler costing procedure seems to be in process-cost accounting; when a choice exists, one should probably lean toward process-cost rather than job-order accounting procedures.

In the sections that follow, we'll try to describe and illustrate the "actual" cost procedures in accounting for raw materials, direct labor, and finally factory overhead under job-order and process-cost conditions.

Use of Subsidiary Ledgers

In job-order cost accounting raw materials, as they are purchased, are charged to a raw materials account in our general ledger. Because a manufacturing company may use a great number of raw material items, it is necessary to do some extremely detailed accounting in order to keep track of the raw materials purchased, used, and remaining in inventory at a given point in time. So far we have been examining transactions through the accounting procedures that lead to your periodic financial statements and we've been making debits and credits to *general ledger* accounts only. But, what would happen if we made debits for every kind of raw material to the same general ledger account? Wouldn't that account become a genuine mess? Suppose we consume 3,000 different raw material items, could we ever record them in a single ledger account and hope to tell later from that account how much we've bought of each? Used of each? And have left over of each? Clearly not, so we must find some escape—and the escape is to use subsidiary ledger accounts.

Here's how. As raw materials are purchased, the cost of all of them is debited to a single Raw Materials account in the general ledger. (Credits are made to Accounts Payable.) We don't need to make an entry in the Raw Materials account each time we buy some. We can delay making this entry until the end of each month and then record it as a grand total, just so the account will be brought up to date for statement purposes. *But,* let's systematically record *each* purchase of raw material on a card form (with a separate card for each kind of stuff we buy), and let's make entries on these cards the moment we receive and accept a batch of raw material. Therefore, if we stock 3,000 different kinds of raw materials, we'll have 3,000 such cards, and we'll call them our *subsidiary ledger* for raw materials.

Each of the subsidiary ledger cards needs three columns: one to show debits for purchases, the second to show credits for materials issued as authorized by our requisition system, and the third to show our "running balance" of the item. Hence, at any time we should be able to go through our raw materials subsidiary ledger cards and find out the complete story of each kind of material that we use. On the other hand if we're concerned only with our total (for financial statement purposes), we find this in our regular, general ledger account for raw materials which is posted up-to-date through monthly journal entries that record debits for all the raw materials purchased and credits for all the raw materials requisitioned. If you've followed me, you will recognize that at the end of the month we could take an adding machine tape of the balances of the raw materials subsidiary accounts, and its total should agree with the balance of the general ledger "control" account for raw materials. It may be appropriate at this time to point out that most of the accounts in our general ledger are control accounts—each receiving aggregate rather than detailed debits and credits, and each being "supported" by a set of cards (or other specially designed forms) on which we keep track of details just as is done with raw materials. Each set of supporting forms is known as a *subsidiary ledger*. (Accountants usually call them *subledgers*.) Control and subsidiary accounts are used very extensively in cost accounting, as we shall see.

Raw Materials Cost Accounting

When raw materials are purchased (have been received, examined, and found to be acceptable), the quantities and dollar amounts of each kind are immediately posted in the received (debit) columns of the raw materials subledger accounts. As each entry is made in a subledger card, the third (balance) column is also updated to show the revised quantity on hand and dollar balance. These entries are the same whether we are operating under a process or a job-order accounting system. The technical accounting can be depicted in the following journal entry:

Raw Materials—Control (end of month only)...................... xxx
  (also to subsidiary ledger cards in detail as each purchase is made)
     Accounts Payable—Control (end of month only)................ xxx
      (also to subsidiary ledger accounts in detail as each purchase is made)
To record purchases of raw materials during a given month.

Employees are allowed to draw raw materials from the storeroom upon presenting a "requisition," which has been signed by someone in authority and which identifies the job or department to be charged. As currently as feasible, the quantity of each raw material shown on each requisition is "priced" and entered in the issued (credit) column of the appropriate subsidiary ledger card. Pricing is done by looking at the appropriate subsidiary ledger card to see what the particular raw material cost per unit is. (This cost may be determined on an average-cost basis or on a FIFO basis.) Regardless of whether we are using job-order or process costing, the credit entries to withdraw raw materials from stores are the same. At the end of the month the requisitions are totaled and one aggregate credit entry is made to the general ledger control account.

The debit entries made to record consumption of raw materials do depend upon the type of cost accounting. If we are in a process-cost situation, the debit is made against the department (which we may call simply the *process*) that called for the materials. Assume that we make a product which is homogeneous and which is manufactured in a continuous flow through processes known as Cooking, Decorating, and Packaging. Pro forma entries to depict a month's raw materials issuances would be as follows:

Cooking Process.. xx
Decorating Process... xx
Packaging Process... xx
    Raw Materials—Control...................................... xx
    (and subledger accounts)
To record June consumption of raw materials by our three departments.

The three accounts debited in the entry shown above would also, in a sense, be control accounts because we would surely want to maintain detailed information on the costs incurred by each process. Such detail is generally kept on what might be called *process cost sheets* which would be specially designed for every company. At the least, a process cost sheet would have three debit columns—one (or more) each for the costs of raw materials, labor, and factory overhead costs.

Under job-order cost circumstances, raw materials are requisitioned for application to specific jobs. The monthly summary debits for materials used will go to a control account called Work in Process, which controls a very important subsidiary ledger consisting of a cost sheet for each job that we are working on. Thus a, requisition for raw material gives rise to immediate credits to raw material subledger accounts and immediate debits to the cost sheets representing the various jobs; at the end of month a summary entry is made (for total of all raw materials requisitions) crediting Raw Materials and debiting Work in Process. In journal form such an entry is as follows:

Work in Process—Control (end of month)......................... xxx
   (also, to subsidiary job cost sheets in detail as materials are requisitioned)
    Raw Materials—Control (end of month)...................... xxx
    (detail to subledger cards currently)
To record raw materials usage for month.

Direct Labor Cost Accounting

Direct labor is that labor cost which can (conveniently) be traced to a specific job and which can readily be added to the cost of a specific job. The term is particularly appropriate in the case of job-order costing to distinguish it from indirect labor which, obviously, cannot be attached to a specific job but has to be prorated over all jobs that benefit from it. In the case of process accounting, where costs are accumulated by departments rather than by jobs, any labor within a given process or department could be called direct, since the costing base in process accounting is the total output of the department for a month rather than a number of differentiated jobs—but, even here, accountants are inclined to limit the term *direct labor* to that which actually works on the thing being made. Again, the term *productive* is common in practice to designate labor that really does something to the product versus the *nonproductive* folks who do such things as boss and render ancillary services.

In any case, in this section we're concerned only with direct or productive labor. The whole trick here is to keep track of how much time each productive worker devotes to each job or task and feed this information to payroll clerks, who translate the time into money terms, and then feed it on to the cost clerks who copy the amounts onto the affected job-cost sheets or process-cost sheets. The secret here is time keeping via time clocks or timekeepers, and code numbers for the jobs being worked on and for processing operations, all inscribed on time tickets. The fact is that so many variations in mechanics are possible that what is said here is intended only to convey the underlying aim of direct-labor costing, which is to trace as much of your labor cost as feasible to the things which are produced by it, so that your job-cost sheets or process-cost sheets will accumulate accurately, within tolerance limits, the "actual" raw materials and direct labor costs.

In journal entry form the direct labor costs, under a job-cost system, are recorded as depicted in the following journal entry.

Work in Process (end of month only) xxx
   (also to subsidiary job-cost sheets in detail currently from direct labor
   time tickets)
      Wages Payable (or Payroll) xxx
To record direct labor payroll for month.

In journal-entry form the direct labor (productive labor) costs in a process manufacturing situation are:

Cooking Process xx
Decorating Process xx
Packaging Process xx
      Wages Payable (or Payroll) xx
To record productive labor payroll for the month, all of which has currently **also** been recorded on process cost sheets.

Factory Overhead Cost Accounting— Process Costing

As we continue to explore actual cost accounting, we find that the handling of factory overhead costs under job-order conditions differs sharply from under process-cost conditions. In process-cost accounting you need only allocate your overhead costs to your producing departments. In job-order cost accounting you allocate your overhead costs to producing departments and *then* must *apply* them to the individual jobs that pass through the departments. Since these jobs are not homogeneous we cannot simply apply the same amount of overhead cost to each job.

First, let's consider the simpler situation—process costing. What we seek to do, when we use "actual" costs, is to find the overhead costs of operating each service department and each producing department. We might refer to this step as our primary overhead allocation. The allocation procedure is highly dependent on the exercise of judgment. Some overhead costs are quite surely and easily traceable to the various departments, fairly directly; others, however, need to be prorated—and proration very often is largely a matter of judgment. Let's make a few journal entries to illustrate the "primary" allocation of overhead costs (factory expenses).

(1)

Cooking	xx	
Decorating	xx	
Packaging	xx	
Power	xx	
Maintenance	xx	
Supplies		xx

To record supplies expense incurred during the month by all departments, as determined by summation of requisitions for supplies.

(2)

Cooking	xx	
Decorating	xx	
Packaging	xx	
Power	xx	
Maintenance	xx	
Wages Payable		xx

To charge all departments with their indirect labor costs for the month, as determined by time and payroll records.

(3)

```
Cooking.............................................................  xx
Decorating..........................................................  xx
Packaging...........................................................  xx
Power...............................................................  xx
Maintenance.........................................................  xx
      Machinery—Allowance for Depreciation.........................        xx
```
To charge each department with one month's depreciation on machinery belonging to each department.

These first three entries illustrate factory expense allocations that are reasonably straightforward—the allocations are based on objective measurements. The next group will depict some that are, at best, "reasonable."

(4)

```
Cooking.............................................................  xx
Decorating..........................................................  xx
Packaging...........................................................  xx
Power...............................................................  xx
Maintenance.........................................................  xx
      Factory Building—Allowance for Depreciation..................        xx
```
To record depreciation of factory building for the month and to allocate it to the various departments *on the basis of the number of square feet occupied by each.*

(5)

```
Cooking.............................................................  xx
Decorating..........................................................  xx
Packaging...........................................................  xx
Power...............................................................  xx
Maintenance.........................................................  xx
      Prepaid Insurance............................................        xx
```
To record expiration of property insurance for the month and *to allocate directly* that part which is attributable to machinery in each department and, *on the basis of floor space,* to allocate the remainder.

As you recognize immediately, each of the two allocations reflected in entries 4 and 5 must, of necessity, be judgmental. Let's call it *the assessing* of each department with what we believe to be its equitable share of the particular cost. The cost accountant has a whole bag of tricks to be used in these primary allocations. What he always seeks is a common denominator (floor space, value of machinery, direct labor cost, etc.) which he can use to make the allocations with a semiclear conscience. Let's add right here that allocations of this sort may stir up ill will—particularly when some very cost-conscious department head does an excellent job of economizing only to be socked with heavy charges through the semiarbitrary allocation procedure. He's quite likely to squeal, and don't blame him. This is why so-called *responsibility* accounting has been invented—a plan under which each department head is charged with, and held responsible for, only those factory expenses *which he is able to control*. More of this later.

We've illustrated primary allocation. What should we do with the expenses we've charged against Power and Maintenance? Since, obviously, we do not run those departments for their own sakes, we must now make a secondary allocation—their costs must be reallocated to the producing departments.

In our highly simplified situation, we have recognized only two service departments and, earlier, assumed that Maintenance not only serves the three producing departments but also serves Power. Thus, our first step should be to divide the maintenance total among the other four departments and then divide Power (including what it was charged from Maintenance). Did you ask what we do when some of the power is used by maintenance? A good question. Where service departments serve each other reciprocally, this is known as *mutual service*. The more common solution is the allocation of them, one at a time, on a downstream basis. First allocate the service department that provides the most widely used (or, maybe, the most costly) services; then, allocate the next most widely used; and so on, in each case ignoring all backwashes. Thus, if A serves B more than B serves A, allocate part of A to B but ignore the B-to-A backflow. Continue the procedure until all service department costs have been disgorged into producing department accounts.

An alternative procedure involves use of simple algebraic equations which work out very prettily but which leave you wondering, in view of the arbitrary allocation bases, if it's all worthwhile.

Factory Overhead Cost Accounting— Job Order

It would complicate things beyond belief even to try to apply each factory overhead cost separately to the various jobs produced under job-order conditions. Remember that we keep a separate job-cost sheet for each job and that the direct raw materials and direct labor costs of each job are currently recorded on the cost sheets as the work progresses. But this can't be done with factory expense, for three major reasons. First, by definition, factory expenses are those manufacturing costs which simply cannot be traced directly to an individual job; second, even if they could be so traced, we probably wouldn't do it because there are so many different items of overhead that the clerical cost would be exorbitant; and third, the overhead cost (unlike direct labor and direct materials) that happens to be incurred at the same time that specific jobs are being worked on is by no means likely to be the amount that is assignable to those specific jobs.

To get to the point: Under "actual" cost accounting (1) we estimate what the actual *total* factory overhead will be for the coming year; (2) we estimate what our total direct labor hours, or total machine hours, will be during the coming year; (3) we then divide the estimated hours into the estimated overhead total to get a *burden rate* per hour; and (4) as a given job progresses, we keep track of the hours spent on it and charge that job with the actual hours times the burden rate. Thus is factory overhead charged to jobs in a job-order system. Let's analyze this procedure.

The burden rate is based upon an estimate of total factory overhead and total hours (of machine use or of direct labor) *for the entire coming year,* because use of a year's average burden per hour makes so much more sense than it would to charge a given job (or group of jobs) with the overhead expenses that just happened to occur while they were being worked on. An obvious case in point would be maintenance costs. It is quite typical that important maintenance programs are scheduled for times when plant activity is at its lightest, and it would be totally inequitable to charge such cost to the few jobs that happened to be "in the works" at the time. Some factory expenses do, of course, increase and decrease along with fluctuations in production activity (these we call *variable* overhead) but many occur simply with the passage of time (these tend to be the *fixed* overhead costs such as manager's and supervisor's salaries, property taxes, depreciation, etc.). In short, the most equitable solution to finding a burden rate appears to be to use the estimated total for the coming year divided by the estimated hours.

An important refinement of our discussion of overhead rates is the development of a separate overhead rate for each production department. Many companies use what we have just been describing—a single plant-wide rate. However, there's no doubt that improved accuracy results when a job is charged with high overhead during its stay in a high-overhead department and low overhead while it's in a low-overhead department. The development of departmental rates requires, first, estimating the overhead costs for all departments, including service departments; then allocating the estimated service department costs to the producing departments; and, finally, dividing each producing department total by its estimated labor or machine hours or whatever other application base may be used.

Now let's follow through hypothetical factory overhead entries and assume use of departmental rates.

(1)

Factory Overhead—Control... xx
   Service Department 1... xx
   Service Department 2... xx
   Producing Department 1... xx
   Producing Department 2... xx
   Producing Department 3... xx
      Miscellaneous Credits... xx
To record *actual* factory overhead costs in general ledger control account and in subsidiary ledger department accounts.

(2)

Factory Overhead—Control... xx
   Producing Department 1... xx
   Producing Department 2... xx
   Producing Department 3... xx
      Factory Overhead—Control... xx
      Service Department 1... xx
      Service Department 2... xx
To transfer actual overhead costs from service departments to producing departments on the basis of actual services rendered.

(3)

Work in Process... xx
   (Also to subsidiary job-cost sheets in detail as jobs are finished; charges are based on hours worked on each job in each department multiplied by the burden rate in each department.)
      Factory Overhead—Control... xx
      Producing Department 1... xx
      Producing Department 2... xx
      Producing Department 3... xx
To charge Work in Process and the individual jobs with burden, at departmental hourly rates, as determined at the beginning of the year, and to credit the actual overhead accounts for the same amounts.

(4)

Income Summary.   xx
   Producing Department 1.   xx
      Factory Overhead.   xx
      Producing Department 2.   xx
      Producing Department 3.   xx
To transfer end-of-year leftover balances of overhead in each department to
Income Summary.

Entry 4 illustrates end-of-year disposal of the overhead cost residuals
in the various departments. As you have no doubt anticipated, we never
assign to jobs, through use of our burden rates that we set up at the
beginning of the year, exactly the amount of overhead that is actually
incurred in any given department through the year. Obviously, if, as
the year progresses, we recognize we've made a significant error in setting
our burden rates, we simply change them to give us more realistic job-
order costs. But, because the application of overhead costs to jobs involves so much estimate and probability of errors, some companies are
content to set departmental or plant-wide rates on the basis of a factory
expense study and leave them unchanged for several years.

Process Variations

In the illustrations of process accounting it was assumed that the company produces a single, homogeneous product. Surely this is only a special situation and there are many where process-cost techniques can
be applied even though a lot of different products are turned out. Thus,
in a canning plant different products are canned as the seasons change,
and in a rubber-tire plant tires of various sizes and specifications are
produced simultaneously. In short, wherever there are "runs" of products
of standard specifications, or of varying mixes of standard operations
and materials, process-cost methods can be and should be applied. The
techniques involve inventive modifications of the basic principles and
procedures described earlier.

Internal Cost Statements

The reports which cost accountants prepare for management use are,
of course, designed according to the ground rules of each situation. Two
major reports tend to be widely used—the statement of costs of goods
manufactured (and sold) and schedules of departmental overhead costs.
In addition to these there are unlimited varieties of reports on departmental labor and raw material usage. Following are pro forma examples

of the two major reports:

OUR COMPANY

Cost of Goods Manufactured and Sold

Year Ended December 31, 19X1

Materials used:		
Inventory, January 1.......................................	$xxx	
Purchases...	xxx	
	$xxx	
Inventory December 31....................................	xxx	$xxx
Direct labor...		xxx
Factory overhead:		
(List actual items and amounts)—actual.....................	$xxx	
Less: Amount not applied ("unapplied").....................	x	
Factory overhead applied to production......................		xxx
Total manufacturing costs....................................		$xxx
Add: Work in process on January 1..........................		xxx
		$xxx
Less: Work unfinished on December 31.......................		xxx
Factory cost of goods manufactured..........................		$xxx
Add: Finished goods on hand on January 1...................		xxx
		$xxx
Less: Finished goods on inventory December 31...............		xxx
Factory cost of goods sold (see income statement)............		$xxx

OUR COMPANY

Schedule of Departmental Overhead Costs and Variances

Year Ended December 31, 19X1

	Service 1	Service 2	Producing 1	Producing 2	Producing 3
Supplies...................	$xx	$xx	$ xx	$xx	$xx
Indirect labor..............	xx	xx	xx	xx	xx
Other expenses (detail)......	xx	xx	xx	xx	xx
Totals....................	$xx	$xx	$ xx	$xx	$xx
Allocation of S1............	xx	xx	xx	xx	xx
Totals........		$xx	$ xx	$xx	$xx
Allocation of S2............		xx	xx	xx	xx
Production totals...........			$ xx	$xx	$xx
Overhead applied to job.....			xx	xx	xx
Unapplied overhead (overapplied)—Variances...			$(xx)	$xx	$xx

TEST PROBLEM

Shown below are a number of spaces for making journal entries to record the flow of costs through a departmentalized job-order system. For each journal entry the explanation is given but the accounts and amounts to be debited and credited have not been entered. On the basis of each explanation, it's up to you to fill in the debit and credit entries. Then prepare a statement of cost of goods manufactured. As usual, solution is given in the appendix.

TEST PROBLEM Solution Space

Debit   *Credit*

(1)

Record purchase of $100,000 of raw materials on account and indicate subledger record.

(2)

Record $97,000 of raw material requisitions for materials going into work in process. Show subledger entries also.

(3)

Record $364,000 of direct labor and wages payable going to work in process. Show subledger notation for work in process. (Note for later use: $174,000 of direct labor was performed in Production 1 and $190,000 in Production 2.)

(4)

Record $643,000 of overhead to Factory Overhead—Control, charging $127,000 of this to Service 1; $94,000 to Service 2; $236,000 to Production 1; and $186,000 to Production 2. Make your credit to Various Accounts.

(5)

Transfer $127,000 from Service 1 as follows: to Service 2, $34,000; to Production 1, $63,000; to Production 2, $30,000. Make general ledger debit and credit to Factory Overhead for total.

192

(6)

Transfer balance in Service 2 ($128,000) to: Production 1, $64,000 and Production 2, $64,000. Both debit and credit Factory Overhead—Control for $128,000.

(7)

Charge Work in Process $614,000, and indicate posting to subledger job-cost sheets, for overhead applied in Production 1 at the rate of 200% of direct labor in Product on 1, which was $174,000, and at the rate of 140% of direct labor in Production 2, which was $190,000.

(8)

Cost of goods finished as shown on job-cost sheets was $960,000.

(9)

Close unapplied overhead remaining in Production 1 and Production 2 to Income Summary.

OUR COMPANY

Statement of Cost of Goods Manufactured

Year Ended December 31, 19X1

Raw materials used		$
Direct labor		
Factory overhead—actual	$	
Less: Unapplied overhead	————	————
Total cost of manufacturing		$
Add: Work in process, January 1		————
		$
Less: Work in process, December 31		————
Cost of goods finished		$

Chapter Thirteen

Cost Standards

What's a Standard?

Now that we've spent an entire chapter exploring "actual" cost accounting, we're about to examine the proposition that actual cost accounting isn't as actual as it seems. Paradoxically, standard cost accounting is really more actual than is actual cost accounting.

Perhaps we can go directly to the point. Cost accounting focuses on finding the *cost of* an activity or a thing, such as a product. Certainly we'd like to avoid wild guesses and get as near to the *actual* cost of the activity or thing as we can (without wasting money in the effort). Now, standard cost accounting holds that when we set out to make or do something involving cost outlays we may be less efficient than we should be; and if we're below par in efficiency, we are wasting time or money, or both. Under standard cost philosophy we assert that the *costs of* inefficiencies should be separated from the *costs of* the activity or thing we're working on. Actual cost accounting makes no real attempt to separate out these wastes, and they become incorporated indistinguishably as part of the actual cost of the product or activity. Under standard cost accounting the *actual* cost of a product can include *only the costs that are applied effectively* and all excesses are *costs of waste* rather than costs of product. Such excesses are called *variances* and almost the whole aim of standard cost accounting is to sort out, to detect, variances (wastes) and report them to management *immediately* for remedial action. So, "actual" costs are not actual costs, standard costs are actual costs!

Now, what's a standard? This is a scientific (engineered) *predetermi-notion of what something should cost.* If you know in advance what something should cost, then this serves as your model, or standard, against which you compare your actual outlays; and your differences (materials, labor, overhead) are accounted for not as *cost of* the thing, but as variances (usually wastes).

Illustration of Standards— Standard Cost per Unit

Because you're interested in concepts rather than bookkeeping complexities, we'll deal with a relatively simple situation. Assume that our company makes just one product and that it is all done in a one-room, one-department plant. A committee of company personnel including our cost accountant, our production manager, our engineer, our purchasing agent, and any other persons who can make a contribution, is set up to fix a standard cost per unit of our regular product. Here's what they finally develop:

OUR PRODUCT
Standard Cost per Unit

Raw material, 50 pounds of material A @ $1..........	$ 50.00
Direct labor, 10 hours @ $4........................	40.00
Burden, 10 hours @ $6.............................	60.00
Total standard cost of one unit...................	$150.00

We'll refer to these figures repeatedly in the discussion that follows.

Raw Materials Standards

The standard cost specifications for our product allow us to consume 50 pounds of material A, no more and no less. The 50-pound quantity should be based on extremely careful analysis of all factors. First, the 50 pounds should be based on that *quality* of raw material that we'll buy. We might buy a cheaper material, but this would perhaps cause us to waste more and thus need to use more; use of a poorer quality of material might lead to more labor and more overhead cost. Therefore, our engineers pick the raw material of quality that they believe will minimize our costs, and they determine how much (the standard quantities) we should use in producing one unit (or one batch) of our product.

The standard quantity of raw material to be used does not contemplate zero scrap, but it does contemplate an allowance for scrap that aligns with other aspects of the work. You can't saw a board in two without producing some sawdust; you can't cut shoes out of a hide without some left-over, worthless clippings, and so on. But the important point is that the 50 pounds in our illustration should be "tight" enough to exclude needless (waste) scrap, yet "loose" enough to allow our labor and machinery to work efficiently.

Thus, our engineers finally conclude that we should allow a standard quantity of 50 pounds of raw material per unit, even though the final product may weigh only 45 pounds, since the standard must include a scrap allowance if called for under the circumstances.

In the meantime our purchasing expert has been making a thorough study of the market for our raw material. (And has kept the engineer posted so his computation can incorporate purchase-price alternatives.) For the quality selected, the price varies somewhat in relation to the quantity ordered. After taking into consideration the costs of storage, it is concluded that the price of $1 per unit is optimal and a *standard price* of $1 is agreed upon.

Needless to say, all prices fluctuate and a standard may soon become out of date. However, it is necessary to compromise here. We want our standard costs to be current but to change them with every fluctuation in market price would be expensive and would actually sacrifice one major advantage of standard costs—the avoidance of varying prices for the same things as they flow through the factory. So it appears that most companies, even though they may avow that they employ current standards, do not adjust their standard prices more than once a year.

Raw Materials Accounting— Standard Costs

The big objective of standard cost accounting is cost minimization or cost control. Everybody realizes that the longer a leak goes untended, the greater the loss. The rewards of a standard cost system are realized in proportion to the quality of the job of setting the standards and the speed with which variances from standard are reported to those in a position to stop the leaks. In many situations variances in materials and direct labor costs are reported daily. Contrast this with old-fashioned actual cost systems which claim victory if their relatively unhelpful reports reach management sooner than the second week after the end of each month.

To speed the disclosure of materials variances and, equally important, to relate them insofar as possible to the persons responsible for them, the favored practice is to recognize variances in purchase prices at the point of receipt of the materials and variances in quantities consumed at the point of requisitioning or as soon thereafter as possible. In other words, materials variances fall into two general types—price and quantity. Price variance on a purchase of materials is the amount paid above or below the standard price. It is recognized at the point of purchase as follows:

(1)

Raw Materials (at standard)...............................	35,000	
Materials Price Variance...................................	3,500	
Accounts Payable......................................		38,500

To debit Raw Materials at the standard price of $1 per pound for purchase of 35,000 pounds of material A at $1.10 and to charge the variance of $.10 per pound to Materials Price Variance.

Note in entry 1 that material A will be inventoried at its standard price of $1; it will be carried through the accounts to its ultimate disposition as part of cost of goods sold at the same $1 price. If all purchases of material A throughout the year are also recorded at $1, this eliminates any need to use FIFO or average-cost schemes for pricing the requisitions, since $1 is the standard price on all requisitions. This saves bookkeeping.

At the end of the year, whatever amount has been accumulated in the Materials Price Variance account may either be closed out to our Income Summary account as an expense for the year or, if the amount is significant, a proportionate part of the variance may be added to the standard cost inventory for position statement purposes. Actually, materials price variances, whether on the debit or credit side, are not really losses and gains but, theoretically, attach to the materials that have gone on out and to the ending inventory.

The cost of raw materials used is, of course, two-dimensional—quantity times price. If we cleanse the materials for all price variances as we buy them and put them in the storeroom, the price dimension has been translated from actual to standard. This means that we need only look for quantity variances, the other dimension, as the materials are drawn from stores and pass on to work in process, finished goods, and, finally, cost of goods sold. Techniques for finding quantity variances on a "real-time" basis (that is, as they occur) must be worked out by accountants and production men within each particular set of conditions. For our purposes of understanding the basics, let's assume that in our one-cylinder plant we requisition, at the beginning of each day, enough material A for the planned production of our product for that day. Pretend we set out to produce 1,000 units today. We might issue a requisition for 50,000 pounds of material A, which is the standard quantity for 1,000 units. But, let's not let our standard cost system overpower our production system. We know, actually, that we'll produce somewhat more or, maybe, somewhat less, than 1,000 units; also, we've set our material quantity standard fairly tight, so we'll likely have a quantity variance of, say, 5 percent. Let's be on the safe side, to avoid running out of material a half hour before quitting time, and requisition an extra 10,000 pounds. (We can always return the stuff to stores at the end of the day if necessary.)

Now we go to work and turn out as many of our product as we can, and end up making 1,040 units. We then find we have 4,000 pounds of unused material A, which we dutifully cart back to stores and get credit for (possibly an adjustment or correction on the original requisition). We're now ready to make an entry for the day's usage of raw materials, as follows:

(2)

Work in Process.	52,000	
Materials Quantity Variances.	4,000	
Raw Materials.		56,000

To record consumption today of 56,000 pounds of material A at standard price of $1 per pound, for production of 1,040 units of our product at 50 pounds per unit, or 52,000 pounds standard quantity, for variance of 4,000 pounds at $1.

It is, of course, unlikely in practice that a journal entry would be made each day; but a simple three-column form could be used to keep track of the three elements of the entry, one line for each day, and at the end of the month one grand entry could be made for the totals. In the meantime, the daily output and variances would be reported to the appropriate persons.

Regretfully, we cannot explore the myriad of production situations under which materials quantity variations may be accounted for—this is what thick cost accounting textbooks are for. However, it should be appropriate for you to inquire about the accounting recognition of such variances in your company and learn how the variances are analyzed once they're disclosed. For example, in a multidepartment situation with more than one kind of material, the quantity variances may be broken down by departments (to "lay the blame") and by kinds of material as well. Such data can be systematically produced in endless detail on a computer.

Direct Labor Accounting—
Standard Costs

Some of the same concepts that we have outlined in the section on raw materials apply equally to direct labor. Again, let's stick to basics.

Direct labor costs, like raw materials cost, is two-dimensional. We are again concerned with quantity (hours) and price (wages). The major difference is that we can't stock up on labor hours in our store-room as we can with materials, so we don't issue requisitions.

Assume continuation of our example in which, today, we produce 1.040 units with standard labor content of 10 hours each and standard wage rate of $4 per hour. This means our standard labor cost for today is 1,040 × 10 × $4, or $41,600. Actually, however, we used 10,730 hours of labor and the employee's earnings were $43,630. Right away you recognize that we missed our target by $43,630 minus $41,600, or $2,030. How do we analyze this "gross" variance into its quantity and price components?

First, let's find the wage (price) variance. For working 10,730 hours the employees earned $43,630. Is $43,630 more or less than the standard wage total for 10,730 hours? Merely multiply 10,730 by $4 and compare. We find 10,730 times $4 is $42,920, which shows that we are paying a wage variance of $43,630 minus $42,920, or $710.

Second, do we have a quantity variance? The answer is "yes," and in the case of labor it's usually called an *efficiency variance*. Having cleansed all labor hours for the wage variance, we merely find the differences between actual and standard hours and multiply by the standard wage rate of $4. Thus, our labor efficiency variance is 10,730 actual hours minus (1,040 times 10) 10,400 standard hours, or 330 hours which at $4 per hour gives an efficiency variance of $1,320. Added together, the efficiency variance of $1,320 and the wage variance of $710 equals our gross labor variance of $2,030 for the day.

In journal entry form the recognition of gross labor liability, standard cost, and variances for the day is recorded as follows:

(3)

Work in Process.............................	41,600	
Labor Wage Variance.......................	710	
Labor Efficiency Variance....................	1,320	
Wages Payable..........................		43,630

Again the techniques for determining the standard labor time (with scientific time-study methods), the standard wage (which can be an average wage for each type of labor in each department), and the real-time-efficiency variances must be developed by experts within your particular environment, and cannot be elaborated upon here. It can only be added that in competitive industry it makes real sense to have a standard cost system for all aspects of manufacturing costs in order to operate profitably in an atmosphere of thin profit margins.

Factory Overhead Accounting— Standard Costs

One of the better inventions in accounting in recent years is the *flexible overhead budget*. Sure, we take liberties with all budgets and they become flexible in a certain sense, but this one works on an entirely different principle. What happens so sensibly under a flexible overhead budget is that at the end of each month (or other period) you determine what your output *has been* for that month and then determine what your factory overhead *should have been* in the production of that actual output.

For the moment let's assume that your factory overhead is all completely variable and that your scientific analysis of costs shows your overhead, at optimum level, to be $1 per standard direct labor hour. Then if your output for the month just ended was such as to justify 2,000 direct labor hours, your overhead cost *should have been* $2,000. In other words, the flexible budget doesn't tell you how much you should allow for overhead cost for the coming month based on your prediction of what will be produced in a given department; rather, it works entirely by hindsight. When the month is ended you count your actual output, compute allowable overhead at that level, and compare allowable with actual.

Actually, as you well know, some overhead costs are quite variable, some are quite sticky, and some fall in between. So, a flexible budget for a department is a list of all the overhead costs that department will incur and, in a series of columns representing various levels of activity for a month, the dollar amount of each overhead item at each activity level. The activity levels can be designated as percentages of capacity, or direct labor or machine hours, units of output, or any other sensible measure of departmental activity. Commonly the activity levels are within the normal operating range and at intervals of 10 percent, which means that if you operate at, say, 86 percent of capacity you'll have to estimate the dollar allowance for each overhead cost, because it falls between your 80 percent and 90 percent column. A highly condensed example of a flexible budget is shown in Figure 1.

FIGURE 1
DEPARTMENT 1
Flexible Overhead Budget for One Month

Expenses	Capacity, %					
	50	60	70	80	90	100
Variable (list them)....	$24,000	$28,800	$33,600	$38,400	$43,200	$48,000
Nonvariable (list them)..	24,000	24,000	24,000	24,000	24,000	24,000
Totals................	$48,000	$52,800	$57,600	$62,400	$67,200	$72,000
Direct labor hours......	6,000	7,200	8,400	9,600	10,800	12,000
Standard burden rate per direct labor hours..						$6.00

Let's utilize the budget in Figure 1 as a continuation of the example of Our Company. Assume that the actual amount debited to Factory Overhead this month turns out to be $68,000, made up of nonvariable expenses of $24,000 and variable expenses of $44,000. How do we evaluate these figures?

First, is the $68,000 total more or less than the amount justifiable by our actual activity for the month? To answer this we use hindsight to develop a budget. We note in the Figure 1 budget that the variable expenses regularly are scheduled at $4 per direct labor hours while the nonvariable remain stable at a total of $24,000. We worked 10,730 direct labor hours *but* we should have worked only 10,400 (which is the number of units produced, 1,040, times the standard number of direct labor hours, 10, per unit). Should we expect our variable overhead actually to fluctuate with the allowed standard direct labor hours, or with the actual direct labor hours? It would seem that one must acknowledge it as good performance if the production workers keep the variable overhead costs down to $4 per *actual* labor hours, because they could hardly be expected to avoid variable overhead costs that result from all labor hours, including those in excess of standard labor hours. So, our overhead budget for 10,730 direct labor hours is $24,000 of nonvariable plus variable equal to $4 times 10,730 actual direct labor hours, or $42,920. The difference between the budget of $42,920 and the actual variable overhead of $44,000 is $1,080, which we label our budget variance.

Let's examine the overhead variance further. If we turned out 1,040 units of product and have a standard overhead cost of $60 per unit, our standard overhead cost for the month is clearly $60 times 1,040, or $62,400, while our actual total was assumed to be $68,000. It would appear that we have a gross variance of $5,600. We have identified $1,080 as so-called *budget variance*. Can we pinpoint the remaining $4,520 of gross variance? Yes.

We worked 10,730 direct labor hours to produce what we should have with 10,400 hours, and in our budget we have allowed $6 per *actual* hour. So, if we wasted 330 hours, we can ascribe $1,980 of overhead cost to inefficiency. We do, in fact, always calculate an overhead *efficiency variance* as the number of hours wasted (330) times the standard overhead rate ($6).

So, now we have accounted for $1,080 plus $1,980, or $3,060 of our $5,600 gross variance. Where is the remaining $2,540? The answer is so-called *idle capacity variance*. This variance deals with nonvariable costs only and it's easy to compute. We worked 10,730 hours as compared with capacity of 12,000—the plant was idle for 1,270 hours this month. Our cost of being ready to work (our plant, or nonvariable, costs) is exactly $2 per hour at capacity ($24,000 divided by 12,000 hours), and 1,270 wasted hours at $2 each equals our $2,540 of idle capacity variance.

The calculation of these overhead variances is summarized in Figure 2. It should be noted that many companies use partial standard costs and do not fully analyze their gross overhead variances.

FIGURE 2
Schedule of Overhead Variances

Budget variance:			
Actual total overhead for month.........................		$68,000	
Budget for 10,730 direct labor hours:			
Variable (10,730 × $4)......................	$42,920		
Nonvariable................................	24,000	66,920	$1,080
Efficiency variance:			
Actual labor hours at standard rate (10,730 × $6)...........		$64,380	
Standard labor hours at standard rate (10,400 × $6).......		62,400	1,980
Idle capacity variance:			
Nonvariable overhead rate per hour at capacity ($24,000 ÷ 12,000) = $2			
Hours of unused (idle) capacity (12,000 − 10,730) = 1,270 @ $2......			2,540
Gross overhead variance ($68,000 − $60 × 1,040).................			$5,600

Standard Cost Applications

The concept of standard costs can be applied in almost any spending situation, including administrative and selling departments. Of course the setting of standards is likely to be most accurate where you are making only one simple product on a mass output basis and have loads of experience to rely on. Standards can always be set, no matter how great the uncertainty; however, the greater the uncertainty the more careful you must be in your interpretation of the resulting variances. Quite obviously an inaccurate standard produces variances that are equally inaccurate, and management must simply adjust its reactions to the existing condition. Where standards can be set with great accuracy, small variances have much more meaning than they do with standards that are based on rough estimates.

It follows that the bookkeeping for standard costs is a small part of the battle. The most important job is to analyze the variances as to their causes and to take remedial action before the leaks have become costly. The inventive construction of a standard cost system of accounting provides, insofar as possible, for the automatic assignment of variance *responsibilities* to departments and even to individuals within departments.

TEST PROBLEM

The problem that follows is quite similar to the one used for illustrative purposes in this chapter. You are given the standard cost specifications of a hypothetical product and a series of transactions, from which you will trace the flow of costs through a standard cost system in journal entry form.

The standard cost specifications for The Product, which is always manufactured in batches of 100 units, are as follows:

Standard Cost per Batch

Raw materials, 5,000 square feet @ $.50..............	$2,500
Direct labor, 300 hours @ $3.......................	900
Factory burden 300 (labor) hours @ $5..............	1,500
Standard cost, 100 units (one batch)................	$4,900

The standard burden rate was determined on the basis of budgeted overhead costs at capacity of 8,000 direct labor hours for a month, as follows:

Variable costs, 8,000 hours @ $3..................	$24,000
Nonvariable costs................................	16,000
Total at capacity, 8,000 hours @ $5................	$40,000

Required:

In the spaces which follow, make journal entries to record the information already shown in the explanation to each entry. Assume these to be summary entries for one month.

TEST PROBLEM Solution Space

(1)

To record purchase of 12,000 square feet of raw material at $.52 per square foot. Raw material price variances are recorded at point of purchase and the materials are put in inventory at standard.

(2)

To record requisitions for 102,000 square feet of raw material used to produce 20 batches of finished product. (Make a debit, at standard cost, directly to Finished Goods.)

(3)

Finished Goods
Labor Wage Variance
Labor Efficiency Variance
    Wages Payable
To record $18,910 of wages payable for 6,100 hours of direct labor, in the production of 20 batches. (Again, make a debit directly to Finished Goods for the standard cost of 20 batches.)

(4)

Factory Overhead
    Various Accounts
To record all kinds of factory overhead costs incurred during the month, $35,000, made up of variable costs of $19,000 and nonvariable costs of $16,000.

(5)

Finished Goods
Overhead—Budget Variance
Overhead—Efficiency Variance
Overhead—Idle Plant Variance
    Factory Overhead
To charge Finished Goods with standard overhead cost of goods finished and to allocate the gross variance to three variance accounts.

Chapter Fourteen

Internal Management Accounting

The Concept of Management Accounting

Nobody is quite sure where accounting, in its narrowest sense, leaves off and where management, in the active sense, begins. First, we ought to agree that any accounting that is not helpful in some way should be scrapped. In all of its phases "useful" accounting is useful to some sort of management, whether it be the officers and subofficers of the company, the investors and potential investors, the creditors and potential creditors, or one or more government agencies. Each of these users of accounting data manages its relationships with the enterprise, in part at least, on the basis of accounting reports—all of which thereby qualify as management-serving.

For the purposes of this chapter we are limiting management to insiders only—that is, the whole spectrum of persons on the corporate organization chart who have responsibilities for reaching decisions that will influence costs and revenues, or be influenced by them. And we'll define as management accounting the accumulation, classification, storage, reporting, and interpreting of cost and revenue data to provide management with the optimum amount of useful information to help in the formulation of decisions.

Certain management accounting procedures are continuous in nature. The accounting documents and ledger accounts are so organized that the data are accumulated and reported continuously without any special call for help by the management who will receive the information. We'll consider these very briefly under the headings of responsibility accounting, standard costing, and direct costing.

Responsibility Accounting

In the last 15 years a lot of fuss has been made over a very obvious, prosaic idea. The idea is this: You can't very well hold a man responsible for costs which he can't control; so let's not charge such costs against him in the first place. If you agree with this proposition you will next agree with the converse, that in making cost allocations we should examine each one, determine who was responsible for it, and then charge the cost against his department. It is probable that almost every cost incurred by an enterprise can be traced to someone as the responsible party. In general, operating costs are recurring, so it follows that a fixed pattern of cost assignments usually will be established—at least with respect to most costs.

An important accompaniment to "responsibility" cost assignments is a structure of departmental budgets, preferably flexible budgets, so that at the end of each quarter, or each month, the actual costs charged against each department can be viewed in comparison with the amount budgeted for the attained level of activity.

As a postscript to the definition of responsibility accounting, it must be added that the responsibility basis should be the guiding factor in the primary spreading of expenses. In many situations the expenses of service departments can, secondarily, be transferred to the producing departments on a responsibility basis. However, this will not always be true and some costs may then remain in service departments. These must also be assigned to producing departments on a "best judgment" basis in order to complete the job of costing the goods manufactured in the producing departments; but such "judgmental" allocations, since they are beyond the control of the producing departments, should be excluded from any reckoning of the performance efficiencies of the producing departments.

The concept of responsibility accounting also works very well in the effort to control your selling and administrative expenses. What is needed is an organization chart clearly defining departmental responsibilities and identifying the responsible department heads, so that one or more ledger accounts can be set up for each and the expenses can then be assigned and the departmental efficiencies evaluated. A budget may, again, be developed for each department; however, since it is quite difficult to measure performance where there is no objective unit of output, the budget in the case may simply be a forecast, planned expense allowance for each month in advance.

Standard Costing

Because Chapter 13 was devoted to standard costing, the subject is mentioned here only to have it prominently included among the internal management accounting devices.

As may not have been made fully evident, the management value in standard costing is found in the reporting and analysis of variances. This process reflects one of the old, well-worn principles of managerial control—the principle of exceptions, which holds that we report to busy management only the exceptions (variances from standard). If everything is "nominal," as the astronauts say, no report is necessary. Why flood the boss with "bed sheets" full of figures that merely show that nothing untoward has happened? A corollary to this is that in any report to management it may be possible for the accountant to underline, or otherwise emphasize, each item or figure that he believes calls for action. Keep those reports condensed, and put details in supporting schedules.

In standard cost accounting it is possible to devise an infinite number of variance accounts. For example, you could have a separate materials price variance account and a separate quantity variance account for each kind of material, and you could then subdivide each into departmental accounts. Probably this would be absurd in almost any situation, but the point is that the variances are worth recognizing and reporting *only if they're actionable.* In other words, it doesn't do much good to report month after month a variance which simply cannot be rectified.

Direct Costing

The last of the routine management accounting processes that we'll examine is direct costing. As in the case of standard costing and responsibility accounting, the ledger account system may be so structured that the routine accounting is conducted on a continuous rather than an ad hoc basis.

"Direct costing" is a misnomer. We have always reserved the term *direct cost* to identify a cost that can be traced directly (without apportionment) to some end product. What the accountant now means, however, when he speaks of direct costing, is that in accounting for manufacturing costs he will feed into the inventory accounts (which are current assets) only *costs that vary with the amount produced.* The fixed (nonvariable) costs, because they will be incurred whether we produce anything or not, will be charged off against income in the period in which they are incurred. The fixed costs, under this scheme of things, are often referred to as *period* costs for this reason.

Direct costing (in my estimation) is great for one important reason: If it is practiced, it means that the company has studied the behavior patterns of its various kinds of costs and is in a position to deal intelligently with them. As has been noted several times, costs may vary with the level of production or with some other activity measure, or they may remain relatively nonvariable. In between the costs that are completely variable and those that are completely fixed, lie the behavior patterns of all other costs. Some rise, in a curved fashion, slower or faster than the activity measure to which they are related—these are commonly termed *semivariable costs.* Others rise in stair-step fashion as activity increases—these are commonly termed *semifixed costs.* Knowledge of cost behavior is of critical importance to the preparation of budgets, whether flexible or not, and is also critical in the fashioning of some of the decisions we are about to discuss.

On the other hand, direct costing doesn't appear to fare well theoretically in the preparation of periodic financial statements. In other words, the very basic direct cost notion that the fixed costs are period costs is hard to defend. In short, in compiling the costs of goods manufactured, is it reasonable to assert that the manufacturing process causes no depreciation, no property taxes, no insurance, and no supervisory costs? To take an extreme example, assume that for a given year a company, for whatever reason, chooses to refrain from all selling activity and devote its full resources to the making and stockpiling of goods for sale in future periods. Would it make sense to suggest that the company has operated all year at a loss equal to its nonvariable manufacturing costs? Are these losses rather than costs of manufacturing? Frankly, I hope you'll reject direct costing for annual statement purposes (it has not received the blessing of the income tax folks as of this date) and stick to its opposite form which is universally known as *absorption* or *full absorption* costing.

Differential Costs and Related Decisions

Most of the remainder of this chapter will be devoted to cost aspects of decisions that may need to be faced from time to time in an ad hoc fashion—decisions which are not based on routine cost accumulation and reporting but rather call for selective cost groupings. In other words, we're now concerned with what is so often referred to as the need for different costs for different purposes.

The term *differential costs* has gained much prominence in recent years and it will probably become increasingly recognized as a cost concept to be reckoned with.

Differential cost means the total addition to costs caused by any addition to output. It's that simple. If your total costs that would be incurred in a given period by producing, say, 20,000 units would be $100,000, and your total if you were to produce 25,000 would be $115,000, then the differential output is 5,000 units, the corresponding differential cost is $15,000, and the unit differential cost for that particular set of assumptions is $3. Thus, differential cost is the added cost of doing something extra. The concept has numerous decision-making applications but it should be applied with caution. Let's consider a few examples.

Our company in a given year produced and sold 100,000 units of its product. Total manufacturing costs were $1,000,000 (for an average unit cost of $10); total selling and administrative costs were $300,000. Our plant capacity for a year is 150,000 units, and we learn that next year the federal government will be in the market for 50,000 units, on which we are invited to bid. We immediately make a cost behavior study and determine that 30 percent of all our costs are nonvariable and the remainder are, for all practical purposes, variable. From this we conclude that our differential (you may prefer to call it *incremental*) cost of making and selling 50,000 incremental, or differential units would be 50 percent of the variable costs we incurred at the 100,000-unit level, or 50 percent of 70 percent of $1,300,000, which is $455,000, or $9.10 per unit (as compared with an average total cost of $13 per unit at the 100,000-unit level). Knowing this differential cost puts management in a position to increase total profits by supplying the 50,000 units to the government at any price above $9.10 (assuming, of course, that we can continue to sell the 100,000 through regular channels and at regular prices). In other words, the unit cost with which management should primarily be concerned in this case is the unit differential cost. It should always be borne in mind, in working from a differential cost base, that to seek volume increases by cutting prices invites price cuts by one's competitors, so the differential cost approach to pricing must be applied with great care.

Another interesting application of differential costs exists where a company, say the one we have just been considering, has made sales only for cash or has followed an ultraconservative policy in making credit sales. Assume that we produce 100,000 units as before and sell them all for cash at $15 each for a before-tax profit of $200,000. Query: What percentage of bad debts could we afford were we to allow customers to charge their purchases, assuming we continue to sell 100,000 for cash and, as the result of permitting credit sales, believe we can sell an additional 50,000 units? The answer lies in a differential cost calculation. If we produce and sell 50,000 more units our total differential cost, as in the earlier example, will be $455,000; and this is the net amount we must receive to break even on the additional sales. The gross dollar amount of the additional sales will be 50,000 × $15, or $750,000, which indicates that we could incur bad debts of $750,000 minus $455,000, or $295,000, and not be worse off. Our incremental bad debt loss could be as high as $295,000 divided by $750,000, or more than 39 percent! Needless to say, the temptation to begin selling on credit might be great under these circumstances; and similar calculations to test the wisdom of more generous extension of credit, where credit is already being granted on a limited basis, may encourage policy changes. Extreme care should most certainly be used in calculating the differential costs (and don't overlook increases in bookkeeping costs for accounts receivable) and the probable effects of any such policy changes.

In our next topic, the make-or-buy decision, we'll consider another possible differential cost situation.

Should We Make It or Buy It?

A great many articles have been published on the subject of "make or buy," and we surely cannot treat it exhaustively here. We're now concerned with questions such as: Should we start making this particular part which up to now we have been buying ready-made from an outsider? Should we set up a garage for maintenance of our trucks and service cars or should we continue to have this done outside? We're paying out a lot of money for printing and duplicating services; shouldn't we set up our own shop? We've been buying our tools and dies from specialty shops that seem to be making a good profit; why don't we make our own tools, dies, jigs, and fixtures? And, a much more far-reaching, make-or-buy type of question: Should we continue to sell through wholesalers, should we deal directly with retailers, or should we even set up our own retail outlets?

Underlying every make-or-buy survey is the belief, or maybe only the suspicion, that "our supplier is getting fat off us" and "we could just as well be making that profit ourselves."

Certainly a most fundamental question in approaching any of make-or-buy decision is: Which will be the more economical policy for us? And, a most critical aspect of any economy study, of course, is the matter of costs.

In make-or-buy analysis, the adage, "use different costs for different purposes" seems to be most relevant. The fact that so many articles appear on the subject suggests a condition of uncertainty, and this is no doubt the case. For our purposes two somewhat opposing schools of thought will be presented.

The first school recommends the differential cost approach to make-or-buy. To illustrate it, let's assume we have been buying part X and we feel that our earnings might be improved were we to produce the thing ourselves. We call on our cost accountant to estimate our costs were we to make part X. He presents the following, condensed schedule:

PART X

Estimated Production Costs

(per 100 units)

Materials (including costs of ordering, receiving, storing, etc.)		$ 1,142
Direct labor (details in supporting schedule)		3,260
Variable overhead (at 120% of direct labor)	$3,912	
Fixed overhead	2,608	6,520
Total estimated cost of 100 units		$10,922

It takes but a moment to make a superficial, differential cost analysis of these data. Our *total* cost per 100 units is $10,922, which is higher than the total cost $(100 \times \$90 = \$9,000)$ of buying them; but our total cost includes $2,608 of fixed costs which are excluded in determining differential cost (that is, the costs that would be incremental to our present total were we to make rather than buy). We determine our differential cost to be $10,922 minus $2,608, or $8,314, and this "clearly indicates a potential saving (earnings increase) of $9,000 minus $8,314, or $686, on every 100-unit batch of part X." Let's get busy and make those parts!

It is possible that many differential cost analyses go no farther than this, and it is equally possible that many of the decisions are faulty. Let's look at the full cost approach to the same question.

In general the full cost approach to make-or-buy rests on the contention that fixed costs are a fact of life. The only basis of excluding them in make-or-buy decisions is if *you clearly have excess, unused capacity;* that is, if you feel that not only your plant assets but also your supervisor and managerial personnel are not fully occupied and, even more important, that in the foreseeable future the plant and managerial personnel *will continue to be inadequately occupied* unless you take on such activities as the manufacture of your own component parts. Stated differently, the only reason for excluding fixed costs is because you are clearly incurring them *and they're going to waste,* and you see little or no prospect that you can step up the volume of your regular activities enough to soak up the reserve energies and reserve capacity of your personnel and plant.

The great risk of taking on the manufacture of something you've been buying—that is, doing this on the basis that you can exclude fixed costs from your tally of costs to make—is that new fixed costs will "creep" into the picture. This creep effect is most likely to result if you take on a sideline manufacturing or service operation and later increase your mainline activities. Then you don't have enough plant and personnel capacity to go around and the fixed costs creep in. And then you're likely to find that it's much more of a problem to disengage from an old activity than it is to add a new one.

The conclusion to be reached from the full cost approach to make-or-buy is that one should not take on (except, perhaps, temporarily to fill in short-term dips in activity) sideline activities unless the supplier's price exceeds your *total costs plus the rate of profit* that you make on your mainline activity.

Needless to say, a make-or-buy decision, even though it relies heavily upon cost analyses, also must take other noncost matters into consideration. For example, we might decide to make part X simply because this is the only way we can assure ourselves of a steady supply and good quality. On the other hand, it might be politically expedient to farm out as much as we can in order to maintain good public relations.

Thus, the make-or-buy question is not a simple one even in what may appear to be simple situations. In general one might very well lean in the "buy" direction and insist that any decision to "make" be vigorously documented.

Decisions to Acquire Plant Assets

How often is a new structure, a new unit of machinery, or other capital asset purchased or constructed on the recommendation of a wise old production manager with no objective analysis of the need and no concrete assurance that the capital outlay is a wise one? Admittedly some plant additions are made simply because they're unavoidable; they may even be required by legal action, as in the case of antipollution equipment. In many instances, however, financial management, equipped with relevant information, should be in a position to endorse or veto a capital outlay on the basis of logical analysis. The present custom is to refer to such analysis and planning of fixed asset acquisitions as *capital budgeting*.

Capital budgeting is not a precise tool and its employment does not assure the avoidance of mistakes, since estimates of future cash flows form a major portion of the analysis; but the chances are overwhelming that employment of systematic capital budgeting will reduce the number and cost of mistakes significantly.

Basically, the two major aspects of capital budgeting are: (1) the ranking of capital outlay requests in the order of their probable value to the firm and (2) the determination of which outlays give promise of being worth making.

Underlying all capital budgeting techniques is our old friend, "net cash flow." Here's a quick review. If we invest $100 in a depreciable asset that will produce cash savings, or cash proceeds, of $50 per year, the gross cash flow is $50 annually. The net cash flow is the $50 minus any and all *cash expenditures* needed to produce the gross inflow. Let's assume cash outflows will amount to $10 per year; then the net cash flow is $40 per year. Note specifically that depreciation does not enter into this calculation. The $40 net flow hopefully will provide for "recovery" of depreciation, and any excess will be profit.

Three principal forms of analysis are applied in capital budgeting. The first of these is the so-called *payback period*. The payback period analysis is strictly a "no-go" check. What it does is to rule that a particular capital asset shall *not* be acquired unless its payback period is less than a prescribed number of years. If, for example, we insist that every capital asset we buy must have a payback period no longer than 4 years, we aren't using this procedure to determine what assets should be acquired; we're merely ruling against all that do not meet the payback schedule. The example is the preceding paragraph, with an annual cash flow estimated at $40, has a 2½-year payback period, so it would meet a 4-year test readily. However, a payback period under 4 years does not in itself constitute justification for the purchase of any asset. Quite obviously, if other things were equal, we might turn down a proposed 2½-year payback asset if we were short of funds and had alternative outlays with payback periods shorter than 2½ years. Again, a rule-of-thumb payback requirement is strictly a no-go tool—it rules that we *shall not* acquire an asset with a payback period of greater length, but it gives little help in choosing *which* assets with shorter payback periods should be chosen. In fact, it is doubtful that the payback method really has much to commend it for any part of the capital budgeting decision, because it overlooks so much that is of far greater importance. Nevertheless, the payback device is a popular one and it should be well understood by executives.

The remaining two tools both depend on use of compound interest arithmetic, and they are closely related.

The great objection to the payback method is that it pays absolutely no attention to the "tail of the dog." Let's assume that we drill two wells, A and B, and both produce enough water, oil, or gas to pay back our full drilling cost in exactly 4 years. Are the wells of equal value? Certainly not if well A goes dry at the end of 4 years and well B continues to produce. In other words, the tail period (after payback is complete) is an important element in any capital budgeting decision. Of course, like most aspects of capital budgeting, the tail period will probably be a matter of estimate; but it certainly wouldn't make sense to choose well A, because of its 4-year payback, if it appeared probable that well B would pay back in 5 years and then would continue to flow for another 5 years.

Hence, we need some device for evaluating two factors at the same time—the *size* of the flow and the *persistence* of the flow. It should be added that the timing of peaks and valleys in the flow is also a matter of concern, though very difficult to predict with any assurance of reliability.

One method of evaluating both size and duration of flow is to reduce the estimated future net cash flow to a single present-value figure. This is the *present-value method*. To employ this procedure with respect to a proposed acquisition requires estimating (1) the periodic net cash flow and (2) the number of periods that the flow will persist. For practical purposes it will probably be acceptable to assume that the flow is the same every year, although a more sophisticated (more certain?) prognostication may be employed. Also, finding the present value of something means that you "discount" it at an acceptable interest rate. When the estimates have been made and the net cash flow has been discounted to a single present-value figure, this amount must be larger than your proposed commitment (that is, worth more than the amount you are proposing to commit in the fixed asset investment).

To illustrate the present-value procedure, assume you are contemplating investment of $100,000 in an asset that you believe will produce net cash flow of $30,000 per year throughout a 5-year life. All that needs to be done is to refer to compound-interest tables and find the present value of the flow at your required rate per annum (say 12 percent), and compare it with the $100,000 initial instrument. The effect of the discounting operation is to put the *series* of periodic payments on effectively the same time base (namely, the date of the initial investment) as the initial investment. The present value of $1 per period for 5 periods, discounted at 12 percent per period, is approximately $3.61. The present value of $30,000 per period, discounted at 12 percent, is 30,000 times $3.61, or $108,300. The fact that the present value of the cash-flow annuity exceeds the amount of the proposed investment gives us a green light for this outlay, provided that it meets whatever other tests need to be considered.

A third test, which is something of a complement to the second, seeks to determine what is the rate of return that is represented in the estimates we have made. In other words, if our $100,000 investment will return

$30,000 of net cash flow each year for 5 years, how good an investment is this in terms of rate of return? The solution again calls for use of compound interest tables. Now we are seeking to determine what discount rate will equate the periodic cash flow with our initial investment. Because most interest tables do not go above 10 percent, it will be satisfactory to divide the cash flow by 2 and assume the resulting $15,000 is the semiannual cash flow for 10 periods. If $100,000 is the present value of cash flow of $15,000 per period for 10 periods, then we divide $100,000 by $15,000 to find the present value, at the same discount rate, of a $1 per period cash flow—this needs doing because interest tables are usually set up in terms of $1 per period. Upon dividing we find a present value of $6.67 and we seek for a figure in our present-value table on the 10-period line that approximates $6.67. The present value of $1 per period for 10 periods at 7 percent is $7.024, at 8 percent it is $6.71, while at 10 percent it is $6.144. This indicates that our rate of return is a bit over 8 percent per half year, or around 17 percent per year compounded semiannually.

To summarize this very abbreviated discussion of capital budgeting, any proposed capital addition may well be subjected to the three tests outlined in this section: (1) determination of the payback period; (2) determination of the estimated cash flow per period throughout the asset's life and comparison of the present value of this cash flow, discounted at our required interest rate, with the expected amount of the investment; and (3) determination of the actual rate of return that is implied in the cash flow that we have predicted. If the proposed investment meets all three of these tests and does it as well as, or better than, any competing opportunities to invest the funds, it should be safe to proceed with the investment.

Miscellaneous Topics

It is clearly impossible to outline, let alone describe exhaustively, all the devices that accountants and other quantitative information men have invented. Today's buzz words include MIS (management information systems), which is a very interesting computer-oriented story in itself. Also, the mathematicians have worked up many interesting business applications under the label operations research. These include linear programming, Monte Carlo method, Bayesian analysis, simulation, etc. Much of this is in its infancy, although the third generation of computers seems to be stimulating the aging process to a point where reliability is greatly enhanced.

TEST PROBLEM

Here's a short one on capital budgeting. Our Company is considering purchase of a machine with a 10-year life which should reduce annual labor costs by $10,000. Operating costs of the machine, excluding depreciation, will be about $3,000 per year. List price of the machine is $41,000. Should we buy it? We require a maximum payback period of 6 years and our minimum rate of return is 10 percent. Added information: The present value of an annuity of $1 for 10 periods at 10 percent is 6.144.

TEST PROBLEM Solution Space

Computation of payback period:

Computation of present value of machine at 10 percent discount:

{ Chapter Fifteen }

Federal Income Taxes

Almost every business decision affects and is affected by federal income tax considerations. Ideally, therefore, every businessman would be an expert in this area. But this is obviously impossible because the *Internal Revenue Code* itself is a complex, detailed, often inconsistent tome of over a thousand pages, to say nothing of the regulations issued by the Treasury Department and the myriad of court cases touching on the subject. Nevertheless, every businessman should have sufficient insight or knowledge of the federal income tax law to recognize, in general, that a given course of action may bring about certain tax consequences; and he should recognize those situations in which he should seek help from tax experts. The purpose of this chapter is to help the businessman develop the required insight. It cannot pretend to instruct you in the art of corporate tax return preparation, but from it we hope you will gather a general conception of the overall corporate income tax responsibility.

This chapter was prepared by Professor Harold E. Arnett.

General Principles of Taxation

The rudimentary structure of the *Internal Revenue Code* applicable to the taxation of corporations consists of the same elements as does traditional accounting net income. Your corporation will be taxed on the amount of its revenues minus its expenses and other deductions. But the structure is not so rudimentary once the provisions having special impact on the amount and timing of revenues and deductions are examined. Much of this chapter will be directed toward scrutiny of these special features, but first some general principles of corporate taxation should be considered. Having knowledge of these basic principles will make it possible for the reader to understand the discussion of code provisions which follow. More importantly, knowledge of these principles will make it possible for managers, when making decisions, to anticipate situations where tax consequences are likely to be, even when knowledge of specific code provisions is lacking.

In the broadest sense, business income includes all wealth flowing into the business during a specified period of time as a result of its activities, that is, all wealth inflows except returns of capital and the investment of new funds by the capital suppliers. Income can be realized in the form of money received; and it can also appear in the form of services, or property, as well as differences in values. It was established as early as 1913 in various court cases regarding taxation that most of the income flowing in was to be included in the taxation base, since income was, and is, defined as "gain derived from capital, from labor, or from both combined, including profit gained through the sale or conversion of capital."

Even though "deductions" are a matter of legislative grace and nothing can be deducted unless it falls within one of the allowable categories in the code, it was also established early that taxable income is a net concept—that returns of capital are not taxed. From this gradually evolved the principle that all *necessary, ordinary,* and *reasonable* expenses incurred in generating income may be deducted in arriving at the taxation base. In general these terms mean:

1. An expense is *necessary* when it is of the kind usually found in like undertakings, that is, when it has a direct association with the business activity.

2. An expense is *ordinary* when it is applicable to the current year;

for example, if a machine that has a life of longer than one year is purchased, the cost of the machine cannot be deducted fully in the year of acquisition, regardless of whether the taxpayer is on the cash or accrual basis of accounting. The cost *must be allocated* in a rational fashion and deducted as expense over the years served by the machine.

3. An expense is *reasonable* when it is in line with the amount paid for like services or is in an amount consistent with the benefits to be received from the expenditure. These criteria do not come into play very often, but they do take on significance with regard to those things which are difficult of proof or, because of their nature, are open to question as to their necessity and relationship to business activities (such as entertainment expenses and the costs of belonging to social clubs). Most expenses, however, are not incurred unless the manager of the business anticipates favorable results, and therefore they usually are not questioned.

As is true in accounting, the transaction view predominates in taxation. This means, simply, that taxable income or deductible loss does not usually arise until a completed transaction has taken place. This is the basis for *realization* in the code. Hence, increases in value which have not been realized through the sale or other disposition of the item are not taxed, nor are unrealized losses usually deductible. This has led to what might be called the *cash availability principle* in taxation.

Simply stated, this principle means that taxes usually do not have to be paid until the cash to be derived from the transaction has either been received or is evidently receivable in the near future.

Rule-of-thumb Guideline in Business Decisions

As businessmen know, it is generally desirable to postpone tax payments as long as possible because of the income that is to be earned on the tax dollars during the period of postponement. For example, if the choice is to pay $100 in taxes either today or one year from now, the latter would be the better choice because during the period of delay the funds could be used to earn, say, 8 percent in the business; otherwise stated, there would be an opportunity cost of $8 ($4 net of taxes at a 50 percent rate) if the taxes were paid today.

This brief example indicates the importance of tax planning. Once an event is consummated, the businessman has no choice but to follow the dictates of the code. In order to minimize opportunity costs and also to take advantage of tax-limiting code provisions, tax planning is essential, that is, making things come out tax-wise in the most advantageous way. As stated, business decisions do affect taxes and, consequently, tax effects are a major consideration in business decisions. Coupled with the desire to postpone tax payments as long as possible, businessmen are faced with a combination of three subgoals: *to minimize revenue reported, maximize expense deductions,* and *minimize the tax rates applied.* The remaining sections of this chapter will be devoted to specific areas of the tax formula in which the effects of these decisions can be realized most readily. Revenue minimization will be considered first.

Revenue Minimization

Some provisions in the code allow a corporation to realize certain types of income which is only partially taxable and some which is fully exempt. Dividends received from another domestic corporation are subject to a special deduction of 85 percent; that is, only 15 percent flows through to taxable income. This might make it desirable to invest temporarily idle funds in high-grade stocks rather than in corporate bonds whose interest is taxable. Interest on state and municipal securities on the other hand is generally tax-exempt. Furthermore, a 100 percent deduction is generally allowed for dividends received from an affiliated corporation which does not or cannot file a consolidated return.

It may be desirable to carry life insurance on the lives of key employees, with the corporation as the beneficiary. Proceeds of such insurance, received by reason of the death of the insured, are fully tax-exempt. Further, dividends on life insurance contracts are not taxable if they are received before any receipts of the policy proceeds, unless they exceed the amount that the taxpayer has paid in premiums (which are not deductible expense).

The cash availability principle can work to the taxpayer's disadvantage in some instances if care is not taken. Generally speaking, collection in advance of amounts which are not restricted as to use are taxable in the year received even though the corporation uses the accrual method of accounting. For example, if rent is received in advance for 5 years on the final day of a given taxable year, the full amount must be included in taxable income in that year; that is, it cannot be spread (accrued) ratably over the 5-year period. Obviously, this could be avoided simply by having the renter spread his payments over the 5-year period. The Internal Revenue Service announced on August 6, 1970, its intent to recognize certain circumstances where accrual basis taxpayers who receive advance payments may defer the inclusion of such payments in their income. However, these new rules generally will apply only for prepayments for goods and services where the goods are to be delivered or the services performed during the year immediately following receipt of the cash. Thus, though the IRS has changed its philosophy considerably, the practical consequences may not be substantial.

A difference exists between what is good financial accounting and the tax requirements regarding the acquisition of new property where similar, old property is traded in. Gain or loss on such trade-ins, if any, should be recognized for financial purposes when the event occurs in order to avoid misstatements of asset values and of income with consequent possible misinterpretation of the statements. From a tax viewpoint, however, *losses* on such exchanges are never recognized; rather, they serve to increase the "basis" of the new property acquired. *Gains* are recognized only if "boot" is received, and this is rare since the value of the property given up would have to exceed the value of the property received for this to happen. Gains not recognized serve to decrease the basis of the new property.

Since cash is generally given in an exchange, and not received, these tax rules again reflect the cash availability concept; and tax generally is not immediately payable on resulting gains. It should be noted, however, that tax depreciation during the life of the acquired asset will differ from the amounts recorded in the books (assuming good accounting procedure), and tax allocation of the sort discussed in Chapter 18 may become necessary. As a matter of fact, it is quite common for small and medium-sized businesses to take the path of least resistance and follow the tax rules in keeping their regular accounting records.

The installment basis, a special tax method, can be used by persons selling real or personal property on a deferred payment basis. It is a cash basis of recognizing revenue, in contrast with the traditional accrual basis. This basis again reflects the cash availability concept, since it recognizes that those who receive debt obligations in a transaction may not immediately have enough cash to pay tax on the gain. Taxable income is then recognized in each year as collections are made, in an amount equal to the percentage of the payments actually received during the year which the gross profit is of the selling price, i.e., the gross profit percentage. The effect, of course, is to spread the profit (and the tax) on an installment sale over the years of collection. The installment method does not result in any saving of total tax dollars expended. However, it does allow the taxpayer to defer the spending of tax dollars and thus to earn money on the dollars during the period of postponement. It, therefore, makes good financial sense to use this method whenever possible. It should be noted that selecting the installment method for income tax purposes does not prevent reporting all the income in the year of sale (that is, on the accrual basis) for financial statement purposes, although, again, a tax allocation problem would be created.

Numerous other items in the code could be discussed, but these should be sufficient to drive home application of the principles stated early in the chapter as they relate to revenue minimization.

Expense Maximization

If one side of the coin is revenue minimization, then expense maximization is the other. A primary concern in expense maximization is to take all the expenses legally possible and to take them as early as possible. It is not the intent here to detail all possible such expenses, nor is it necessary. Keeping in mind the basic principle discussed at the beginning of this chapter that all necessary, normal, and reasonable expenditures can be deducted in arriving at taxable income, the business executive ought to be able to "guess" reasonably accurately, when making decisions, whether an expenditure is likely to be deductible, or, at least, to know when he needs advice from tax experts on such matters.

The goal here is to emphasize the importance, generally, of taking the maximum deductions as early as possible. A number of major items will be discussed in this context. First we'll consider depreciation.

Property, except land, *held for the production of income* or used in a trade or business, is generally depreciable. Nonbusiness property (property not used for income production) cannot be depreciated for tax purposes. The theory of depreciation is quite simple. If a piece of property is expected to have a useful life of 5 years, a full deduction of its cost cannot be taken in the year of acquisition because the services in the asset are not all used up in that year. The property was purchased in the first place because of the expectation that it could be used during the period of its useful life to produce income for the owner. Since expenses can be deducted only as incurred in producing or attempting to produce income, it naturally follows that the cost of the asset can be deducted only in the form of depreciation over its useful life.

If an asset is expected to have any salvage value, that is, if the taxpayer expects to realize something, such as cash or a trade-in allowance, when he disposes of it at the end of its useful life, this value must be subtracted from the amount which could otherwise be recovered by means of depreciation allowances. An asset cannot be depreciated below a reasonable salvage value under any method. However, a code provision allows taxpayers to ignore salvage value up to an amount equal to 10 percent of the cost of personal property where the useful life of the property is 3 years or longer.

Of course, the question of "how" still remains. Many methods of depreciation are possible and allowable for tax purposes as long as the one chosen is used consistently. In other words, the taxpayer could elect a different method for each piece of equipment, but the method once chosen must generally then be used consistently unless permission to change is granted by the Director of Internal Revenue. Moreover, the method chosen must result in deductions of reasonable amount, considering the useful life of the property. For example, a taxpayer would not usually, in the year of acquisition, be allowed to deduct 90 percent of the cost of property having a useful life of 5 years, since this would appear to reflect an unreasonable allocation of the cost.

Since we do not seek to make the reader an expert on depreciation methods for tax purposes, only a few of the major provisions will be covered in order to indicate the importance of exercising caution in selecting the method to be used. There is a definite need for tax planning here as elsewhere.

If the business property has a life of at least 6 years and is tangible personal property (any business property except buildings and their structural components), an amount equal to 20 percent of the cost of up to a total of $10,000 of new investment can be deducted in the year of acquisition, in addition to the regular depreciation amount. This is known as *bonus* depreciation. This deduction does reduce the basis of the property for the regular depreciation deduction. For example, if the property acquisitions cost $10,000, then $2,000 can be deducted in the first year *in addition to the regular depreciation*. (But the regular depreciation deduction must be based on the remaining $8,000.)

The additional first-year deduction is optional, however, so each taxpayer must decide whether there is a greater tax advantage in taking it and spreading the remaining $8,000 over the useful life of the asset in some reasonable way, or in not taking it and spreading $10,000 over the full life. The answer depends on the circumstances of each taxpayer, so no absolute rules can be laid down. We emphasize again that it is usually advantageous to take expense deductions as rapidly as allowed. Again, proper tax planning is essential. Let's explore this further.

Most businesses start their lives with a minimum of cash on hand, so the first thought might be to take advantage of the bonus depreciation deduction in order to minimize current tax payments and preserve cash for business use. Further, the cash retained, by being used in the business, can be used to generate income which would otherwise be lost were the deduction postponed. Similar considerations might also be true in the case of an established business which has a weak cash position; however, in both situations there are other considerations which may indicate that an opposing decision is warranted.

As a general rule, the first few years of the life of a business are devoted to expanding, that is, increasing demand for the product and plowing back funds into the business to increase its productive capabilities. And this may be true of an established business which has lost its share of the market and is attempting to regain it, or which is entering new product lines and the like. In any case, such businesses may be in a lower tax bracket than is likely in the future (particularly in the case of sole proprietorships and partnerships) and the additional 20 percent bonus deduction would offset income taxed at a lower rate than will be true 2, 3, or 5 years hence. This condition, of course, would be an inducement for not taking the extra deduction but instead spreading the full $10,000 over the entire useful life of the property. Which decisions should be made depends on the severity of current cash needs, expectations as to the future growth of the business, and anticipation as to future tax rates as well as other considerations. In any case, it is not a decision to be taken lightly. Needless to say, if the enterprise is currently losing money, there is nothing to be gained by taking the extra deduction.

Much the same is true in deciding whether to use the straight-line method of depreciation or one of the accelerated methods. The straight-line method results in equal yearly deductions over the life of the property, whereas the declining-balance method, for example, results in deductions which are approximately twice as large in the first year but only about half as large in the final year. Which of these, or other acceptable methods, should be used can be determined by giving consideration to things such as those already mentioned with regard to the 20 percent first-year deduction. In other words, even though all methods of depreciation result in the same total deduction over the entire life of the property, differing methods result in varying expense amounts in *each* of the years; and the one chosen should therefore have the most favorable effects on the taxpayer's business operations and result in the maximum long-run tax benefits.

Depreciation Illustration

An expanded example may help to clarify these points and to drive home the basic principles involved. Assume the following:

On January 1, 1965, a corporation buys a new truck for $2,625. The estimated life of the truck is 10 years, and it has an estimated salvage value of $362.50 of which $262.50 is ignored, leaving a balance of $100 to be considered. A 50 percent tax rate is assumed throughout. Table I shows the results of taking the bonus depreciation, while Table II omits it.

TABLE I

Year	Straight-line		Double-declining-balance	
	Depreciation	Tax Saving	Depreciation	Tax Saving
		(50%)		
One—bonus	$ 525.00	$ 262.50	$ 525.00	$ 262.50
—ordinary	200.00	100.00	420.00	210.00
Total year One	$ 725.00	$ 362.50	$ 945.00	$ 472.50
Two	200.00	100.00	336.00	168.00
Three	200.00	100.00	268.80	134.40
Four	200.00	100.00	215.04	107.52
Five	200.00	100.00	172.03	86.01
Six	200.00	100.00	137.63	68.82
Seven	200.00	100.00	110.10	55.05
Eight	200.00	100.00	113.47	56.73
Nine	200.00	100.00	113.47	56.74
Ten	200.00	100.00	113.46	56.73
Total	$2,525.00	$1,262.50	$2,525.00	$1,262.50
Salvage value	$100		$100	

TABLE II

Year	Straight-line		Double-declining-balance	
	Depreciation	Tax Saving	Depreciation	Tax Saving
One	$ 252.50	$ 126.25	$ 525.00	$ 262.00
Two	252.50	126.25	420.00	210.00
Three	252.50	126.25	336.00	168.00
Four	252.50	126.25	268.80	134.40
Five	252.50	126.25	215.02	107.51
Six	252.50	126.25	172.02	86.01
Seven	252.50	126.25	137.61	68.80
Eight	252.50	126.25	150.18	75.09
Nine	252.50	126.25	150.18	75.09
Ten	252.50	126.25	150.19	75.10
	$2,525.00	$1,262.50	$2,525.00	1,262.50
Salvage value	$100		$100	

Since under the declining-balance method, because of the way it is applied, it would be impossible to depreciate the asset down to its salvage value, assume that the corporation switches to the straight-line method at the beginning of the eighth year. (A taxpayer can switch from declining balance to straight line without permission of the Director.) Since, at the beginning of the eighth year the undepreciated balance of the asset is $440.40 ($2,625 less $2,184.60), depreciation for each of the remaining 3 years would be $113.47 ($440.40 less $100 divided by 3), in Table I. The calculations are made in the same fashion for Table II. The figures differ, of course, because bonus depreciation was not taken in Table II.

The bonus depreciation the first year under both procedures is 20% × $2,625.

Straight-line depreciation then is $\dfrac{\$2,625 - (\$525 + \$100 \text{ salvage})}{10}$, or $200 per year.

Since the straight-line rate is 10% $\left(\dfrac{100\ \%}{10\ \text{yrs.}}\right)$, the double-declining-balance rate is 20%. Depreciation for each year is calculated by multiplying this rate times the recorded value of the asset at the beginning of the year. For example, in year one it is 20% × ($2,625 − $525), or $420. In year two it is 20% × ($2,625 − $525 − $420), or $336. For year three it is 20% × ($2,625 − $525 − $420 − $336), or

$268.80. This procedure is followed through year seven. Depreciation for the last 3 years is calculated as indicated above.

A number of observations can be made concerning the data reflected in the tables.

1. Total depreciation is the same in both tables for both methods of depreciation.
2. Hence, for both methods the total tax dollars saved, because depreciation is allowed as a deduction in arriving at taxable income, is $1,262.50. (Statements 1 and 2 also would be true for any other depreciation method used.) In other words, the outflow of dollars for tax purposes is not affected *in total* by the depreciation method used, nor by whether or not bonus depreciation is taken the first year.

One might be tempted to conclude, therefore, that it makes no difference which method is chosen. Such a conclusion would be hasty.

3. Note that deductible depreciation does vary considerably per year, depending on which method is used and upon whether bonus depreciation is taken the first year or not.

Consequently, it does make a difference because a dollar today is more valuable than a dollar sometime in the future. For example, if you invested $1 today in a savings account at a 4 percent rate of return, 1 year from today you would have $1.04. If you left that $1.04 in the account for 1 more year, you would have (theoretically) $1.0816, and so on. Consequently, a dollar today is worth more, mainly because of the use you can make of it.

Let's assume, therefore, that the dollars saved because of the depreciation deduction can be utilized in the business at an 8 percent rate of return and go back and compare the results using straight line as opposed to double-declining balance for both tables. In Table I*a* the tax savings that were listed in Table I under each method of depreciation, including bonus depreciation, are multiplied by 8 percent compound interest factors to compute their total "investment" value—that is, to compute the amount to which they would accumulate if invested at 8 percent for the remaining life of the asset. The multipliers are taken from ordinary compound interest tables. For example, you multiply an amount by 1.999 to determine its future accumulated value after 9 years; you multiply by 1.851 to get accumulated amount in 8 years, etc. Under straight line, the $100 amount is multiplied by 10.637, which is the factor used to find the future accumulated value of nine savings of $100 each.

Here we see that the amount earned at an 8 percent rate of return on

TABLE Ia

Straight-line		Double-declining-balance	
$362.50 × 1.999 = $ 724.64		$472.50 × 1.999 = $ 944.53	
$100.00 × 10.637 = 1,063.70		168.00 × 1.851 = 310.97	
		134.40 × 1.714 = 230.36	
		107.52 × 1.587 = 170.63	
		86.01 × 1.469 = 126.35	
		68.82 × 1.360 = 93.60	
		55.05 × 1.260 = 69.36	
		56.73 × 1.166 = 66.15	
		56.74 × 1.080 = 61.28	
Totals	$1,788.34		$2,073.23
Tax dollars used	1,262.50		1,262.50
Amount earned @ 8%	$ 525.84		$ 810.73

the tax dollars saved using straight-line depreciation is $525.84 and that using double-declining balance it is $810.73, a difference of $284.89. In other words, *significantly* more can be earned on the dollars saved using double-declining-balance depreciation than using straight line, with the facts as given.

TABLE IIa

Straight-line		Double-declining-balance	
$126.25 × 12.488 = $1,576.61		$262.50 × 1.999 = $ 524.74	
		210.00 × 1.851 = 388.71	
		168.00 × 1.714 = 287.95	
		134.40 × 1.587 = 213.29	
		107.51 × 1.469 = 157.93	
		86.01 × 1.360 = 116.97	
		68.80 × 1.260 = 86.69	
		75.09 × 1.166 = 87.55	
		75.09 × 1.080 = 81.10	
Totals	$1,576.61		$1,944.93
Tax dollars used	1,262.50		1,262.50
Amount earned @ 8%	$ 314.11		$ 682.43

Table IIa uses the same form of computation as Ia and makes it clear that, holding other things constant, bonus depreciation should be taken where possible regardless of the method of depreciation used. $211.73 ($525.84 — $314.11) less is earned under the straight-line procedure when bonus depreciation is not taken, and $128.30 ($810.73 — $682.43) less is earned under the declining-balance method. It can also be observed that the drop is much more pronounced under straight-line. This follows because of the larger deductions allowed in the early years of an asset's life under declining balance.

Expenses Maximization—
Further Examples

There are also substantial tax consequences related to the disposition of an asset. Since the analysis is very similar to the discussions above, a detailed coverage will not be given. However, a few generalizations are in order. If an asset is sold, any gain or loss on disposition is recognized at the date of disposition. Such gains are usually taxed at ordinary rates. (The capital gain and loss provisions normally do not apply.) On the other hand, if the asset is traded in on the new one, gains and losses are not recognized at time of disposition. Unrecognized gains decrease the basis of the asset for future depreciation deductions, while unrecognized losses increase it. Thus, keeping in mind the previous discussion regarding the time value of a dollar, it is generally better to *sell* the old asset when a loss will be recognized, since the loss will reduce tax payments and these postponed dollar payments can be used in the business to earn more dollars. If a gain is going to materialize on disposition, on the other hand, it is generally better to trade in the old asset on the new, thereby postponing the recognition of the gain and keeping the dollar outflow for tax payments to a minimum. Certainly these dollars saved now (at date of trade-in) will have to be paid out for taxes in the future because of decreased depreciation deductions allowed; but, in the meanwhile, they can be used to earn profits for the business.

Considerations of inflation and deflation have been ignored in the previous discussion, but they are important considerations. If continued inflation is expected, this is an additional strong incentive to postpone payments of taxes for as long as legally possible since future dollars will be cheaper in terms of purchasing power. It is noted that "purchasing power" for this purpose should be judged in terms of the goods and services dealt in by the business under consideration, rather than in terms of some broad, national concept of changes in the value of the dollar.

Although perhaps not significant in general, two other expenses should be discussed in order to emphasize the general principles that have been considered; these are entertainment expense and the cost of belonging to social clubs.

Entertainment expense, if incurred in relation to business activity, is just as legitimate and just as deductible as any other expense incurred in the production of income. However, because there is a greater likelihood of confusion or commingling of personal expenditures with business expenditures in this type of outlay, the Internal Revenue Service may examine them more closely and challenge them more often than is the case of business expenses that are not likely to be incurred unless absolutely essential to business operations. Therefore, the taxpayer must certainly preserve all records and stand ready to justify both their deductibility and the amounts deducted.

Entertainment expenses are deductible if they are directly related to the taxpayer's business and are of a character reasonably expected to benefit the business. In order to qualify as deductions they must be incurred during or directly before or after business discussions (including business meetings at conventions). These "before-and-after" entertainment expenses have been interpreted as an integral part of the business meeting and therefore are deductible. Included are such things as the expenses of entertaining out-of-town business guests and their wives (or husbands) during the evening before holding business conferences, and costs of entertaining business associates and their wives at a nightclub in the evening.

In order to substantiate the amounts deducted, taxpayers should keep rather detailed records showing dates, amounts, places, persons involved, and relationship to the business. Substantiation is usually considered adequate if the taxpayer maintains an account book, diary, or similar record which includes this information and/or documentary evidence such as itemized receipts, itemized paid bills, canceled checks, or other evidence directly supporting such information. It should also be pointed out in this connection that the taxpayer must *justify* the amount deducted as well as substantiate it. In other words, he must be able to show that the amount deducted is reasonable. This, of course, is a debatable point. When is something reasonable or unreasonable? But it is designed to prevent taxpayers from taking deductions materially beyond amounts which would usually be incurred to obtain the business benefits derived.

Dues and other amounts paid to social clubs, such as country clubs or athletic or sporting clubs, are ordinarily regarded as personal expenses and are not deductible. However, if the club is used, directly or indirectly, more than 50 percent for the furtherance of the taxpayer's trade or business, the dues and fees can be deducted, but only to the extent that the use is *directly* related to the business or trade. For example, assume that a taxpayer belonged to a country club which he used 25 percent for pleasure, 40 percent for entertainment "directly related" to his business, 30 percent for entertainment "associated with" his business, and 5 percent for business meals. Since the club is used, directly and indirectly, more than 50 percent for business purposes, a deduction can be taken for part of the dues and fees. Assuming that these amount to $500, the taxpayer could take a business expense deduction for $225 (that portion attributable to "direct" business use: 40 percent + 5 percent, or 45 percent × $500). As with entertainment expenses, this item usually is carefully scrutinized, so the taxpayer should stand ready to justify and substantiate amounts deducted.

Minimization of Rates Applied

Executives must also be alert to prevent situations where penalty taxes might be invoked, which effectively increase the rate of tax that must be paid. The best example of this is the accumulated earnings tax.

This tax becomes a factor mainly where corporations are closely held, although it can be important in other situations. In typical situations shareholders might arrange to have dividends distributed in years when their incomes are low, or they might arrange for the indefinite accumulation of earnings in order to realize capital gains upon the dissolution or liquidation of the corporation.

This tax is invoked where earnings or profits are allowed to accumulate beyond the reasonably anticipated needs of the business in excess of $100,000. The first $100,000 beyond this point is taxed at 27½ percent and the remainder at 38½ percent. This is in addition to the regular tax payable by the corporation.

Choosing whether or not to file consolidated tax returns is an important decision in terms of total tax that will have to be paid. Some of the possible advantages of consolidated tax returns are: (1) Intercompany dividends can be distributed without the recognition of taxable income; (2) capital losses of one company can be offset against capital gains of another; (3) the operating losses of one company can be offset against the profits of another; and (4) intercompany profits can be eliminated, thus reducing or postponing tax payments.

Summary

It has not been possible in the space available to present anything approaching a comprehensive analysis of income taxes that apply to business concerns. Rather, we have attempted only to set forth some of the more pervasive principles—on the one hand, some of the most widely recognized rules to be observed in attempting to meet the tax obligations honestly, while, on the other hand, seeking in each year the determination of taxable income and tax liability that optimizes the relationship between the ever-present tax burden and the assumed aim of maximizing the earning power of the enterprise. The few illustrations that were presented could be multiplied many times in number and variety.

Chapter Sixteen

Use of Computers in Data Processing

Introduction

The purpose of this chapter is to examine the role and characteristics of computer systems. Our plan is to keep the discussion related, insofar as possible, to what has been presented in the earlier chapters on the subject of data processing. Therefore, we shall deal almost exclusively with the computer function of routine processing of accounting data.

Computerized Accounting Systems—
An Overview

A traditional accounting system may be viewed as being made up of underlying documents, journals, ledgers, and financial statements. In the accounting system data representing environmental events are re-

This chapter was prepared by Professor Robert H. Arnold.

corded, transformed, and communicated to decision makers. The data are transformed to be meaningful and relevant to a decision maker and presented in a format so that they can be assimilated by the decision maker. Data transformed in this manner can be considered "information." In this sense, the accounting system is more than merely a data processing system; it is a management information system.

In processing data in the accounting system, calculations must be made and data stored for later use. Reports must be generated and distributed to decision makers. To accomplish these tasks the system must have the capability to accept and store data and sift and sort them, to carry on arithmetic operations, and to generate certain reports. Traditionally these tasks have been carried on by human beings along with certain bookkeeping machines. Increasingly now various computer systems are being introduced into the operations of the accounting system to perform these tasks.

A computer is a calculating machine with the capabilities to operate at very high speeds, to store data, to perform arithmetic operations, and to compare values. A integral interrelationship between accounting and computer systems is that *they are both data processing systems.*

It is important to appreciate that the principles of accounting which form the key underpinning to the design of any accounting system are in no way affected by the use of a computer. Computer applications alter the physical design, not the logical basis of the accounting system. The computer can, however, have significant implications for management in terms of its effect on the timeliness, the quantity, and the quality of data used in a decision-making situation.

Timeliness is certainly an important attribute of information. It may be viewed as being made up of the time period for which data are gathered and the waiting time until they become available. The high-speed processing capability of the computer can have an effect on the speed with which data can be made available to decision units. The computer system can also reduce data gathering time by rapid transmission of data between different operations of the firm.

The economics of computerized systems in terms of their processing and storage capacities may allow management to receive data which otherwise would not have been generated. A computerized system may also assist in decreasing errors commonly made by humans in the processing of data. For example, in addition to its speed and capacity, a computer is not subject to many of the distractions that are so prevalent in modern-day offices. In this sense the quality of data can be improved by employing a computer system.

Management has always had to face the question of the timeliness, quantity, and quality of data and the costs associated with it. Such factors have played a key role in establishing the cost-benefit equation related to the use of computerized systems.

Like any system, accounting and computer systems can be characterized in terms of the nature of their inputs, processing activities, and outputs. So far in this book we have discussed the importance of underlying documents as *inputs* into the accounting system, the role of journal and ledger accounts in the *processing* of financial data, and the nature of financial reports and updated accounts as the *outputs* of an accounting system.

We may use the same basic framework to study the characteristics of a computer system. This can be illustrated with the help of the diagram in Figure 1, which points out key interrelationships between accounting and computer systems.

FIGURE 1

Accounting system

| Underlying documents | Journal and ledger entries | Financial statements and updated accounts |

| Data preparation and input | Central processing unit | Updated files and hard copy output |

Computer system

Computer Inputs and Outputs

A computer works electronically. Therefore, to make it possible for man to place data into and receive information out of the computer, it is necessary to transform recorded data into electrical impulses. To see how this communication takes place one needs to consider specific media and machines.

PUNCHED CARDS: The punched card is the most familiar medium.

It can be used to enter data into the system and receive information transformed by the computer. Hence, it is known as an *input-output medium.*

Most of the cards used in computer systems are divided into 80 vertical columns. In each column one letter, one number, or a special character such as a period may be stored. Numbers are recorded in a card by punching only one hole in a column for each digit. If alphabetical data are to be recorded, two holes are required in any column for each letter of the alphabet. The cards themselves must be of a predetermined format, so that each unit of information occupies the same position on all cards representing any given transaction.

TAPE INPUT-OUTPUT: Paper tape is also often used as a means of entering data into a computer system or for recording output. This tape, like punched cards, is laid out in rows and columns. A character of information is represented by a punch or combination of punches in a vertical column.

Another type of tape medium is magnetic tape. Magnetic tape is nothing more than a plastic tape coated on one side with a metallic oxide. Data are recorded on magnetic spots on the metallic oxide.

There are relative advantages and disadvantages in using any of these input modes. For example, punched cards are easily understood; and it is possible to delete, add, or sort some cards without disturbing the others. Paper tape has certain advantages because of its continuous length. Magnetic tape is the fastest input mode of the three. It can be erased and reused many times and is thus very economical.

In terms of output, all three of the above modes may be used to record processed data, the output of a computer system. Naturally, the computer can also print specific records or documents such as income statements.

Electronic data processing is significantly altering the traditional methods of maintaining business records. Manually posted records are being replaced by machine records such as printouts, magnetic tape files, and other forms of computer-related records.

INPUT-OUTPUT PERIPHERALS: An important dimension of any computer system is the machinery used to record data on the input or output medium and the equipment which allows these recorded data to be entered into the computer, or represented in a form which a human can understand. One often hears of *key punches,* which are used with punched cards, and *card readers,* which enter data into the computer as punched cards are fed through them. The computer can also punch cards automatically in generating output. Similar recording and reading techniques are used in the case of paper tapes and magnetic tapes.

There are other means for entering in or receiving data from a computer. One such device involves online terminals; another uses various types of character recognition such as magnetic-ink character recognition.

ONLINE TERMINAL SYSTEMS: In so-called *online systems* the computer is directly tied to the men or machines to which it reacts. Individual decision makers may make use of online systems by communicating with the computer through a terminal. The most common type of terminal is a teletypewriter. Other types of terminals allow for "visual communication" through a device resembling a TV screen. Such terminals are called *cathode ray terminals,* or CRTs.

To make online input and output economically feasible within an organization, it is generally accepted that the computer must have multiple access capabilities. So-called *time-sharing systems* have been put into operation that allow for a number of decision makers to employ an online computer facility in such a way that each user can be completely unaware of the use of the facility by others.

Closely related to the concept of online systems is the idea of real-time data processing. In a real-time environment the computer operations supply information to decision makers *in time* for them to carry out their duties effectively and efficiently.

Online input and output can facilitate real-time decision making in at least two ways. It is possible to have direct data entry from the point at which the occurrence of an event was recorded. There is an ever-increasing need for industry to gather data at various remote locations and, through the use of computer communication networks, transmit the data rapidly to a data processing center. The systems that have evolved make use of nationwide communication systems to link data processing centers in order to integrate operations and increase the speed of data transmission. These input-output systems are known as *teleprocessing systems.* Online systems can also help to eliminate user turnaround time between the decision maker and the computer. Turnaround time is the period involved between the data entry and the receipt of the output by the decision maker.

COMPUTER INPUT VIA CHARACTER RECOGNITION: In certain computer systems data can be entered by having the system "interpret characters" which are created by using special ink. The most common example of magnetic-ink character recognition (MICR) is in the processing of bank checks.

Another example of this type of input mode is optical character recognition (OCR). Most OCR devices used in business are designed to read machine-printed characters.

Both online terminals and character recognition devices are nothing more than alternative input-output modes. They have been designed to deal with situations that cannot be better handled by punched cards, paper tapes, or magnetic tapes.

COMPUTER INPUT AND OUTPUT IN ACCOUNTING SYSTEMS: In the accounting systems that have been computerized, the role of underlying documents and the various output forms is not changed. Certain firms have revised them in order to gather and express more or less data about certain events.

The simple fact is that a computer system has its own data input requirements in terms of how the transaction data must be stated. In a computerized system it is necessary, first, to transform the data from underlying documents to machine-acceptable form. Then the output from the system which is initially transmitted in electrical impulses must at some point be interpreted and expressed in a human acceptable form. The processing of the input to the output is done by the central processing unit, or CPU. This element of the computer system is discussed in the next section.

Central Processing Unit

The transformation of data in an accounting system is based on accounting principles. This transformation occurs through the medium of journal entries and ledger accounts. For example, the data on revenues, losses, gains, and taxes are gathered in the income summary, a ledger account, and then expressed in terms of their net effect on retained earnings and presented as output in the form of an income statement.

The processing unit in the computer system is designated as the central processing unit. It is the heart and brains of the system. A set of electronic circuits gives the system its capabilities to carry on arithmetic and certain logic operations. It also controls the actions of other elements of the computer system. To carry on these tasks, the central processing unit operates on two streams of data: (1) the data to be processed and (2) instructions.

In an accounting system the data to be processed are entered into the system on the basis of data gathered from underlying documents. The manipulation of the data within the CPU corresponds directly with that expressed earlier in the book in terms of accounting principles. In fact, it is possible to envision a set of ledger accounts stored within the computer system through which the data flow while being processed. In this sense there is no real difference between a computerized and a noncomputerized accounting system. One merely makes use of a computer to carry on the necessary data-sorting and mathematical calculations required to generate and store relevant financial information. As an inanimate object, the CPU does not inherently have the necessary understanding of accounting principles to carry out the desired processing operations. Because the system cannot think for itself, it is necessary to "communicate" to the machine, in a language which it understands, instructions which leave out no details. The instructions involved are likely to include (1) how the data should be read in, (2) the designation of a storage location in the system, (3) the steps to be taken in analyzing the data, and (4) the format in which the data are to be presented.

Data Storage

The central processor, as with a human being, must have information in internal storage to which it has access before any decisions can be made with regard to the type of computation to be performed. The storage of data in the CPU itself is called *internal* or *primary* storage. Data stored outside the CPU are held in so-called *secondary* storage.

In most computers the primary storage is magnetic-core storage—usually referred to as *core*. A magnetic core is a doughnut-shaped ring which can be magnetized in either of two directions. Data are actually stored by the use of magnetism.

SECONDARY STORAGE: Secondary storage can be either online or offline. Online secondary storage is capable of unassisted communication with the central processor. Attaching additional storage units to the CPU enables one to expand the capacity of the primary storage. The most common auxiliary storage modes are magnetic tape, disks, and drums.

Management is likely to have vast amounts of information stored on such mediums as magnetic tapes in a type of library. When this information is needed, it is entered into the system through some input device with the help of humans. Such storage is offline.

When direct, rapid accessibility to any file record is most desirable, online external storage is chosen. Otherwise the relative cost of online storage might well dictate that data be stored in offline libraries.

The Role of Computer Personnel

Every organization that uses computers in a significant way is faced with the problem of how to handle people who operate the computer system. The human is the most important element of the computer system. All too often the human element in computer operations has been the cause of great frustration to many a management team. We can't, in this chapter, attempt to discuss the multifaceted problems related to staffing and operation of a computer system. It is, however, possible and important to define key roles in the staff making up a computer department.

THE SYSTEMS ANALYST: The role of the systems analyst involves a combination of defining the objectives and requirements of a system and deciding how the design which best meets these needs can be produced. In terms of data processing, decisions must be made as to how the data are to be gathered and processed and the design which best fits these needs. Given this job description, it is obvious that a systems analyst working on a computerized accounting system should have a good understanding of accounting.

THE COMPUTER PROGRAMMER: Various computer languages have been developed which facilitate communication between the human operator and the computer system. Such languages often used in business include Cobol and Fortran.

Very few decision makers know or care to know program languages. They rely on computer programmers to express their thoughts in a form which can be interpreted by the computer. When the computer programmer translates a set of instructions into a computer language, the result is a computer program. Computer programs are made up of the instructions that define the nature of the processing to be done within a computer system. They are often referred to as *software,* while the actual computer equipment is designated as *hardware.*

To be put in final machine-readable form, computer programs are processed by a compiler in the computer system. The compiler transforms instructions written in languages such as Fortran and Cobol to machine language. The compiler itself is a computer program written in machine language. Machine language is extremely complex, and very few computer programmers are capable of dealing with it directly.

Progress is being made in the development of programming languages which are very similar to our native languages. This evolution brings us ever closer to a world of "conversational" computing. As this occurs, decision makers can be expected to interact to a greater extent directly with the computer rather than making use of a computer programmer.

COMPUTER OPERATOR: The majority of the personnel in a computer operation are involved with the preparation of the data for input and in the actual operations of the equipment. This kind of work includes key-punching data onto cards for input and handling offline computer libraries. For example, when certain data are requested and it is "offline" on tape, a computer operator will "mount" the appropriate tape or connect the tape with a tape reader.

Computer Applications: A Case Study

One of the best ways to gain an appreciation of the implications and operations of a computerized accounting system is to consider a case example. The following is a hypothetical case study based on a number of actual experiences with computer system design.

The firm selected is that well-known Acme corporation. For the sake of discussion, assume that the management team of Acme had decided to computerize certain accounting systems related to the recording of sales transactions. In this case, the specific functions affected might be accounts receivable, inventory, and sales analysis. Let us briefly consider certain of the ramifications of management's decision to use a computer. An early operations review of the computerized system was structured in terms of the attributes of a computer, its speed, calculating powers, and sorting capabilities.

SPEED: Before the Acme system was computerized, underlying documents such as sales tickets and shipping orders had been recorded and classified by customer name and stored to the end of the month. At that time calculations were made to determine the total amount purchased by each customer and total sales by product group; also, inventory accounts were updated. Management was concerned, in part, because monthly reports related to sales, receivables, and inventory were generated as much as 30 days after the close of the month or up to 60 days after the first relevant transaction took place.

The computerized system allowed for the data to be effectively and efficiently entered on a daily basis. The speed of the computer also enabled accounts to be updated and related reports generated on a daily basis. The implications of this fact are best illustrated in terms of accounts receivable management:

1. The computerized receivables system reduced the credit cycle by billing faster. The faster billing also seemed to stimulate faster payments by customers and thus resulted in an improved cash flow.

2. The prompt updating of accounts meant that required credit authorizations could be made on the basis of current conditions.

The speed with which the new system could transform input data also affected inventory policies. After introducing the computerized system, management had maintained the same formula for inventory replacement. However, they found that the computer system had resulted in lower reorder points because it was possible now to review inventory levels over shorter periods of time.

CALCULATING POWERS: Before the computer system was introduced, management had often found that the time and cost involved in processing data had restricted the generation of reports relevant to inventory control and credit analysis. Acme corporation has a number of products. It was often difficult merely to keep track of inventory levels. Little or no effort had been made to tie inventory levels to production schedules.

After introducing the computer system with its calculation powers, management was able to keep a continuous record giving information such as description of the items, stock on hand, unshipped sales, reorder points, and items in process. These data helped management not only to keep better control of inventory items but also to improve production operations. With the help of the computer system, management was better able to integrate production schedules with inventory levels.

A good deal of emphasis has been given to tightening controls over receivables. Management found that the new system had the ability to store and analyze credit information on individual accounts and could readily develop a schedule of aged accounts. A decision was made to further analyze each aged group by a number of criteria such as neighborhood and past history and to use this output in establishing future credit policies. It was generally agreed that such information could not have been produced economically by the old system.

The marketing department of Acme found that it could make use of the calculating power of the computer to do market research. For example, greater emphasis could be given to defining sales by particular customer groups and to using this information to establish estimates of market potential.

SORTING CAPABILITIES: In examining the existing system before introducing a computer, the system design group called to management's attention that sales were recorded separately for sales analysis, accounts receivable, and inventory, even though they originated from the same underlying documents. It was suggested that the sorting capabilities of the computer would allow for a more integrated system. The new system was designed so that a single recording of basic data in a common classifying format would allow for making maximum use of the data with a minimum number of human operations. The new input format was designed so that the input could be used to update inventory, product sales, and receivable files.

Two specific input modes were employed in the new system. To deal with over-the-counter sales, Acme acquired new cash registers that have as part of their output punched paper tape. At the end of the day the data on the tape are entered into the system and all transaction data are recorded simultaneously.

Other sales are handled in a slightly different manner. When an order is received, it is recorded on punched cards. These sales data include information that may also be used as computer input to prepare shipping orders and customer invoices.

A Report on the New System

The following results were ascertained by a group that reviewed the new system after a period of operation.

1. Data can be generated more often and more quickly.

2. Data can be sorted into various patterns more readily and thus explored more effectively.

3. Control operations can be facilitated by the nature of the data output from the system.

4. Certain decisions—such as order points for inventory—can be routinized.

5. In general the new system appears to be most effective in cases in which

    a. Operations are repetitive.

    b. Variables involved in the calculations and their interrelationships can be rigidly stated.

    c. There is a large amount of data to be handled.

    d. The data must be handled with reasonable speed and accuracy.

The report suggested that the use of the computer in the area of accounts payable and payroll also appears promising. For example, there are common problems related to accounts payable operations due to the time involved in processing data. These include late payments resulting in lost discounts, multiplicity of procedures resulting in less cash control, and excessive cash balances tied up to meet payable requirements.

The benefits of computerization would include more timely processing, better cash control, and less handling expense. The system should help to eliminate late payments of invoices and reduce clerical staff. Additional management reports may be readily generated on the basis of accumulated information, which should assist management to analyze expense distributions by account classification and vendor.

The calculations involved in handling payroll also appear ideal for computerization, given the findings of the present analysis. For example, the calculating power of the computer can be used to deal with all the arithmetic calculations in connection with payroll taxes. The system can also have as output employee checks or payroll slips.

Chapter Seventeen

Consolidated Statements

What Is a Consolidated Statement?

Basically a consolidated position statement, or income statement, is one in which we have combined the financial data of two or more affiliated companies in accordance with certain rules of the game.

But why in the world should we combine the data of two or more companies? Answer: Under appropriate circumstances a combined (consolidated) statement of two or more companies conveys financial information better than if our financial report presented the statements of each company separately.

For example, if our company, in addition to its cash, inventories, machinery, buildings, etc., owns as a long-term investment all the outstanding capital stock of another company, we could present our company's own (legal) position statement and it would show, among the noncurrent assets, its investment in the other company. This investment would probably be shown at cost, as noncurrent assets are customarily shown. Then, for us to analyze the financial position of our company, we would need to "look behind" the investment; that is, we would also want to see the current position statement of the other company, particularly if the cost of our company's investment in the other company constitutes a significant element among our company's assets.

The task of examining our company's legal position statement and also the legal statement of the other company might be relatively easy. Because our company owns 100 percent of the stock of the other company (that is, we own the whole works), we would probably add together, mentally or on paper, the cash of our company and that of the other (subsidiary) company to determine our overall cash position; we would also add together the assets of each other category, and then add together the liabilities. In other words, ownership of stock in our company at the same time effectively constitutes ownership in the other (subsidiary) company. Now, if the officers and directors of our company, through our company's ownership of all the stock of the other company, can control all the affairs of the other company, just as if that company were a mere branch of our company, why don't we save the reader a lot of bother and combine the statements for him? That's just what we do; only instead of calling the result a combined statement we call it a *consolidated statement.*

You should now be ready for a definition. A consolidated position statement is one which presents the assets, liabilities, and owners' equities of two or more affiliated companies in a single position statement *as if the affiliated companies were a single legal entity.* Let's face it. We're not really dealing with a single legal entity, we're dealing with two or more. So, please observe now, and remember, that every consolidated statement contains an element of fiction: The statements are drawn up *as if* they represented a single entity even though they truly consolidate the data of a parent company and its subsidiary companies.

Once again let's remember that a position statement lists (1) the assets owned by the corporate entity, (2) the liabilities owed to outsiders by the corporate entity, and (3) the (residual) equity of the owners.

Why Isn't a Consolidated Statement a Combined Statement?

To prepare a simple, *combined* position statement for two or more companies would involve nothing more than listing all the cash, all the receivables, and all the "everything else," but then you would not have a consolidated statement. So, please hold on tight as we travel through the next sentences. If we present the separate, legal position statements of two companies, we'll show *all* the assets and *all* the liabilities of each. If we consolidate the two, any debts that one owes to the other will be canceled out (for consolidation purposes only) because when the two are hypothetically brought together *as a single entity,* such debts cease to be owed to or by outsiders.

The key to the preparation of consolidated statements lies in recognizing the need for eliminating mirror items. By *mirror items* we mean items that, figuratively, bridge the space between two separate but affiliated corporations. If you consolidate their statements, you eliminate the space between them and, in so doing, eliminate the bridges. Such a bridge, or pair of mirror items, is the $100 debt that the other company owes our company. On our legal position statement it shows as a $100 account receivable, while on their legal position statement it shows as a $100 account payable. If, then, we consolidate and make up a single position statement, the $100 item is eliminated since it becomes, for this purpose only, strictly an internal debt (within the family). Thus, in the case of your own company, when an employee signs out a tool from the toolroom, he owes something to the toolroom and the toolroom has a claim against him, but since this liability-receivable relationship is all intramural, it would not show up on our position statement.

A consolidated statement is in a true sense a fiction. It brings together what would otherwise be the separate, legal statements of two or more affiliated companies and, in so doing, it shaves off all mirrored items so as to avoid duplication.

Consolidation Buzz Words

The accountant's vocabulary includes a bunch of words that relate primarily to consolidated statement matters. A preview of them will save our stopping for definitions when we look into the actual process of making consolidated statements. Here are some, but certainly not all, of the buzz words. The definitions are loosely presented since few formal definitions exist.

AFFILIATES: Companies are said to be affiliated when they have more or less permanent relationships, usually through stock ownership. For our purposes, when Company A owns an influential portion of the total voting stock of Company B, we will refer to A and B as affiliated companies, or simply as affiliates.

PARENT COMPANY: When one affiliate owns a "controlling interest" in the stock of another company (also an affiliate), the owner company is the parent company. Technically, to be a parent company requires more than 50 percent ownership interest in the affiliate's stock.

SUBSIDIARY COMPANY: This is the affiliate whose stock is owned by a parent company. It is of course possible for Company A to exercise overwhelming influence over Company B while holding less than 50 percent of B stock, but usually no consolidated statement is prepared for these cases.

MAJORITY INTEREST: This refers to the stockholding of the parent company; it must be more than 50 percent of the stock which the subsidiary has outstanding.

MINORITY INTEREST: This refers to shares of stock held by persons, corporations, etc., other than the parent corporation. Thus, if the parent holds a 51 percent majority interest, the minority shareholder, or shareholders altogether, hold the remaining 49 percent, which could be held by any number of minority stockholders, from one to many.

CONTROLLING INTEREST: If the outstanding voting shares of a company are widely scattered, it is possible for the owner of as little as 10 or 20 percent to exercise great influence over election of corporate directors and other affairs of the corporation. However, consolidated statements are not customarily prepared unless the parent affiliate not only has assured *technical* control through ownership of more than 50 percent of the voting stock but also has *realistic* control. Technical 50 percent-plus control is easy to measure; realistic or effective control may depend on other matters and conditions. Thus, you might be justified in excluding from consolidation certain foreign subsidiaries in countries which are under serious economic or political crisis conditions or which do not allow transmittal of funds back to this country. Also separate statements (rather than consolidated statements) may be presented with respect to subsidiaries which are regulated by governmental commissions and which are subject to their unique accounting regulations, such as banks, public utilities, and railroads. In short, a controlling interest requires control in fact as well as technical control.

INTERCOMPANY ITEMS: These are the mirror items referred to earlier. The major examples are:

1. Parent has to make loans (advances) of $100,000 to Subsidiary. On Parent's books the loan is a receivable; on Subsidiary's books (and

on Subsidiary's legal statement) the same loan is a liability. This group of cases are referred to as intercompany debt.

2. Parent owns 51 percent of Subsidiary common stock. On Parent's legal statement this stock is shown as a single figure, labeled Investment in Subsidiary. On Subsidiary's legal statement this stock doesn't show separately but is included as part of the total stock outstanding. (Let's refresh our memories here. Each corporation, even though an affiliate, remains a separate legal entity and its "legal" statement is its own position statement or income statement, not consolidated. A consolidated statement combines the legal statements of two or more affiliated companies.)

3. Parent sells merchandise to Subsidiary. On their respective legal statements the sales by Parent are shown in their entirety as are the purchases of Subsidiary. In effecting a consolidated statement, with the companies' statements combined, these intercompany sales and purchases fade out since, *as a family,* the transactions are the same as if they were mere movements of goods from one department to another within a single enterprise.

4. When one affiliate sells something to another at a profit, the price (cost) of the thing on the buyer's books becomes higher than it was on the seller's books. This markup is reflected (*a*) in a higher price (cost) on the buyer's books and (*b*) in retained earnings on the seller's books. Thus "intercompany profits," so long as the marked-up item remains in the family, constitutes an intercompany item. There are numerous other forms of intercompany items, but these should suffice for your understanding of their nature.

Elimination Entries

So-called *elimination entries* must be made for *all intercompany items.* Thank goodness, they all fit neatly into our basic debit-credit structure. Let's introduce them by an example. In the preceding section, the example given for what was there listed as group (1) items had Parent lending $100,000 cash to Subsidiary. You know that on Parent's books making the loan would be recorded by the following entry:

(1)

Advance to Subsidiary.   100,000
    Cash in Bank.   100,000
To record loan of $100,000 to our affiliate, Subsidiary Co.

On the books of Subsidiary, the receipt of the cash from Parent would be recorded as follows:

(2)

Cash...	100,000	
Advance from Parent...............................		100,000
To record receipt of cash advance from Parent Co.		

In these entries you should clearly recognize the intercompany items (Advance to Subsidiary and Advance from Parent). Now, when the position statements of Parent and Subsidiary are to be consolidated, we must first make the following eliminating entry:

(3)

Advance from Parent.................................	100,000	
Advance to Subsidiary.............................		100,000
To eliminate intercompany items resulting from advance from Parent to Subsidiary.		

The second group of intercompany items listed in the preceding section consisted of intercompany stockholdings; Parent owns more than 50 percent of the outstanding voting stock of Subsidiary. Assume that Parent had bought 90 percent of Subsidiary common stock from the present stockholders of Subsidiary for $1,170,000 cash, at a time when the stockholders' equity section of Subsidiary's legal position statement stood as follows:

SUBSIDIARY CO.
Stockholders' Equity, December 31, 19XX

Capital stock, common, $10 par..................	$1,000,000
Retained earnings..............................	300,000
	$1,300,000

The entry to record this acquisition on Parent's books is:

(4)

Investment in Subsidiary Stock........................	1,170,000	
Cash in Bank....................................		1,170,000
To record purchase of 90% of Subsidiary common stock for cash.		

What entry would be made on Subsidiary books? Of course these would be none. Subsidiary's stock outstanding merely changed hands and there is no direct effect on Subsidiary's assets or equities. However, the mirror item is already on Subsidiary's books in the form of its existing stock-holders' equity and we'll again have to do some eliminating in the process of consolidating. Here's the way it's done:

(5)

Capital Stock Common, $10 par (90%)...................	900,000	
Retained Earnings (90%)...............................	270,000	
Investment in Subsidiary Stock.......................		1,170,000

To eliminate intercompany 90% stock ownership as of date of acquisition.

Entry 5 needs more clarification. When Parent bought up 90 percent of the outstanding stock of Subsidiary, it acquired 90 percent of the Subsidiary stockholders' equity. In a sense, 90 percent of the $1,300,000 stock equity (or $1,170,000) is now "owed" to Parent (and Parent has a sort of claim of the same amount against Subsidiary). This inter-company item is made up of 90 percent of the stock and 90 percent of the retained earnings (at date of the stock purchase by Parent—at "acquisition" date). Before we proceed to the next group, note that the $1,170,000 assumed in our example exactly matched 90 percent of the stock equity as it stood on the books of Subsidiary. Such perfect matching will rarely occur in real life, and we'll run into problems of accounting for the disparities. Entries shown later will demonstrate the handling of these cases.

The third group of intercompany items consists of intercompany sales of merchandise. Assume that Parent, during a given year, makes cash sales totaling $500,000 to Subsidiary. The entries on both sets of books are:

(6)

On Parent's Books

Cash....................................	500,000	
Sales................................		500,000

(7)

On Subsidiary's Books

Purchases..............................	500,000	
Cash in Bank.......................		500,000

The intercompany, or duplicating, items in entries 6 and 7 are Sales and Purchases. The obvious eliminating entries for purposes of consolidation are:

(8)

Sales....................................	500,000	
Purchases............................		500,000

The fourth group of intercompany items includes the "unrealized profit" (the markup) on assets, of whatever kind, sold by one affiliate to another *and remaining in the hands of the purchaser* affiliate as of the date of our consolidated statement. Please bear in mind that the profit is truly realized so far as the selling and buying entities are concerned, but when the position statements (and income statements) of the affiliates are *consolidated,* the profit lodged in any assets is strictly "in house" profit and must be treated as unrealized. If we didn't eliminate this profit, it would make room for some first-class shenanigans; for instance, Parent could buy a ping-pong ball for $.25, sell it to Subsidiary (on account) for $1; without elimination entries, the consolidated position statement would show the ball at "cost" of $1 and would include a $.75 gain in the Retained Earnings account of Parent. For real fun, bounce the ping-pong ball back and forth between Parent and Subsidiary, with each buying it at one price and immediately reselling it at a higher price to the other. We might end up with the world's first million-dollar ping-pong ball!

Now for an illustration refer again to entries 6 and 7, where Parent sold merchandise to Subsidiary for $500,000. We then made an elimination entry 8 to cancel the mirrored sales/purchases of $500,000. Next assume that Subsidiary resells 80 percent of these goods to outsiders before the end of the accounting period. Subsidiary's position statement will still include 20 percent of the $500,000, or $100,000, priced at the intercompany sales price. Now assume that the goods include a markup by Parent of 40 percent of selling price. Clearly, then, the goods remaining on Subsidiary's shelves had a cost *to the family* of only $60,000, and $40,000 of unrealized profit must be eliminated by the following entry:

(9)

Retained Earnings (Parent)...............................	40,000	
Inventories (Subsidiary)...............................		40,000

To eliminate the $40,000 of unrealized profit in Subsidiary inventory.

You might wonder why we don't also eliminate the intercompany profit on the remaining $400,000 of sales from Parent to Subsidiary. The answer is that, to the degree that Subsidiary resells goods bought from Parent, Subsidiary's expenses (cost of goods sold) will be inflated by an amount which matches the profit we allowed Parent to claim. That is, Subsidiary resold $400,000 of the goods which had been marked up by $160,000, so Subsidiary's cost of goods sold is inflated by that amount, which exactly offsets the $160,000 profit that we allowed Parent to claim when we eliminated only $40,000 of the $200,000 gain that Parent booked from the sales. We'll do some further tinkering with this subject in illustrating consolidated income statements.

Where Are Elimination Entries Recorded?

By now you must be wondering how it is possible to record a journal entry in which a debit is made to an account on one entity's books and the related credit is made to an account on another entity's books. For instance, in entry 8 we debited Sales to eliminate intercompany sales from Parent's financial data and we credited Purchases for the same amount to eliminate the mirrored item from Subsidiary's financial data—all to ready the data for consolidation. (We might insert here that a consolidated statement can properly be called a *combined* statement of the financial data of affiliated entities *after* the effects of intercompany transactions have been eliminated.)

The answer to our pending question is that the elimination journal entries are not made in any set of books. The legal accounting records of Parent and the legal accounting records of Subsidiary are not touched in the consolidation process. Each entity may, if desirable, issue its legal financial statements. The entries are entirely hypothetical and need not actually be written down anywhere just so long as you see to it that you eliminate all the intercompany items before you combine the statements.

In actual practice the preparation of consolidated statements is usually done through a work sheet. What you do is list the legal position statement data of Parent in the first pair of columns; list the data of Subsidiary in the next pair of columns; make all necessary debit and credit elimination entries in the next pair of columns; and combine (consolidate) what's left. If your company has one or more subsidiaries, you might ask the accountant in charge of preparing consolidated statements to show you his consolidated working papers and explain them to you.

Because in this book we're concerned with the understanding rather than the mechanics of accounting, our consolidation examples, coming up next, will not utilize work sheets but will employ a journal entry procedure because it is more flexible and useful for our particular purposes.

Consolidation of Position Statements at Acquisition Date

Assume that Parent Co. buys 80 percent of the outstanding common stock of Subsidiary Co. on January 1, 19X1, for $120,000 and that the legal position statement data of the two companies, in condensed form, stand as follows on that date just after Parent Co. buys the stock:

Assets	Parent Co.	Subsidiary Co.
Current.........................	$100,000	$ 50,000
Investment in S Co. (cost)............	120,000	—
Plant (net).......................	80,000	100,000
	$300,000	$150,000
Equities		
Current liabilities..................	$ 40,000	$ 20,000
Capital stock......................	150,000	100,000
Retained earnings..................	110,000	30,000
	$300,000	$150,000

If we wish to prepare a consolidated position statement immediately after the stock acquisition, what elimination entries must we make before we combine the data? For the sake of simplicity, assume that the two companies have had no dealings with each other. Then, the only elimination items are the investment account on Parent's books and 80 percent of the stockholders' equity on Subsidiary's books. The needed elimination entry (with one item temporarily omitted) is:

(9)

Capital Stock—Subsidiary (80%)...........................	80,000	
Retained Earnings (at date of acquisition)—Subsidiary (80%)..	24,000	
Balance to be plugged....................................	16,000	
Investment in Subsidiary............................		120,000

To eliminate intercompany investment and corresponding capital stock and "purchased" retained earnings.

What do we do about the $16,000 plug? The traditional answer to this is that it must represent a mix of two things: (1) unrecognized appreciation (or inflation) assignable to the various assets owned by Subsidiary Co. and (2) goodwill. The accepted rule is to replace the plug with debits to Subsidiary asset accounts, insofar as such write-ups are justified, and charge the balance to consolidated goodwill. So, if we assume that Subsidiary's current assets are up to date but that the plant has a current appraised value of $110,000, we would debit Plant with $10,000 and Goodwill with $6,000 and revise the entry as follows:

(9a)

Capital Stock—Subsidiary...................	80,000	
Retained Earnings—Subsidiary.............	24,000	
Plant......................................	10,000	
Goodwill.................................	6,000	
Investment in Subsidiary...............		120,000

Preparation of a consolidated position statement now requires only that we combine the original data, as adjusted by our eliminating entry. Our consolidated statement (with helpful notations) becomes as shown in Figure 1.

Consolidated Position Statement— Sometime Later

Ten years have passed since Parent acquired its 80 percent interest in Subsidiary and we are now again expected to prepare a consolidated position statement. The position statement data at this moment stand as follows in the books of the two affiliates:

Assets	Parent Co.	Subsidiary Co.
Current............................	$150,000	$ 75,000
Investment in S Co. (cost)............	120,000	—
Plant (net)........................	120,000	150,000
	$390,000	$225,000
Equities		
Current liabilities	$ 60,000	$ 30,000
Capital stock......................	150,000	100,000
Retained earnings..................	180,000	95,000
	$390,000	$225,000

In addition, assume that (1) Parent now owes Subsidiary $10,000; (2) the current assets of Parent include merchandise inventory purchased from Subsidiary on which Subsidiary recorded profit of $5,000; (3) the plant adjustment in entry 9a must be reduced to reflect depreciation of $8,000; and (4) the goodwill adjustment in entry 9a must be reduced to reflect amortization of $1,500. As before, our first step is

FIGURE 1
PARENT CO. AND SUBSIDIARY CO.
Consolidated Position Statement, January 1, 19X1

Assets		Equities		
Current (sum).........	$150,000	Current liabilities (sum)......		$ 60,000
Plant (sum plus $10,000)	190,000	Minority interest (20% of Sub-		
Goodwill (new item)....	6,000	sidiary equity).............		26,000
		Stockholders' equity:		
		Capital stock....	$150,000	
		Retained earnings	110,000	260,000
	$346,000			$346,000

to prepare the necessary elimination (and adjusting) entries. They are:

(10)

Capital Stock...	80,000	
Retained Earnings (80% of amount at acquisition, as before)...	24,000	
Plant...	10,000	
Goodwill..	6,000	
Investment in Subsidiary...........................		120,000

To eliminate intercompany investment, corresponding capital stock, and "purchased" retained earnings, and to recognize the $16,000 amount paid in excess of book value as an adjustment of Plant and Goodwill of Subsidiary.

(11)

Retained Earnings (Parent).............................	9,500	
Plant...		8,000
Goodwill..		1,500

To charge off against consolidated retained earnings the amounts indicated as accumulated depreciation and amortization, respectively, of plant and goodwill adjustments made at date of acquisition.

(12)

Current Liabilities.....................................	10,000	
Current Assets....................................		10,000

To eliminate intercompany debt.

(13)

Retained Earnings (Subsidiary)..........................	5,000	
Current Assets....................................		5,000

To eliminate unrealized Subsidiary profits from inventories of Parent.

Our final "elimination" entry is not actually an elimination. Rather, it consists of splitting the retained earnings of Subsidiary between the minority and the parent company majority interests. We have already reduced Subsidiary's retained earnings by $5,000 in entry 13, leaving a balance of $90,000. Of this, 20 percent belongs to the minority and the rest (less the $24,000 "purchased" at acquisition date) goes to consolidated retained earnings. This may all be put in journal entry form as follows:

(14)

Retained Earnings (Subsidiary)	90,000	
Minority Interest (20%)		18,000
Investment Account (already entered in 9a)		24,000
Consolidated Retained Earnings		48,000

To allocate retained earnings of subsidiary between minority and majority interests.

We are now ready to combine the leftovers in a consolidated position statement, which is shown as Figure 2.

Consolidation of Income Statements

To illustrate the preparation of a consolidated income statement, assume the following income statement data for the tenth year of affiliation:

	Parent Co.	Subsidiary Co.
Sales	$200,000	$100,000
Cost of goods sold	$120,000	$ 60,000
Other expenses and taxes	60,000	30,000
	$180,000	$ 90,000
Net income	$ 20,000	$ 10,000

Assume as before that Parent owns 80 percent of the outstanding common stock of Subsidiary; also that, of the sales of Subsidiary, $90,000 were shipments to Parent; and that by the year-end Parent had resold $40,000 of these goods to outsiders (leaving $50,000 in Parent's end-of-year inventory). The requirement is to prepare a consolidated income statement. For this purpose assume that all goods sold by Subsidiary Co. provide the same rate of profit.

There are several ways in which this problem and cases like it can be handled, and each has its supporters. No doubt all would agree that we should eliminate the $90,000 of sales shown on Subsidiary's books as going to Parent. From here on practices differ, but we'll follow

FIGURE 2

PARENT CO. AND SUBSIDIARY CO.

Consolidated Position Statement, Ten Years Later

Assets		Equities		
Current (sum minus $10,000 and $5,000)....	$210,000	Current liabilities (sum less $10,000)...................		$ 80,000
Plant (sum plus $10,000 less $8,000)...........	272,000	Minority interest (20% of $195,000 less $5,000)........		38,000
Goodwill ($6,000 less $1,500)..............	4,500	Stockholders' equity:		
		Capital stock....	$150,000	
		Retained earnings ($180,000 minus $9,500, plus $48,000).......	218,500	368,500
	$486,500			$486,500

through only one plan and assume that you will discuss it and its alternatives with your accountants if the matter is of interest to you.

If, as the assumption states, the profit margin is the same on all of Subsidiary's sales, then total profit on sales to Parent this year was 90 percent of $10,000, or $9,000. This profit, as we've noted before, represents within-the-family markup and we should trace its impacts on the legal statements and eliminate them in a logical manner. The tip-off is the statement that Parent has resold $40,000 of the goods to outsiders. This means that $4,000 of the $9,000 profits has been carried into the Parent cost of goods sold account, and the remainder, $5,000, must still be lodged in Parent's inventory. Next, if we eliminate part ($90,000) of Subsidiary's sales, don't we then have to eliminate the same proportion (nine-tenths) of Subsidiary's cost of goods sold? Yes. And if the other expenses of Subsidiary were proportionately related to the sales made to Parent, the same share (nine-tenths) of them will also be eliminated. Now we have all the necessary elements of our elimination entry, which comes out as follows:

(15)

Sales (of Subsidiary, 90%)....................................	90,000	
Cost of Goods Sold (of Subsidiary, 90%)..................		54,000
Other Expenses and Taxes (of Subsidiary, 90%)..........		27,000
Cost of Goods Sold (of Parent, 4/9 of $9,000)..............		4,000
Merchandise Inventory (of Parent, 5/9 of $9,000)..........		5,000

To eliminate intercompany sales and related expenses, as well as related profit.

FIGURE 3
PARENT CO. AND SUBSIDIARY CO.
Consolidated Income Statement, Tenth Year of Affiliation

Sales (sum minus $90,000 eliminated)............................		$210,000
Expenses:		
Cost of goods sold (sum minus $54,000 and $4,000).......	$122,000	
Other expenses and taxes (sum minus $27,000)..........	63,000	185,000
Total net income (sum less $5,000 unrealized)......................		$ 25,000
Minority interest (20% of $10,000 less $5,000 unrealized).............		1,000
Consolidated net income.......................................		$ 24,000
Proof of consolidated net income:		
Earnings of Parent...		$ 20,000
Parent's share of Subsidiary earnings (80% of $10,000 less $5,000)....		4,000
		$ 24,000

The resulting consolidated income statement may now be prepared. It is shown as Figure 3, with informal notations added for purposes of clarification.

Consolidated Statements—Conclusion

We have only scratched the surface of the world of consolidated statements. The mere mention of consolidated statement problems to the young man about to take his CPA exams will usually bring on a cold sweat. He has practiced doing consolidations of horrendous complexity and he fully expects the worst. CPA examiners delight in setting problems involving a flock of, rather than only two, affiliates; or problems involving subsidiaries and sub-subsidiaries. Sometimes, where only a couple of affiliates are involved, each owns some of the capital stock of the other (mutual holdings); ownership interests may change in mid-year; bonds are issued at a discount by one affiliate and are purchased in the open market at a different price by another affiliate, etc.

One nice thing about the consolidation problems of a given company is that once consolidated statements have successfully been prepared, their repetitive preparation in future years, or months, becomes pure routine.

All we've attempted to accomplish here, of course, is to present an outline of some of the typical problems along with one pattern of solution. From this point on you should be able to think along with your accountants in terms of consolidated data as well as the data of the individual affiliates.

TEST PROBLEM

On January 1, 19X1, Our Company acquires 90 percent of the outstanding common stock of Their Company for $82,000 cash. On this date the position statement data of the two companies (condensed) stand as follows after the stock purchase:

	Our Company	Their Company
Current assets.......................................	$ 50,000	$ 30,000
Investment in Their Company (at cost).....................	82,000	
Plant assets (net)..	118,000	70,000
	$250,000	$100,000
Current liabilities......................................	$ 20,000	$ 20,000
Capital stock..	180,000	50,000
Retained earnings......................................	50,000	30,000
	$250,000	$100,000

Required:

(1) Assume that there have been no intercompany transactions and that goodwill accounts for the payment in excess of book value. Prepare elimination entries and a consolidated position statement as of January 1, 19X1.

(2) Next, assume that each company earns $20,000 during 19X1; that Their Company pays cash dividends of $12,000 (of which 90 percent is added to Our Company's earnings), and at year-end Their Company owes Our Company $5,000. Also, assume that $500 of consolidated goodwill must be amortized. The position statements at the end of 19X1 contain the following:

	Our Company	Their Company
Current assets.......................................	$ 83,800	$ 41,000
Investment in Their Company (at cost).....................	82,000	
Plant assets (net)..	115,000	67,000
	$280,800	$108,000
Current liabilities......................................	$ 20,000	$ 20,000
Capital stock..	180,000	50,000
Retained earnings......................................	80,800	38,000
	$280,800	$108,000

Prepare elimination entries and a consolidated position statement as of the end of 19X1.

TEST PROBLEM Solution Space

(1) Elimination entries on January 1, 19X1:

Debit   *Credit*

Capital Stock
Retained Earnings
Goodwill
    Investment in Their Company

Our Company and Their Company
Consolidated Position Statement
January 1, 19X1

Assets		*Equities*	
Current	$	Current liabilities	$
Plant		Minority interest	
Goodwill		Stockholders' equity:	
		Capital stock	$
		Retained earnings	
	$		$

(2) Elimination entry on December 31, 19X1

Debit   *Credit*

(1)

Capital Stock
Retained Earnings
Goodwill
    Investment in Their Company

(2)

Retained Earnings
    Goodwill

(3)

Current Liabilities
    Current Assets

Our Company and Their Company
Consolidated Position Statement
December 31, 19X1

Assets		*Equities*	
Current		Current liabilities	$
Plant		Minority interest	
Goodwill		Stock equity:	
		Capital stock	$
		Retained earnings	
	$		$

Chapter Eighteen

Income Tax Allocation

Why Bother?

It's a tough enough job just to determine how much income tax your company owes at the end of any year—why complicate things by attempting to "allocate" your taxes to periods other than the ones in which they become due?

This question has led to countless arguments among accountants and nonaccountants; it has been the subject of hundreds of lawsuits; and it has, in general, helped to keep the profession of accounting from becoming deadly dull.

Most people who are untrained in accounting, and accountants who may not have studied the subject of income tax allocation, will automatically vote against allocation, and the results of this ingenuous position taking are often seriously inequitable. Judges and regulatory commissions, lacking a trained accountant's perception of tax allocation, gravitate naturally toward unfortunate rulings, usually opposing allocation.

The answer to the question, why bother? can be reduced to a brief statement, which will require elaboration, but here it is: The determination of periodic enterprise income rests upon the process of matching costs with revenues on a logical basis. Such matching is virtually synonymous with *accrual basis,* rather than *cash basis,* accounting. Income tax allocation is synonymous with accrual accounting; nonallocation is synonymous with cash basis accounting. Therefore, we must allocate. To summarize, the question is: Why isn't the income tax that we actually have to pay the amount of income tax that we should show as our current income tax expense in our income statement? The answer is that the income tax burden must be matched (accrued) with the items of revenue and expense which generate it; to treat the tax as an expense in a given year only because we pay it, or owe it, makes no sense at all.

What Conditions Make Interperiod Allocation Necessary?

We would have almost no tax allocation problems if the rules for measuring taxable income were made to conform to the "generally accepted principles" of accounting, or if the principles governing accounting were made to conform to the tax rules. Either of these changes, however, is only a creature of the dream world. The tax folks are too anxious to get their hands on the taxpayers' hard cash to allow them full exercise of sound accounting principles; at the same time, the taxpayers would be most reluctant to give up certain tax-deferring opportunities which do not fit well into their accounting records and reports. So, tax allocation is needed when either the revenues or the expenses that we record in our books and financial statements differ from the amounts that we report (honestly) on our tax return. It should be added that we're not concerned with accounting or reporting errors, nor are we concerned with possible tax evasion. The differences are almost entirely the result of timing. Thus, a particular $10,000 may be recognized as revenue in our books in one year and may be shown on our tax return as revenue in either an earlier or a later year; and the same may be true with certain expense outlays. For purposes of completeness, we'll divide this part of the discussion into four segments, as follows:

1. Cases in which *revenues* show up in our books and financial statements *before* they are subject to tax (that is, before they are reported on our tax returns).

2. Cases in which *expenses* show up in our books and financial state-

ments *before* they are used as tax deductions (that is, before they are reported on our tax returns).

3. Cases in which *revenues* show up in our books and financial statements *after* they have been taxed (that is, after they have been reported on our tax returns).

4. Cases in which *expenses* show up in our books and financial statements *after* they have been used as tax deductions (that is, after they have been reported on our tax returns).

General Principles of Interperiod Allocation

The all-encompassing principle of tax allocation requires that we employ the accrual method (not the cash method) of recognizing income taxes. Corollaries, or subprinciples to this general principle, with more detail added, may be phrased as follows:

1. If income is recorded in the books and financial statements before it has been subjected to income tax, we must accrue an appropriate amount of tax in order to avoid overstatement of income.

2. If taxes are paid on "income" before being properly recognized in the books and financial statements, the tax charges, from the standpoint of our books, have actually been "prepaid" and should be so shown in our financial statements pending recognition of the income.

Revenue Recognized before It Is Taxed

The weight of accounting opinion nowadays favors comprehensive use of accrual accounting; more specifically, it favors the recognition of sales revenue at the time a sale is made, even though it may be an installment sale, so long as collection of the sales price is reasonably assured. On the other hand, the government allows the cash basis of accounting for installment sales in determining *taxable* income (subject, of course, to meeting technical tax rules). What this means is that on an installment gain you are able to defer the actual payout of tax money beyond the point of sale by taking advantage of the tax provision which says your income may be taxable in proportion to the fraction of the sales price that you actually collect each year.

Let's take a fairly clear-cut example. Assume that we sell for $20,000 an asset which cost $5,000, and assume that the buyer pays 10 percent down (and no more during the year of sale). Our entry at the time of sale, using accrual accounting, is:

(1)

Installment Account Receivable	18,000	
Cash	2,000	
Asset—Cost		5,000
Gain on Sale of Asset		15,000

Assume that the tax rate on this kind of gain is 25 percent; however, since we've collected only 10 percent of the selling price, only 10 percent of the gain is taxed this year, for a total tax of $375. When we recognize this tax liability, our entry is:

(2)

Income Tax Expense	375	
Income Tax Payable (or Cash)		375

Now the question is, would it be "fair" reporting to show this portion of our income statement as follows?

Gross gain on sale of asset	$15,000
Less: Tax on collected portion	375
Net income from sale of asset	$14,625

Quite obviously this is a misleading presentation, because we have claimed the entire gross gain in this accounting period but have charged against it only the "cash" portion of the income tax that presumably will have to be paid. This situation clearly calls for a tax allocation (accrual) entry to charge against the gain recognized this period the tax that will become payable on the total gain. The obvious solution is to *accrue* the 25 percent tax on the remaining 90 percent of the gain in the year of sale. Such an entry is made as follows:

(3)

Income Tax Expense	3,375	
Accrued Future Tax Liability		3,375

To accrue 25% tax on $13,500 of installment gain recognized in the accounts but subject to tax only in the future as cash installments are collected.

With entry 3 on the books, the income statement will now show the following:

Gross gain on sale of asset	$15,000
Less: Income tax expense (including $3,375 deferred on installment basis)	3,750
Net income	$11,250

This discussion is necessarily abbreviated. Its aim, however, is to introduce the concept of tax allocation to you. Upon further reading, and discussion with your accountants, you will find that the tax allocation entry "preferred" by the Accounting Principles Board of the American Institute of Certified Public Accountants requires a credit to a "deferred credit" account rather than to the liability account shown in entry 2. The question always remaining, of course, is: Just what is a deferred credit?

The conclusion would appear logically to be that whenever revenue that will sometime be taxed is recognized in the accounts as earned before the period in which it actually becomes subjected to tax, a charge should be made to the tax expense account to accrue the future tax so that the current period's statement will not be distorted; the related credit probably is an accrued liability, although the Institute's Board prefers to label it a deferred credit.

Other cases in which revenue may be booked before it is taxed occur in connection with accounting for long-term construction contracts, or in the technical handling of leaseholds on the books of the lessor.

Expenses Recognized before They Become Tax Deductions

The Internal Revenue decision makers have steadfastly refused to allow businesses to deduct expenses of a conjectural or strictly estimated nature, such as estimated future inventory losses and estimated outlays for product warranties; however, the accrual of such expenses is thoroughly logical and necessary on a timely basis in order to avoid overstatements of income. What this boils down to is that such expenses are shown on the income statement as reductions of earnings but income taxes, in fact, are not correspondingly saved. Again the question is, Do we show on our income statement only the income taxes we actually pay (or owe), or do we allocate the taxes to make them match up with the revenues and expenses that we have booked, knowing that the differences are almost entirely matters of timing and will eventually wash out? The answer, again, would appear to be that when we pay a tax in one year that really should be matched against the income of the next, or later, period, we should hold the tax charge in abeyance until its proper time for appearance in the income statement. This is done by treating the tax as being "prepaid" or, as the Accounting Principles Board prefers to call it, "deferred."

For an example, assume that our company accrues $100,000 of product warranty expense in the year in which the sales of these products are recorded as revenues; also, assume that our income tax rate is 40 percent. The warranty entry and the tax entries would then be:

(1)

Product Warranty Expense.............................. 100,000
    Accrued Liability for Product Warranty................   100,000
To accrue as warranty expense and liability the percentage of sales that has been found by experience to be reasonable.

(2)

Prepaid (Deferred) Income Tax Charge.................... 40,000
    Income Tax Expense.................................   40,000
To reduce the cash tax expense account, and treat as prepaid, 40% of the amount accrued as warranty expense which is not currently tax deductible.

Other examples of expenses booked before they become tax deductible could easily be cited. However, the conclusion would appear to be sound that under circumstances in which expenses are recognized in the books before they are deductible, the tax payment made as the result of such nondeductibility should be set up as a prepayment or deferred charge, to be transferred to tax expense as the accrued expenses materialize in the form of actual outlays.

Revenue Taxed before It Is Recognized

Apparently under most circumstances the government assesses income taxes on collections of cash that a business firm may make in advance of rendering a service. Thus, rents collected in advance, dues in advance, subscriptions in advance, payments for correspondence lessons in advance, etc., all may be taxable in the period of receipt (i.e., on a cash basis), rather than in the period when the services are rendered and the revenue is recognized in accordance with sound accounting principles.

Needless to say, the accountant resists showing advance cash collections as revenue. His entry to record these takes the following general form:

(1)

Cash... xxx
    Liability for Amounts Collected in Advance from Customers......   xxx

As the services are rendered, whether in later periods or the current one, he records the earning (realization) of revenues as follows. (Assume that we're dealing with rents collected in advance.)

(2)

Liability for Amounts Collected in Advance from Customers.   xxx
    Rent Revenue.   xxx

If entry 1 occurs in one year and entry 2 in the second, then the income tax will be payable in Year 1 on revenue that is not recognized until Year 2.

Fortunately, again, we can resort to the accrual methods of accounting. To do this, the tax which we pay in Year 1 (on the revenues to be earned in Year 2) is debited to a prepaid (or deferred) tax account; like any other prepayment, it is treated as an asset to be written off as it is used up. In the second year, when the rent revenue is recognized, the amount in the prepaid tax account is transferred to the tax expense account so that it will become matched with the rent revenue in the second year's income statement.

The general conclusion, thus, for all cases in which income taxes must be paid prematurely on cash advances from customers or clients is to hold the tax in a prepaid expense (or deferred charge) account as an asset to be written off in the period or periods in which the services are rendered to the customers and their advances are transferred from liability to revenue accounts.

Expenses as Tax Deductions before They are Recognized

This final category of interperiod tax allocation cases has created much more controversy than the others. The circumstances are these: We own a depreciable asset which has an assumed 5-year life. On our books we use the straight-line depreciation method, while we use the sum-of-years'-digits method for tax purposes. The result is that our tax deduction for depreciation during the first 2 years is greater than our book depreciation, and during the final 2 years it is less (in the third year they are identical). Over the full 5 years, the depreciation totals are, of course, alike. The timing, however, differs as between book and tax depreciation. The respective annual depreciation charges are shown in Figure 1 for an asset assumed to have cost $900.

FIGURE 1
Book and Tax Depreciation

Year	Book (straight-line)	Tax (SYD)	Differences
1	$180	$300	$ + 120
2	180	240	+ 60
3	180	180	—
4	180	120	— 60
5	180	60	— 120
Total	$900	$900	$ —

If we assume that our company has net revenue (after deducting everything except depreciation and tax) of $300 per year and an effective tax rate of 25 percent, its actual income tax liabilities for the 5-year period would be as shown in Figure 2.

FIGURE 2
Our Company's Tax Liabilities

Year	Revenue before depreciation	Tax depreciation	Taxable income	25% tax
1	$ 300	$300	—	—
2	300	240	$ 60	$ 15
3	300	180	120	30
4	300	120	180	45
5	300	60	240	60
Total	$1,500	$900	$600	$150

Were our company to present its income statements without allocation of taxes, it would of course show a relatively high net income in the first two years and a relatively low net income in the final two years. The customary buzz words for a presentation of this sort are "flow through"; that is, we ignore the inconsistent relationships between the taxes we pay, as compared with the revenues and expenses that we record, and merely let the cash tax consequences flow through. In Figure 3 are shown the income statement data for the 5 years on a flow-through basis.

FIGURE 3
OUR COMPANY
Comparative Income Statements on Flow-through Basis

	Years					
	1	2	3	4	5	All
Net revenue (before depreciation and tax)..	$300	$300	$300	$300	$300	$1,500
Depreciation per books..................	180	180	180	180	180	900
Net before tax........................	$120	$120	$120	$120	$120	$ 600
Tax (actual)...........................	—	15	30	45	60	150
Net income............................	$120	$105	$ 90	$ 75	$ 60	$ 450

Surely anybody making an analysis of Our Company's progress as reflected in its net income trend would be quite pessimistic because of the persistent decline. This is exactly what is wrong with flow through; again, it consists of an unfortunate mix of accrual accounting for all data except taxes, which are naïvely recognized on a cash basis. One of the more popular inequities which regulatory commissions throughout the country have imposed upon our public utility companies has been to require them (1) to use one of the rapid depreciation methods for tax purposes, (2) to use straight-line depreciation in their books, and (3) to use the flow-through scheme for determining income subject to regulation. The early effects of such requirements are, of course, an apparently inflated amount of earnings, which the commissions then proceed to chisel down with no promise of compensatory adjustment as the tide reverses itself in later years.

Next, let's apply tax allocation techniques to these same data. In Year 1, $300 of the asset's cost was written off as a tax deduction (leaving only $600 for future write-offs in the next 4 years). On the other hand, only $180 of cost was written off in the accounting records. If we present a flow-through income statement (as in Figure 3), do we properly disclose the fact that in this first year we have, in a sense, borrowed some $120 of depreciation deductions from our future? Does it put the reader on notice that our remarkably low tax bill was achieved at the expense of higher tax bills in the future? Wouldn't it be more honest to accrue an appropriate amount of income tax charge against the $120 of apparent earnings, on the ground that because we are using up $300 of depreciation deduction now we'll be obligated to pay commensurately more taxes in future years? All these questions would appear to point in the direction of tax allocation. Stated most simply, our *cash* tax has, indeed, been delayed (deferred) but it has not been evaded or *avoided;* our tax burden should be accrued on the basis of our pretax book income. In the present instance the tax charge has been only temporarily reduced and the amount of this temporary reduction is found by multiplying our tax rate (25 percent) by the amount of *extra* depreciation taken for tax purposes ($120). We should accrue against this year's earnings 25 percent of $120, or $30 as deferred income tax. The entry is:

(1)

Income Tax Expense..............................   30
    Deferred (or Accrued) Income Tax Credit.........   30

In Year 2 the amount deferred is 25 percent of $60 (which is tax depreciation of $240 minus book depreciation of $180), or $15. In Year 3 no allocation entry is needed. Then, in the final two years the situation turns around. The difference between tax depreciation and book depreciation becomes negative, so our allocation entries are the reverse of those made in the first two years, or as follows:

(2)
Year 4

Income Tax Expense..............................   45
    Cash (or Tax Payable).........................   45
To record tax liability for Year 4.

(3)

Deferred (or Accrued) Income Tax Credit............   15
    Income Tax Expense...........................   15
To reverse deferral of 25% of $120 — 180.

(4)
Year 5

Income Tax Expense..............................   60
    Cash (or Tax Payable).........................   60
To record tax liability for Year 5.
Deferred Income Tax Credit......................   30
    Income Tax Expense...........................   30
To reverse deferral of 25% of $60 — 180.

If tax allocation entries are recorded in the fashion illustrated, the income statements for the 5 years should produce the same amount of net income each year, since all other things were unchanged. In Figure 4 the income

FIGURE 4
OUR COMPANY
Comparative Income Statements (on full accrual basis)

	Years					
	1	2	3	4	5	All
Net revenue (before depreciation and tax).	$300	$300	$300	$300	$300	$1,500
Depreciation, straight-line ($900/5)......	180	180	180	180	180	900
Net revenue before tax................	$120	$120	$120	$120	$120	$ 600
Income tax:						
Cash.............................	$ 0	$ 15	$ 30	$ 45	$ 60	$ 150
Accrual..........................	30	15	0	(15)	(30)	0
	$ 30	$ 30	$ 30	$ 30	$ 30	$ 150
Net Income........................	$ 90	$ 90	$ 90	$ 90	$ 90	$ 450

statements are presented again with the effects of the tax allocation entries clearly disclosed (as they should be).

There are those (including myself) who believe that the same allocation results could be obtained more logically if the amounts of additional tax accrued in the first two years and the tax reductions of the last two years, were treated instead as adjustments of the straight-line depreciation accruals. The theory is that, in consuming $300 worth of tax depreciation in the first year, we "sapped" the asset of some of its future cash-flow power and this should be reflected as additional depreciation. Were this plan adopted, our income statements would show as tax expense the amounts actually owed each year, while the periodic depreciation would be the $180 of straight-line charge, increased by $30 and $15, respectively, in the first two years, and decreased by $15 and $30, respectively, in the last two years; net income would be the same—$90 for each year.

Tax Allocation and Permanent Differences

So far we have looked at tax allocation procedures where differences between the books and the tax returns are only differences in timing; in other words, the cumulative difference eventually reduces to zero for all practical purposes. There are some situations, however, where certain items of income or expense recorded in the books are never to be included in the income tax determination. Quite obviously we here have no problem of allocation; no allocation entries are to be made because the two (books and tax returns) never catch up with each other. This is the case with all permanent differences.

Arguments against Tax Allocation

Some persons feel that no tax allocation entry should be made in the case of depreciation differences because the company could, by continually expanding at a uniform or accelerating rate, permanently delay part of its tax payments; then "flow through" (so they argue) is the only proper course. The Accounting Principles Board strongly rejected this view, pointing out that it would be much like arguing that a growing company should treat its current liabilities as part of retained earnings because the total is always bound to increase! This is only the beginning of the argument, and we'll leave it to you to have some enjoyable discussions with your accountants about it.

Tax Allocation within a Period

Yes, even within a single year taxes may require allocation. This happens in the relatively unusual cases where income determination items are shown partly in one place and partly in another. If, for example, your income statement reports an extraordinary gain, the gain will be shown at the bottom of the statement. Quite logically, the gain should carry with it its full share of operating expenses and income taxes; so, just as income may be shown in two different places in the income statement, taxes may also be split.

Also, on rare occasions we may make charges or credits directly to Retained Earnings to record corrections of earnings carried forward from prior years. To the degree that such entries enter into the income tax determination, a portion of the tax (sometimes a negative portion) should be allocated to them. One obvious result of such allocations is that the tax remaining in the income statement approximates the amount chargeable against the income reported therein (by excluding the amount attributable to the entry in retained earnings).

TEST PROBLEM

(1) Assume that our tax rate is 40 percent. If Our Company uses the accrual method to record installment sales, with a resulting net income (before taxes) of $100,000, while we use the cash (installment) method for tax purposes, with a resulting taxable income of $40,000, we should make the following tax allocation entry:

Debit
    Credit

(2) If we accrue product warranty expenses of $100,000 that are not allowable tax deductions until we actually incur the expenses, we should make the following tax allocation entry:

Debit
    Credit

(3) If we collect $100,000 in rents and earn only $60,000 of this amount this year, we should make the following tax allocation entry at the year-end:

Debit
    Credit

(4) If we record total straight-line depreciation of $100,000, while reporting $250,000 for tax purposes, we should make the following entry:

Debit
    Credit

Chapter Nineteen

Business Combinations

How Business Combinations
Are Achieved

Nothing has created more interest, for those who enjoy a good fight, than the battle during recent years among accountants and financiers, low and high, over the manner in which we should account for various types of business combinations. It has been said repeatedly that many mergers simply would not be carried out if the companies were not permitted to account for them the way they want to. This is sad! In any case, let's apply accounting analysis to the major patterns of combinations so we can see what the argument's all about.

The heart of the ruckus can be boiled down to two words—pooling and purchase. For years and years, given the requisite arrangements, companies have been allowed to decide how they will account for a combination, whether as a purchase or as a pooling, and the resulting financial reports could be vastly different, depending on the choice of method. Then the Accounting Principles Board set out to narrow this range of choice to the point where some people cried that poolings, for all practical purposes, would be choked off entirely. The end result was a compromise which throws the doors wide open for poolings *if the combining transactions qualify* but which insists that there shall be no freedom of choice in the accounting once the transaction has been consummated in a given form.

In the process of developing its principles, the Accounting Principles Board adopted the word "acquisition" to replace "purchase"; from now on, we'll employ the terms *acquisitions* and *poolings*.

The Physiology of an Acquisition

The management of A Co. has an excess of working capital and wants to employ it by acquiring the business (the net assets) of B Co. There are several ways in which this can be done. For purposes of discussion we'll assume that the position statement data of the two companies stand, at the moment of decision, as shown in Figure 1.

FIGURE 1
Position Statement Data at Time of Acquisition

Assets	A Co.	B Co.
Current...........................	$ 700,000	$100,000
Plant.............................	500,000	500,000
Total.........................	$1,200,000	$600,000
Equities		
Current liabilities....................	$ 100,000	$ 50,000
Bonds payable.......................	400,000	—
Capital stock, par $1.................	500,000	450,000
Retained earnings....................	200,000	100,000
Total........................	$1,200,000	$600,000

For our first variation, assume that A Co. bargains directly with B Co. and they agree that A Co. is to pay B Co. cash, in the amount of $650,000, for the net assets of B Co. (which consist of the asset total of $600,000 offset by the liability total of $50,000).

On the books of A Co. we can delay the difficult part of the acquisition entry a few minutes by making the following initial entry:

(1)

Investment in Net Assets of B Co.—Cost....................	650,000	
Cash in Bank.......................................		650,000

To record purchase of B Co. net assets, with book value of $600,000, for $650,000 cash.

We could now leave B Co. to its own devices if we wanted to since it will have no subsequent effect on A Co. Just for the sake of this excursion, though, let's assume that B Co., now flooded with cash and nothing else, elects to dissolve. The entries, including the sellout, are:

(1*a*)

Cash...	650,000	
Current Liabilities....................................	50,000	
Current Assets.......................................		100,000
Plant..		500,000
Gain on Sale of Net Assets (or Retained Earnings).........		100,000

To record sale of all net assets to A Co. for cash.

(2*a*)

Capital Stock.......................................	450,000	
Retained Earnings (with $100,000 added)................	200,000	
Cash in Bank......................................		650,000

To record distribution of cash to stockholders in liquidation.

In the meantime, A Co. must face the problem of recognizing on its books and statements the net assets acquired from B Co. The easy way out would be simply to debit the various asset accounts for the same amounts at which they were carried on the books of B Co., credit liability accounts also for the amounts formerly owed by B Co., then credit the investment account with the amount of its $650,000 balance and make a "plug" entry to Goodwill to make the entry balance. Such an entry would appear as follows:

(2)

Current Assets (in detail)...............................	100,000	
Plant (in detail).....................................	500,000	
Goodwill (plug to balance)...........................	100,000	
Current Liabilities (in detail)........................		50,000
Investment in Net Assets of B Co.—Cost...............		650,000

To replace investment account with accounts for specific assets and liabilities acquired from B Co., at B Co. book values, and to charge Goodwill for the amount paid ($100,000) in excess of the book value of the net assets.

Needless to point out, entry 2 balances because we *made* it balance with the goodwill plug, but the entry makes no sense whatsoever. There is not the slightest reason (other than indolence or stupidity) for continuing the book values of B Co. on the books of A Co. following their purchase for cash. It would make equal sense, if you were to buy your neighbor's car for $2,000, for you to record it on your books at $3,500 with an allowance for depreciation of $2,000 (a net of $1,500) and charge the $500 difference to Goodwill simply because the neighbor had originally paid $3,500 for the car and had, to date, recorded $2,000 of depreciation.

The point is that we should, at least initially, record assets at cost. When we buy a basket of assets (cum liabilities) for $650,000, it should mean that we have appraised the lot and can allocate the purchase price to them on a reasonable basis including, perhaps, a lump sum for goodwill (which is often simply debited with the amount that is left over).

For a more sensible solution, assume that the current assets are found to be worth approximately their B Co. book values, while the plant assets are appraised at $530,000 and Goodwill is valued at $70,000. Now the entry to clear the Investment account becomes:

(3)

Current Assets (in detail).	100,000	
Plant (in detail).	530,000	
Goodwill.	70,000	
Current Liabilities (in detail).		50,000
Investment in Net Assets of B Co.—Cost.		650,000

To replace the investment account with specific asset and liability accounts at their current values.

For another variation, assume that A Co. issues bonds payable to B Co. for $650,000 instead of paying cash. The acquisition and investment-clearing entries (assuming the same values as before) then become:

(4)

Investment in Net Assets of B Co.	650,000	
Bonds Payable.		650,000

(5)

Current Assets.	100,000	
Plant.	530,000	
Goodwill.	70,000	
Current Liabilities.		50,000
Investment in Net Assets of B Co.		650,000

The same end results can be obtained if the acquisition is made through the purchase of the outstanding capital stock of B Co. and the company is then liquidated; or B Co., after purchase, can be "kept alive" as a subsidiary, and the combining of assets and liabilities then is accomplished only in consolidated statements. The first entry, in either case, records purchase of the capital stock. Assume that a total of

$650,000 cash (or, it could be in bonds) is paid. The purchase entry is:

(6)

Investment in B Co. Common Stock......................	650,000	
Cash in Bank.......................................		650,000

Purchase of 100% of B Co. common for $650,000.

(7)

Current Assets..	100,000	
Plant...	530,000	
Goodwill..	70,000	
Current Liabilities....................................		50,000
Investment in B Co. Common Stock...................		650,000

Dissolution of B Co.

Under the new rules of the game, a business combination must be recorded as a purchase, or acquisition, in all cases except where the merging is accomplished by the issuance of voting common stock in exchange for the common stock of the other company. In the examples that we have examined so far, A Co. might have accomplished an acquisition by issuing preferred stock or consideration of any other form except common stock, instead of cash or bonds, and the entries would follow the pattern shown. When preferred stock is issued instead of cash or bonds, it may be necessary to find a "fair market value" for the stock so that the resulting valuations of current and noncurrent assets will be the same as if cash had been paid.

Impact of Acquisition Transaction on Income

The accounting for a business combination by the "acquisition" route may have a very drastic effect on net income. Prior to acquisition, B Co. might be reporting annual earnings of, say, $60,000 per year, or a rate of return of 10 percent on total assets; however, this amount is based on book values at historical cost. If, as we assumed, the price paid for the assets places them at a total valuation of $700,000, the rate of return drops to $60,000 divided by $700,000, or 8.6 percent, as the result of increasing the "rate base." But this is not all. If the depreciable asset valuations are stepped up and the useful lives are assumed to be unchanged, then the periodic depreciation charges are increased and the net income declines by the amount of the depreciation increase less the related reduction in income taxes. Furthermore, and this could be the real hitch, we came up with goodwill in the amount of $70,000. Accounting logic requires that this asset be amortized over a reasonable (10–40 year) period. In our example, 10-year amortization of the $70,000 of goodwill would reduce the net income by $7,000 per year (with no income tax relief). Thus, from a 10 percent return before acquisition, the purchased business might provide less than 8 percent on the basis of revised asset valuations, depreciation, and amortization. For this reason businessmen and a lot of accountants have argued stoutly for the continued privilege of recording business combinations by what is known as the *pooling-of-interests,* or *pooling,* method whenever certain prerequisites are met.

Before moving on to the subject of poolings, we should stop to ask whether the apparent undesirable consequences of the acquisition method of recording a combination are in any way undeserved. The answer would appear to be that acquisition, or purchase, accounting rules are entirely realistic. In a nutshell, if one pays a high price for an enterprise, whether the payment is made in the form of cash, bonds, or some other type of security, it is only realistic to reflect the high cost in the accounts and in the subsequent financial statements. Any accounting device that actually obscures the cost or other sacrifice made to acquire the enterprise is subject to severe condemnation.

The Physiology of a Pooling of Interests

In the process of effecting a business combination, if one company acquires the outstanding voting common stock of another by a payment of cash or by exchanging preferred stock, bonds, or anything at all other than voting common stock, just forget any pooling of interests; you can't do it that way. But you can pool by issuing your *common stock* in exchange for the common of the other company, and this is then the only way you can do it.

What do we mean by pooling? It means that we don't put up-to-date values on the assets acquired (we don't attempt to determine what they cost us); we bring them onto our books and statements at their old book values. To use the current expression, when we pool the assets of one company with another "they do not have a new basis of accountability." This is to say that when our company issues common stock to the stockholders of your company in exchange for all your common stock, the assets of your company end up in the pool at their present book values per your books.

The underlying theory of pooling is that, in a sense, two or more companies simply elect to join forces—to pool their resources. To do this the stockholders of one company give up their stock in exchange for stock of the other company; they continue to be stockholders, but now in the expanded entity.

In order to emphasize the very important differences betwen the treatment of a combination as an acquisition and as a pooling of interests, we'll use the same initial position statements that we used in the purchase examples. For your convenience they are repeated in Figure 2.

FIGURE 2
Position Statement Data at Time of Pooling

Assets	A Co.	B Co.
Current	$ 700,000	$100,000
Plant	500,000	500,000
Total	$1,200,000	$600,000
Equities		
Current liabilities	$ 100,000	$ 50,000
Bonds payable	400,000	—
Capital stock, par $1	500,000	450,000
Retained earnings	200,000	100,000
Total	$1,200,000	$600,000

To bring B Co. into the family, A Co. now persuades the stockholders of B Co. to accept 1⅑ shares of A Co. common for each share of B Co. stock they now hold. In other words, A Co. issues 500,000 shares of $1 par stock in exchange for 450,000 shares of B Co. stock. It matters not what is the value of A Co. stock in the market (or what is the apparent "opportunity cost" incurred by A Co. upon trading its shares for those of B Co.). The easiest way to visualize the accounting treatment of the transaction is, as before, to record it in two successive entries, as follows:

(8)

Investment in B Co. Stock (book value)	550,000	
Capital Stock, par (500,000 shares)		500,000
Retained Earnings (plug, maximum $100,000)		50,000

To record acquisition of all outstanding common stock of B Co. by exchange of our common stock, treated as a pooling of interests.

Entry 8 requires further explanation. We now hold all the B Co. stock and we've recorded it at $550,000, which is the book value of the stock-holders' equity on B Co.'s position statement. We could pick up all of B Co.'s retained earnings had we issued only $450,000 in our stock, but what we did is substitute $500,000 par of our stock for $500,000 of the B Co. stock equity, leaving another $50,000 of B Co. equity to be carried into our accounts as retained earnings.

So we see that a pooling of interests has two unique characteristics. First, regardless of how much stock we give for the stock of B Co., we record the investment at $550,000—the book value of the stock received; second, to the extent that the par or stated value of the stock which we issue amounts to less than the total stock equity of B Co., we pick up B Co. retained earnings for such difference. The limit on the second point is that we cannot pick up more retained earnings than the amount shown on B Co.'s position statement; if we have to fill a still larger gap, we do it with capital surplus, that is, Capital in Excess of Par (or Stated Value).

The next step may be to dissolve B Co. now that we hold all the stock (or we may keep B Co. alive and report periodically by means of consolidated statements). The entries to record dissolution are simple because the B Co. values are already represented in our investment account. To record liquidation, the following entry is made:

(9)

Current Assets (at book value)	100,000	
Plant (at book value)	500,000	
Current Liabilities		50,000
Investment in B Co. Stock		550,000

To record dissolution of B Co. and recognition of B Co. assets and liabilities on our books at their B Co. book values.

Impact of Pooling Transaction on Income

No goodwill and no new or higher asset values! With these handicaps eluded, we avoid subsequent shrinkage in the earnings of the B Co. assets that we've taken over, since we don't change the amount of depreciation nor do we have any goodwill to amortize.

In order to gain some notion of the effects of the two kinds of combinations, we can compare the postcombination balance sheets resulting from our assumed acquisition and pooling transactions. Shown side-by-side, the position statements are displayed in Figure 3.

FIGURE 3
A Co.
Comparative Position Statements Immediately Following Combination with B Co.

Assets	Combination Treated as: Purchase	Pooling
Current..........................	$ 150,000	$ 800,000
Plant............................	1,030,000	1,000,000
Goodwill.........................	70,000	—
Total........................	$1,250,000	$1,800,000
Equities		
Current liabilities...................	$ 150,000	$ 150,000
Bonds payable......................	400,000	400,000
Capital stock, par $1................	500,000	1,000,000
Retained earnings...................	200,000	250,000
Total.........................	$1,250,000	$1,800,000

Some of the differences that result from following one course of action as compared with the other are fairly obvious upon examining Figure 3. First, the pooling procedure caused no significant drain on working capital, which in our example amounts to $650,000 (the sum of the precombination working capital of A Co., $600,000, and B Co., $50,000). Combination via acquisition, on the other hand, required an outlay of $650,000, which directly reduced the combined working capital. This apparent advantage of pooling may not be especially attractive where the acquiring company (A Co.) enters the transaction primarily as a means of investing idle funds. Also, many acquisition-type combinations are financed with freshly borrowed funds or by issuing various types of securities, other than voting common stock, directly in exchange for the voting stock of the acquired company.

The second major difference, of course, lies in the effects upon earnings after combination. The expenses of A Co. with the net assets of B Co. taken in at cost will be higher than the sum of each prior to acquisition, and the increase results directly from the fact of purchase rather than pooling. As demonstrated in Figure 3, under acquisition treatment the very same assets are marked up by $30,000 and also goodwill appears. If we assume future revenues to be the same under either treatment, then net income will be lower under purchase treatment by the amount of the increased depreciation (less income tax saving) and goodwill amortization (not deductible for tax purposes). The downward influence of purchase on recorded net income is further evidenced in relating the earnings to the earnings' base. If we exclude working capital from the reckoning, we find in Figure 3 that the rate of return under acquisition accounting must be related to noncurrent assets totaling $1,100,000 as compared with $1,000,000 under pooling treatment.

Finally, businessmen seem to have an almost emotional objection to listing goodwill on the position statement. There is no logical basis for this objection in cases where the acquiring company has clearly expended funds for goodwill. To submerge the cost of goodwill in such a case is tantamount to telling an untruth.

Pool versus Purchase Accounting

Until recently the accounting rules for recording transactions involving business combinations have been, to put it mildly, permissive. A large segment of the membership on the Accounting Principles Board have struggled for years to outlaw pooling entirely but, under heavy pressure from the minority which was aided and abetted by the Financial Executives Institute, the Board compromised and agreed to *require* use of pooling accounting in all cases where, as in our example, A Co. issues voting common stock (only) in exchange for the voting common of B Co.

Prior to the issuance of Opinion No. 16 on this subject, the accounting was an unhappy gallimaufry of permissiveness, abuse of freedom of choice, and fancy-dan accounting. The value of securities issued in exchange for assets was not reflected in the recording of the assets on the acquirer's books. There have been many cases of "instant profits" where such assets were almost immediately resold at large (but perhaps unreal) gains. Thus, A Co. issues valuable common stock in exchange for the common of B Co.; next, B Co. is dissolved so that its assets become assets of A Co. at the amounts at which they were carried on the books of B Co. (in no way reflecting the worth of what A Co. exchanged for them); then A Co. immediately sells them and reports a fat gain in its current income statement! It is not appropriate here to examine the content of Opinion No. 16 in any depth but, with what has been presented in this chapter as background, it is strongly recommended that you now obtain a copy of that document from the American Institute of Certified Public Accountants and read it carefully if you have any current or potential interest in participating in a business combination. You will note that the Board has gone far toward shutting off the opportunities for abuse of the combination transaction. At the same time, over objections of the majority, it has acceded to the demand for an open-door policy with respect to poolings-of-interests accounting. The one feature which appears to have caused the most serious objections to the pooling procedure is, as it is commonly stated, "under pooling the assets of the absorbed companies have *no new basis of accountability.*"

TEST PROBLEM

The condensed position statement data of Our Company and Your Company stand as follows:

Assets	Our Company	Your Company
Current..............................	$100,000	$ 80,000
Noncurrent..........................	400,000	320,000
	$500,000	$400,000
Equities		
Current liabilities......................	$ 50,000	$ 40,000
Capital stock, par $10..................	300,000	200,000
Retained earnings.....................	150,000	160,000
	$500,000	$400,000

The current market value of the common stock of Our Company is $40 per share and of Your Company is $19 per share. Management of Our Company believe that the stockholders of Your Company would be willing (a) to exchange all their common stock in the ratio of two shares for one share of Our Company (which is better than the market ratio), or (b) to exchange all their common for 6 percent 20-year, convertible debenture bonds of Our Company on the basis of a $1,000 par bond for each 50 shares of stock. The debentures would be convertible into Our Company common at the rate of 22 shares for each bond, with the bonds not subject to call until after 10 years. The bonds would probably have a market value of par. Assume that the current assets of Your Company are worth approximately the amount of their book value and plant is appraised at $350,000.

Required:

Assume, first, that the combination is effected by the offer described in (a), on a pooling-of-interests basis. (1) Prepare a journal entry to record, on the books of Our Company, the issue of 1,000 shares of common stock in exchange for the 2,000 outstanding shares of Your Company. (2) Next prepare a journal entry to record the dissolution of Your Company.

Assume that method (b) is followed. (3) Prepare an entry to record the initial investment. (4) Then prepare an entry to record the dissolution of Your Company. Assume that the bonds are worth par.

Finally, in comparative form, present the position statement data of Our Company resulting from each of the two combination procedures.

TEST PROBLEM Solution Space

(1)
Pooling

Debit   Credit

Investment in Your Company Common Stock
    Capital Stock, Par $10
    Retained Earnings
    Capital Paid In in Excess of Par Value
To record exchange of 1,000 shares of Our Company common for 2,000 shares of Your Company common, with pooling-of-interests treatment.

(2)

Current Assets
Noncurrent Assets
    Current Liabilities
    Investment in Your Company Common Stock
To record dissolution of Your Company with assets recorded with "no new basis of accountability."

(3)
Acquisition

Investment in Your Company Common Stock
    Convertible Bonds Payable
To record purchase of Your Company common in exchange for our 6% convertible bonds with par and market value of $400,000.

(4)

Current Assets (appraised)
Noncurrent Assets (appraised)
Goodwill (to balance—cost)
    Current Liabilities (per books)
    Investment in Your Company Common Stock
To record dissolution of Your Company and recognition of assets at current value, including goodwill.

OUR COMPANY
Position Statements after Combination

Assets	Recorded as:	
	Pooling	*Acquisition*
Current	$	$
Noncurrent		
Goodwill	—	
	$	$
Equities		
Current liabilities	$	$
Bonds payable	—	
Capital stock, par $10		
Capital in excess of par		—
Retained earnings		
	$	$

290

Chapter Twenty

Recognition of Effects of Inflation

First Let's Set the Scene

We all know, as surely as anything, that with each passing year our dollar buys less and less. In short, we're all conscious of inflation. Believe it or not, most accountants and most businessmen are still unwilling to admit that the accounting data which are being ground out are likely to be seriously deficient, in fact seriously misleading, if they are not modified or adjusted to compensate for the effects inflation has upon them.

The problem with respect to accounting data, as represented in accounting reports, is twofold. First, the only dollars with which everyone is thoroughly familiar are those which we handle today, that is, "current" dollars. If we quote the price of something, we are presumed to be specifying the amount that we would have to pay *in the kind of dollars currently circulating* in order to buy that thing. In other words, it would be quite misleading for us to quote a price and then, when a customer offers to buy at that price, tell him that this was actually the price 10 years ago and he must now pay us double or more for it because all prices have risen. In our accounting reports we commit virtually this same sin whenever we list the amount we paid for some asset (its "cost") and fail to point out that the price we're quoting is actually the price we paid some 10 or more years ago! Second, we compound our misbehavior by the manner in which we indiscriminately fuse together the costs of things purchased at various times.

For a simple example, assume that we buy one unit of equipment for $500; later, when prices in general have doubled, we buy an identical second unit for $1,000. There are at least three ways that we could represent the two pieces of equipment in our position statement. First, we could merely add $500 and $1,000 and report the cost of equipment as $1,500. This, in effect, is saying that the cost price of our equipment total is $1,500 when, in reality, it consists of $1,000 in today's prices plus $500 in yesterday's prices. Surely this is misleading; unfortunately, this is *the* traditional accounting procedure.

Second, we might show the equipment in a schedule such as the following, which includes dates of acquisition and an index of prices at each date:

OUR EQUIPMENT ACCOUNT
Explanation of $1,500 Cost Shown in Our Position Statement

Date of Purchase	Cost	Price Index
Jan. 1, 19X1	$ 500	100
Dec. 31, 19X9	1,000	200
	$1,500	

This is a pretty good method. If the reader understands price indexes, he will interpret the schedule somewhat as follows: "Because the price index measures the purchasing power of money, I would assume that the second piece is not twice as elaborate as the first but rather that it took twice as much money to buy about the same thing." Unfortunately this method suffers from two major drawbacks. It would be too clumsy and impractical if there were more than a half-dozen or so pieces of equipment. Also, it tends to imply that the price of this particular kind of equipment has doubled when, in fact, it is the prices of "things in general" that have doubled; that is, the general purchasing power of the dollar has deteriorated one-half during the period in question.

A third, entirely practical and far superior, method consists simply in listing all the equipment in terms of current dollars. The purchase on December 31, 19X9, is already in current dollars (if we are presenting a position statement as of December 31, 19X9); the cost on January 1, 19X1, can be translated into current dollars by adjusting it for the 100 percent change in general price level. In other words, we are saying that we have invested 1,000 current dollars in a piece of equipment today and we also have a second piece in which we invested *the equivalent of* 1,000 current dollars. In the third form of presentation we have translated the dollars of two different years into dollars of common purchasing power equivalent, or common dollars. Since each 19X1 dollar had twice as much purchasing power as each 19X9 dollar, we had to multiply the 500 dollars of 19X1 by 2 to translate them into the equivalent of 19X9 dollars.

The act of translation into common dollars is not much of a feat. You merely multiply the raw dollar amount by a fraction which consists of the current price index over the old price index, that is, the current index over the index that prevailed at the time of the original transaction. Thus, to translate the $500 cost we multiply by current index (200) over the prevailing index (100), or 200/100, to arrive at $1,000. The $1,000 then is the number of dollars of today's purchasing power needed to be the equivalent of the $500 spent on equipment in 19X1. We'll be using this technique throughout the remainder of the chapter.

A Simple Example

Between 1940 and 1952 the general cost-of-living index rose an average of almost 10 percent per year. Assume that you had loaned the government $750 at the beginning of 1940; to do this you merely purchased a $1,000 bond for $750, to be repaid at maturity value of $1,000 some 12 years later. What was the *real* effect on your economic well-being of your investing $750 in 1940 for a return of $1,000 in 1952? Let's make a series of computations and see which is the most logical.

First, if you invest $750 and later receive $1,000 in return, orthodox accounting reckons your gain as the difference between $750 and $1,000, or $250 (to be reduced, of course, by income tax on the gain).

Second, you might argue that the $250 is really an exaggeration of your true gain since, during the earning period, your cost of living almost doubled. Might we not, therefore, cut the $250 in half as a measure of our real gain? In other words, you didn't really have clear gain of $250 but, rather, only the equivalent of half that much.

On further thought, you realize that the very subtraction of $750 from $1,000 violates the rules of arithmetic because the 750 dollars of 1940 vintage were quite different from the 1,000 dollars of 1952 vintage, and it's just as incorrect to subtract unlike things from each other as it is to add unlike things together. So you proceed to translate the 1,000 dollars of 1952 vintage into their 1940 equivalent. To do this you divide by the prevailing index (200) and multiply by the index to be used for common dollar purposes (100). Your 1,000 1952 dollars translate into 500 1940 dollars, and you then realize that you really didn't earn $250, and you didn't really earn half that amount—you actually *lost* $250 of the 1940 kind of dollars.

Then you think a bit more and conclude that your reckoning should be in terms of up-to-date current dollars; therefore, you translate the 750 dollars of 1940 vintage into their 1952 counterpart. To do this you divide by the prevailing index (100) and multiply by the current index (200). Now you realize that in 1940 you loaned the government the equivalent of 1,500 1952 dollars and you got back only 750 1952 dollars! You didn't earn $250, you didn't earn $125, and you didn't lose $250; you effectively lost $500, and to crown your investment success you paid income tax on your "gain"!

How Do You Translate Old Dollars into Current Dollars?

The process of translating dollars of one generation into equivalent dollars of current vintage is extremely easy. The Bureau of Labor Statistics prepares a monthly index of the cost of urban living in the United States. This index should rate as the best for our translation purposes because it is based on the proposition that we can compare the purchasing power of the dollar at two different points in time simply by finding how much it cost on each date to purchase a wide variety of consumer items, ranging from recreation to housing, etc. What we're concerned with in our financial reports are "people" dollars—dollars that people saved from their earnings and entrusted to our stewardship. It follows that we should render our reports to them in people dollars—dollars that we are employing in our efforts to generate earnings with which to pay people dividends. For this purpose neither the widely heralded gross national product price deflator, nor the wholesale price index, seems appropriate, though each has a respectable number of supporters. In any case, almost any index is better than none. As one of my accountant friends has said, "If you don't take steps to translate the dollar amounts in your statements, you're as much as contending that the index always remains at 100!"

To translate, merely divide the dollar quantum by the cost-of-living index that prevailed when the particular quantum came into existence, then multiply by the current index (presuming you're aiming for a homogeneous dollar statement in terms of today's dollars).

The consumers' price index is based on an average of prices in the years 1957–1959, to which is assigned the base number 100. In a dozen years this index rose to over 140. If we had purchased a piece of equipment in 1955 for $10,000 and wanted to determine how many consumer dollars we would have to get out of it at the end of 1969 in order to break even (that is, to recover our investment in real cost terms), we would use a translation factor consisting of denominator 93.3, representing the prevailing index at date of acquisition, and numerator 131.3, representing the current index at end of 1969. The $10,000 of translated cost becomes more than $14,000.

You might recognize the translation process as very similar to the translation of foreign currencies into the local equivalent, and the principle is indeed the same. Dollars of yesteryear should be just as foreign to income and position statements carrying today's date as would be dollars of Australian, Canadian, or Hong Kong domicile. Few people would be foolish enough indiscriminately to add together raw dollars from Australia, Canada, Hong Kong, and the United States.

The Particulars of Translation Technique

Above all, bear in mind that the translation of raw, heterogeneous United States dollars of different vintages into their homogeneous current equivalent has nothing to do with the actual record keeping. No, the records continue to be kept in original, raw dollars with all entries properly dated. Each translation then involves going back to the index that prevailed on the original date of the transaction; the original dollar amount is then translated each year into the up-to-date level of prices. Thus, the dated raw dollar data must remain in the accounts.

Now let's scan the major statement elements to observe the translation requirements. Assume that we are looking at a position statement dated December 31 of the current year but made up of the traditional mess of heterogeneous dollars. What do we do to make it right?

CASH AND CLAIMS TO CASH: If our position statement shows that we have $50,000 of cash and claims to cash on hand, we'll not tamper with that figure, because dollars now on hand are automatically current dollars. Also, if we have accounts receivable now of $50,000, we don't modify this figure because, again, the amount is automatically stated in terms of today's money (even though it originated at an earlier date). On the other hand, if we want to compare the $50,000 of cash and $50,000 of receivables that we now possess with the corresponding asset holdings of a year ago or at any other date, the old balances do require translation because they were claims to dollars of their own time period. Thus, assume that our comparative position statement shows the following monetary current assets at the beginning and end of a given year in which the price index rose from 118 to 124. Before translating, the raw comparative amounts are:

	Monetary Current Assets January 1	December 31
Cash in banks	$ 59,000	$ 61,000
Accounts receivable	177,000	185,000
Total	$236,000	$246,000

As traditionally reported, our liquid asset position shows $10,000 of improvement. Now, let's make the two totals more comparable. The amounts on December 31 need no adjustment; the amounts on January 1 are multiplied by the fraction 124/118 to produce the following results:

	January 1 raw	Monetary current assets Translation factor	Translated	December 1 raw
Cash in banks	$ 59,000	124/118	$ 62,000	$ 61,000
Accounts receivable	177,000	124/118	186,000	185,000
	$236,000		$248,000	$246,000

Under the assumption that we have made, the misleading signs of progress disappear and we see that our liquid asset position has actually worsened in terms of its ability to buy things:

NONMONETARY ASSETS: All other assets require translation both in "today's" position (unless they were acquired today) and in the comparative position statement. Consider the cost of a long-lived asset, such as a building. Suppose we purchased a building for 1,000,000 1958 dollars. Each year thereafter, so long as the building remains our property, its 1958-dollar cost should be translated into dollars of the date of the statement in which the building's cost is reported. Thus, if the general price index was 80 at time of acquisition of the building, and if the index rose in the next 4 years in the pattern of 83, 87, 92, and 95, the building's cost would be reported in the following amounts in the 4 years following acquisition:

Year	Ledger cost	Translation factor	Cost in current dollars
0	$1,000,000	80/80	$1,000,000
1	1,000,000	83/80	1,037,500
2	1,000,000	87/80	1,087,500
3	1,000,000	92/80	1,150,000
4	1,000,000	95/80	1,187,500

Needless to point out, the translation process must be applied to all assets and the cost of each building (or of all acquired on a given date) must be translated on the basis of the price index that prevailed when the particular building was acquired. This is not as complicated as it appears, provided that the price index that prevails at the time of each asset acquisition is duly recorded in that asset's ledger account so that it can readily be used as the denominator for each subsequent translation.

LIABILITIES: Liabilities that appear in the current position statement require no translation because they automatically represent the number of dollars in today's currency that are needed to pay off the indicated debts; however, for proper comparison of today's liabilities with those of a year ago or with some other earlier date, the liabilities of earlier dates must be translated into their today equivalent. Thus, if we owed $1,000,000 a year ago when the index stood at 100 and we owe

$1,050,000 today at index 110, our debt position, viewed by itself, has actually improved because the year-ago debt is the equivalent of a debt of $1,100,000 today.

STOCKHOLDERS' EQUITY: The capital stock account, unlike a true liability account, must be translated from the date of origin to today's date because we must show in it the amount needed in current dollars just to break even. If investors contributed $1,000,000 when the cost-of-living index stood at 80, then 15 years later at index 120 the original investment must be shown at $1,500,000, because this is the number of today's dollars the stockholders would have to be paid in order for them to break even.

RETAINED EARNINGS: The retained earnings figures developed from untranslated data will differ radically from the homogeneous dollar amount. Since retained earnings is actually a pool or a series of layers of earnings retained through time, the amount each year will consist of the preceding year's amount modified by the increment resulting from the operations of the current year and by the losses or gains resulting from the company's monetary working capital and noncurrent liability changes. This will be elaborated upon in the comprehensive illustration to follow.

CURRENT REVENUES AND EXPENSES: Revenues and expenses of the current year, unless they are clearly bunched in some one or two seasons of the year, for all practical purposes can be translated into year-end, homogeneous (common) dollars by using the year's average, or midpoint, index as the denominator and the end-of-year index as the numerator. This does not hold true, however, for at least two items—depreciation and cost of goods sold. The numerator for both of these, as always, is the current index, but the denominators must be those which prevailed in the cases of the assets being depreciated, and those which prevailed with respect to the opening and closing inventories in the case of the cost of goods sold. These will both be illustrated.

Common Dollar Reporting— Comparative Data

As we'll see later, an income statement covering a period of a year or less in raw dollars may not be seriously misleading *provided* that the depreciation of assets acquired some years ago is not significant in amount relative to the net income. On the other hand, where raw net

income after all charges is, say, $1,000,000 and the amount of deprecia-
tion that is included in the expenses is also $1,000,000, quite obviously
a 20 percent price-level adjustment upward for depreciation causes an
equal 20 percent decline in reported earnings. It is not at all unusual for
the depreciation charge for the period to be considerably larger (double
or more) than the net income, so the leverage effect can be very serious.

Even if we are presenting data that do not include depreciation, we
must not overlook the fact that any such data when reported in comparative form can be mighty misleading. To illustrate this point, just examine
the data shown in Figure 1. In column 1 Our Company reports its
sales revenue for each of the past 10 years, and in column 2 gives the
reader assistance in interpreting the sales data by showing the cumulative
percentages of growth throughout the 10-year period. In column 3 you'll
find inserted the translation factor needed to translate the sales for each
year into homogeneous dollars as of the end of 1969. Column 4 then
shows the translated data, and column 5 lists the percentages of growth
in uniform dollars. Needless to say, the translated data significantly
change the growth pattern. It is common practice for corporations to

FIGURE 1
OUR COMPANY
Comparative Sales Revenue for the Years 1960–1969
(in thousands of dollars)

Year	(1) Sales	(2) Cumulative growth, %	(3) Translation factor*	(4) Common dollar sales	(5) Common dollar growth
1960	$100,000	100	103.1	$127,352	100.0
1961	102,000	102	104.2	128,528	100.9
1962	105,000	105	105.4	130,802	102.7
1963	108,000	108	106.7	132,900	104.4
1964	112,000	112	108.1	136,037	106.8
1965	117,000	117	109.9	139,784	110.0
1966	120,000	120	113.1	139,310	109.4
1967	124,000	124	116.3	139,993	109.9
1968	130,000	130	121.2	140,833	110.6
1969	138,000	138	127.7	141,890	111.4

* The numerator of the translation factor for each year is the consumer price index at
the end of December, 1969, or 131.3. The denominator in each year is the average index
number for that particular year.

present 10-year comparisons in raw dollars for purposes of showing growth. It seems perfectly amazing that such data have gone unchallenged all these years! Some companies have followed the practice of issuing a small, say, 2 percent, stock dividend each year while keeping the cash dividend per share unchanged. Pity the poor stockholder who believes in such circumstances that his fortunes are improving by 2 percent each year when, in actuality, over the past 10 years he would have required an increase of approximately 3 percent just to break even. As an aside, note that interest rates of about 10 percent per annum take on quite a different complexion when they are properly adjusted for price-level changes in the neighborhood of 6 percent or more per year.

Common Dollar Reporting— Comprehensive Illustration

Let us repeat that common dollar reporting adds little if any to the burdens of accounting. All account data are kept in their original raw form since each year they must be retranslated for statement purposes in terms of the general price index at the end of the year.

Our illustration will utilize a pair of assumed comparative position statements as of the beginning and end of a given year, and an income statement for the same year. The purposes of the illustration are, first, to demonstrate the technique and, second, to show again how important it is that modern accounting statements be supplemented, if not replaced, by statements that are in homogeneous or common dollars of the kind in current circulation. The raw data are presented in Figure 2.

The first schedule that should be prepared is the one for determining monetary working capital inflation loss since the amount as determined must be appended to the income statement to account for the whole change in retained earnings during the year. The necessary schedule is shown as Figure 3. Remember that monetary working capital is the net balance of cash and receivables less current liabilities.

Next we prepare the common dollar income statement as shown in Figure 4.

Finally, the comparative position statements are prepared as demonstrated in Figure 5. Note that the retained earnings balance in common dollars at the end of 1968 is a "plug" figure since it represents the net result of all past earnings, dividends, etc.

FIGURE 2

PROBLEM DATA
OUR COMPANY
Comparative Position Statements as of December 31

Assets	1968	1969
Cash..	$ 20,000	$ 25,000
Receivables (net).................................	30,000	35,000
Inventories.......................................	10,000	15,000
Land...	10,000	10,000
Buildings and equipment...........................	50,000	50,000
Allowance for depreciation.........................	(20,000)	(25,000)
	$100,000	$110,000

Equities		
Accounts and notes payable.........................	$ 10,000	$ 15,000
Capital stock.....................................	70,000	70,000
Retained earnings.................................	20,000	25,000
	$100,000	$110,000

Income Statement, Year Ended December 31, 1969

Sales and miscellaneous revenues......................		$ 60,000
Expenses and taxes:		
Merchandise cost of sales...........................	$ 40,000	
Salaries and wages................................	8,000	
Depreciation (1958 assets, $2,000; 1965 assets, $3,000)...	5,000	
Taxes...	2,000	55,000
Net income (all retained).............................		$ 5,000

Notes to statements:
(1) Our Company was established in 1958 and all the capital stock was issued then at par.
(2) Merchandise purchases in 1969 were $45,000.
(3) Depreciation of $5,000 in 1969 came $2,000 from 1958 assets and $3,000 from 1965 equipment.
(4) Relevant consumer price index data are:

Date or Event	Prevailing Index
Company started in 1958..	100
Land purchased for $10,000....................................	100
Building and equipment purchased, 1958, $40,000..................	100
Equipment purchased, 1965, $10,000.............................	110
Depreciation of 1958 assets to December 31, 1968, $15,000.............	100
Depreciation of 1965 assets to December 31, 1968, $5,000..............	110
Inventory held on December 31, 1968, FIFO.......................	123
Index on January 1, 1969..	124
Average index for revenues and expenses in 1969....................	128
Inventory held on December 31, 1969, FIFO.......................	130
Index on December 31, 1969.....................................	131

FIGURE 3

OUR COMPANY

**Working Capital in Raw and Common Dollars
to Determine Inflation Loss**

	Raw	Translation* factor	Common dollars
Monetary working capital, 1/1/69........	$ 40,000	124	$ 42,258
Add: Sales and other revenues...........	60,000	128	61,406
	$100,000		$103,664
Less:			
Merchandise purchases................	$ 45,000	128	$ 46,055
Salaries and wages..................	8,000	128	8,188
Taxes............................	2,000	128	2,047
	$ 55,000	xx	$ 56,290
Computed balance, 12/31/69............	$ 45,000		$ 47,374
Actual balance, 12/31/69..............	45,000		45,000
Inflation loss.........................	—		$ (2,374)

* The numerator is 131, the December 31, 1969 index, throughout the solution to the problem.

FIGURE 4

OUR COMPANY

**Income Statement for Year Ended December 31, 1969
in Raw and Common Dollars**

	Raw	T/F*	Common
Sales and other revenues....................	$60,000	128	$61,406
Cost of goods sold:			
Inventory, Jan. 1, 1969..................	$10,000	123	$10,650
Purchases.............................	45,000	128	46,055
Total......:.........................	$55,000		$56,705
Inventory, Dec. 31, 1969.................	15,000	130	15,115
	$40,000		$41,590
Salaries and wages........................	8,000	128	8,188
Depreciation—1958—$2,000.................	2,000	100	2,620
—1965—$3,000.................	3,000	110	3,572
Taxes....................................	2,000	128	2,047
	$55,000		$58,017
Net income before inflation.................	$ 5,000		$ 3,389
Inflation loss..............................	—		(2,374)
Net income...............................	$ 5,000		$ 1,015

* Translation factor numerator is 131 throughout.

FIGURE 5

Our Company

Comparative Position Statements in Raw and Common Dollars
as of December 31

	1968			1969		
Assets	Raw	T/F*	Common	Raw	T/F*	Common
Cash..............	$ 20,000	124	$ 21,129	$ 25,000	131	$ 25,000
Receivables (net)....	30,000	124	31,694	35,000	131	35,000
Inventories.........	10,000	123	10,650	15,000	130	15,115
Land..............	10,000	100	13,100	10,000	100	13,100
Buildings and equipment—1958.......	40,000	100	52,400	40,000	100	52,400
—1965.......	10,000	110	11,909	10,000	110	11,909
Allowance for depreciation—1958......	(15,000)	100	(19,650)	(17,000)	100	(22,270)
—1965......	(5,000)	110	(5,955)	(8,000)	110	(9,527)
	$100,000		$115,277	$110,000		$120,727
Equities						
Accounts and notes payable...........	$ 10,000	124	$ 10,565	$ 15,000	131	$ 15,000
Capital stock.......	70,000	100	91,700	70,000	100	91,700
Retained earnings...	20,000	xx	13,012	25,000	var.	14,027
	$100,000		$115,277	$110,000		$120,727

* Translation factor numerator is 131 throughout.

Concluding Comment

It may seem too bad to have plowed through 20 more or less tough chapters on accounting only to find that modern accounting statements are badly deficient if they fail to take into account the persistent erosion of our monetary unit. Fortunately the accounting profession, more and more, is showing signs of recognizing the great importance of this problem. Statement 3 of the Accounting Principles Board (we thought it would never happen!) was adopted unanimously by the 18 members in June of 1969. Though the recommendation to employ price-level translation in the presentation of financial data is lukewarm, there can be little doubt that, at last, we're on our way to much better accounting. The recommendation, in part, reads:

> The Board believes that general price-level financial statements, or pertinent information extracted from them, present useful information

not available from basic historical-dollar financial statements. General price-level information may be presented in addition to the basic historical-dollar financial statements, but general price-level financial statements should not be presented as the basic statements. The Board believes that general price-level information is not required at this time for fair presentation of financial position and results of operations in conformity with generally accepted accounting principles in the United States.

{ Appendix }

Solutions to Tests

Chapter 1

DENTON BREAD CO.
Balance Sheet as of December 31, 1972

Assets

Current:

Cash..	$ 9,200		
Accounts receivable (less $500 allowance for uncollectibles)....	11,500		
Raw materials inventory (at cost).........................	5,000		
Miscellaneous supplies..................................	1,000		
Prepayments...	500	$ 27,200	

Plant:

Land (cost)...	$ 5,000		
Buildings (cost)..............................	$ 50,000		
Machinery and equipment (cost)................	60,000		
	$110,000		
Less: Accumulated depreciation.................	3,400	106,600	111,600
			$138,800

Equities

Current liabilities:

Wages payable...	$ 1,600		
Taxes payable...	3,000		
Interest payable.......................................	200	$ 4,800	
Mortgage payable, 20 year, 8%..........................		30,000	
Total liabilities.......................................		$ 34,800	

Stockholders' equity:

Capital stock, par $10..................................	$100,000		
Retained earnings.....................................	4,000	104,000	
		$138,800	

Chapter 2

TARRANT CO.

Income Statement for the Year 19XX

Revenues		
Sales (Less: Uncollectibles of $24,000).............................		$5,603,483
Other income...		13,680
		$5,617,163
Revenue deductions:		
Expenses:		
Cost of goods sold.................................	$3,980,000	
Selling...	592,000	
Administrative...................................	614,250	$5,186,250
Income taxes..		154,000
		$5,340,250
Income before extraordinary item..................................		$ 276,913
Uninsured flood loss..		125,000
Net income..		$ 151,913
Retained earnings at beginning of year:		
As previously reported...		$1,500,000
Adjustment for litigation losses of prior years......................		75,000
As restated...		$1,425,000
		$1,576,913
Cash dividends on common stock, $1 per share......................		100,000
Retained earnings at end of year..................................		$1,476,913
Per share of common stock:		
Income before extraordinary item.................................		$2.71
Extraordinary item (flood loss)...................................		(1.22)
Net income..		$1.49

COMMENT: Technically the income taxes in this problem should be "allocated" in relation to the extraordinary charges for flood and litigation losses. Tax allocation is examined in a special chapter on that subject (Chapter 18).

Chapter 3

DECATUR CO.
Funds Statement, Year Ended December 31, 19X2

Sources of funds:

Net income	$30,000	
Add back: Depreciation	10,000	
Funds flow from operations		$ 40,000
Sale of land		15,000
Issue of capital stock		50,000
		$105,000

Applications of funds:

Cash dividends	$ 25,000
Purchase of plant	50,000
Reduction of mortgage	10,000
Net increase in working capital (schedule)	20,000
	$105,000

Schedule of Working Capital Changes

	19X1	19X2	Increase (Decrease)
Current assets	$80,000	$100,000	$20,000
Current liabilities	40,000	40,000	—
Working capital	$40,000	$ 60,000	$20,000

Chapter 4

EMPIRE CORP.
Ledger

Cash in Bank		
(1) 100,000	(2)	1,000
	(3)	30,000
	(6)	10,000

Capital Stock	
	(1) 100,000

Accounts Receivable	
(5) 60,000	

Retained Earnings	
	(12d) 13,875

Merchandise		
(4) 50,000	(7)	35,000

Sales		
(12a) 60,000	(5)	60,000

Store Equipment		
(3) 30,000	(8)	125

Merchandise Cost of Sales		
(7) 35,000	(12b)	35,000

Accounts Payable	
	(4) 50,000

Miscellaneous Expenses		
(2) 1,000	(12c)	11,125
(6) 10,000		
(8) 125		

Income Summary		
(12b) 35,000	(12a)	60,000
(12c) 11,125		
(12d) 13,875		

(9) EMPIRE CORP.
Trial Balance (before closing), July 31, 19XX

| | Balances | |
Account Title	Left	Right
Cash in bank...	$ 59,000	
Accounts receivable.....................................	60,000	
Merchandise..	15,000	
Store equipment..	29,875	
Accounts payable..		$ 50,000
Capital stock...		100,000
Retained earnings.......................................		—
Sales...		60,000
Merchandise cost of sales................................	35,000	
Miscellaneous expenses..................................	11,125	
	$210,000	$210,000

(10) EMPIRE CORP.
Income Statement for July, 19XX

Sales..		$60,000
Expenses:		
Merchandise cost of sales................................	$35,000	
Miscellaneous..	11,125	46,125
Net income (and earnings retained).................................		$13,875

(11) EMPIRE CORP.
Position Statement, July 31, 19XX

Assets			Equities		
Current:			Current liabilities:		
Cash in bank....	$59,000		Accounts payable.........		$ 50,000
Accounts			Stock equity:		
receivable......	60,000		Capital stock....	$100,000	
Merchandise			Retained		
inventory.......	15,000	$134,000	earnings........	13,875	113,875
Store equipment.............		29,875			
		$163,875			$163,875

BLITZ CO.

Work Sheet for the Year Ended December 31, 19XX

	Trial balance Debit	Trial balance Credit	Adjusting entries Debit	Adjusting entries Credit	Income statement Debit	Income statement Credit	Balance sheet Debit	Balance sheet Credit
Cash in bank	2,500			(1) 25			2,475	
Accounts receivable	40,000						40,000	
Allowance for bad debts		100		(2) 600				700
Merchandise	40,000			(3) 30,000			10,000	
Plant	100,000						100,000	
Allowance for depreciation		35,000		(4) 4,000				39,000
Accounts payable		20,000						20,000
Interest accrued payable				(5) 1,000				1,000
Income tax accrued payable				(6) 650				650
Bonds payable		25,000						25,000
Capital stock		50,000						50,000
Retained earnings		13,400						13,400
Sales		60,000				60,000		
Bad debts			(2) 600		600			
Cost of goods sold			(3) 30,000		30,000			
Selling expenses	10,000		(4) 3,600		13,600			
Administrative expenses	11,000		(1) 25		11,425			
			(4) 400					
Interest expense			(5) 1,000		1,000			
Income taxes			(6) 650		650			
Net income for year					2,725			2,725
Totals	203,500	203,500	36,275	36,275	60,000	60,000	152,475	152,475

BLITZ Co.
Income Statement, Year Ended December 31, 19XX

Sales		$ 60,000
Less: Bad debts		600
Net sales		$ 59,400
Expenses:		
Cost of goods sold	$30,000	
Selling expenses	13,600	
Administrative expenses	11,425	
	$55,025	
Interest expense	1,000	
Income taxes	650	56,675
Net income (and earnings retained)		$ 2,725

BLITZ Co.
Balance Sheet, December 31, 19XX

Assets

Current:			
Cash in bank		$ 2,475	
Accounts receivable	$40,000		
Less: Allowance for bad debts	700	39,300	
Merchandise		10,000	$ 51,775
Plant (cost)		$100,000	
Less: Allowance for depreciation		39,000	61,000
			$112,775

Equities

Current liabilities:			
Accounts payable		$ 20,000	
Interest accrued payable		1,000	
Income taxes accrued payable		650	$ 21,650
Bonds payable			25,000
Total liabilities			$ 46,650
Stockholders' equity			
Capital stock		$ 50,000	
Retained earnings, January 1	$13,400		
Earnings retained, 19XX	2,725	16,125	66,125
			$112,775

Chapter 6

(1) Cash	500	
Sales		500
(2) Accounts Receivable	600	
Sales		600
(3) Cash	196	
Sales Discounts	4	
Accounts Receivable		200
(4) Cash in Bank	5,000	
Notes Payable		5,000
(5) Interest Expense	100	
Notes Payable	5,000	
Cash in Bank		5,100
(6) Cash	800	
Allowance for Depreciation	1,100	
Retirement Loss	100	
Machinery		2,000
(7) Sales—Bad Debts	500	
Accounts Receivable—Allowance for Bad Debts		500
(8) Accounts Receivable—Allowance for Bad Debts	120	
Accounts Receivable		120
(9) Cost of Goods Sold	9,000	
Merchandise		9,000
(10) Insurance Expense	300	
Prepaid Insurance		300

Chapter 7

JAN. 10

Raw Materials	19,600	
Accounts Payable		19,600

Purchase of 25,000 pounds @ 80 cents, terms 2/10, n/30.

JAN. 19

Accounts Payable	19,600	
Cash in Bank		19,600

JAN. 20

Raw Materials	17,640	
Accounts Payable		17,640

JAN. 31

Accounts Payable	17,640	
Loss from Lapsed Discounts	360	
Cash in Bank		18,000
Work in Process	30,032	
Raw Materials		30,032

Consumption of all but 22,000 pounds with FIFO cost of $17,640 plus $1,568 (which is 2,000 units of the first purchase at 80 cents less 2%).

Chapter 8

Straight-line procedure:

YEAR 1

Depreciation...	1,700	
Allowance for Depreciation..................................		1,700

YEAR 2

Depreciation...	1,700	
Allowance for Depreciation..................................		1,700

YEAR 3

Depreciation...	1,700	
Allowance for Depreciation..................................		1,700

YEAR 4

Allowance for Depreciation..	5,100	
Cash..	3,000	
Retirement Loss...	1,900	
Machinery...		10,000

Sum-of-years' digits procedure:

YEAR 1

Depreciation...	2,833	
Allowance for Depreciation..................................		2,833

COMPUTATION: $1 + 2 + 3 + 4 + 5 = 15$. Depreciation for first year is then $\frac{5}{15}$ of $8,500. Second year will be $\frac{4}{15}$ of $8,500, or $567 less. The amount declines by $567 each year, leaving a salvage of $1,500 at the end of year 5 if the asset is not retired earlier.

YEAR 2

Depreciation...	2,266	
Allowance for Depreciation..................................		2,266

YEAR 3

Depreciation...	1,700	
Allowance for Depreciation..................................		1,700

YEAR 4

Allowance for Depreciation..	6,799	
Cash..	3,000	
Retirement Loss...	201	
Machinery...		10,000

Chapter 9

(1)

Cash in Bank..	11,250,000	
Capital Stock Common—Stated Value $2............		500,000
Capital Paid In in Excess of Stated Value....... ...		10,750,000

(2)

Capital Stock Common—Stated Value $2...............	2,000,000	
Capital Stock Common—Stated Value $1............		2,000,000

(3)

No entry. Unissued stock has no effective financial significance and no basis for entry.

(4)

Treasury Stock Common—Cost........................	3,000,000	
Cash in Bank.....................................		3,000,000

(5)

Cash in Bank..	1,750,000	
Treasury Stock Common—Cost....................		1,500,000
Capital Paid In in Excess of Stated Value............		250,000

(6)

Capital Stock Preferred.............................	1,000,000	
Retained Earnings.................................	100,000	
Cash in Bank.....................................		1,100,000

(7)

Cash in bank......................................	1,050,000	
Capital Stock Preferred—Par......................		1,000,000
Capital Stock Common—Warrants..................		40,000
Capital Paid In in excess of Par....................		10,000

(8)

No entry called for.

Stockholders' Equity:

Capital stock preferred—6%, $100 par...........................		$ 1,000,000
Capital paid in in excess of par.................................		10,000
Capital stock common, no par, stated value $1, authorized 3,000,000 shares, issued 2,000,000...................	$ 2,000,000	
Capital paid in in excess of stated value...............	19,500,000	
Capital stock common—warrants......................	40,000	
Retained earnings...................................	7,000,000	
	$28,540,000	
Less: Capital stock common in treasury at cost (50,000 shares)..	1,500,000	27,040,000
		$28,050,000

Chapter 10

MARCH 15

Retained Earnings.. 200,000
    Retained Earnings Reserved for Possible Fire Loss............   100,000
    Retained Earnings Reserved for General Contingencies........   100,000

APRIL 15

Retained Earnings.. 500,000
    Capital Stock, Par $5....................................   100,000
    Capital in Excess of Par   400,000
To record 10% stock dividend or 20,000 shares at market value of $25 per share.

Chapter 11

(1)

Cash.. 97,000
Bonds Payable—Discount................................... 18,402
    Bonds Payable—Par.....................................   100,000
    Common Stock Warrants................................   15,402
Issue of 100 bonds with warrants attached, each to buy one share of common stock at $20.

(2)

Bond Interest Expense...................................... 3,500
    Cash...   3,500
Payment of coupon 1 at 7%.

Bond Interest Expense...................................... 460
    Bonds Payable—Discount...............................   460
To accumulate one-fortieth of the original bond discount.

(3)

Common Stock Warrants.................................... 15,402
Cash.. 2,000
    Capital Stock—Par.....................................   10,000
    Capital Paid In in Excess of Par.........................   7,402
To record issue of 100 shares of common stock at $20 cash plus one warrant per share.

Chapter 12

(1)

Raw Materials—Control......................................	100,000	
(also subledger cards, received column, for each kind of material)		
Accounts Payable—Control..............................		100,000

(2)

Work in Process—Control....................................	97,000	
(also individual subledger job-cost sheets)		
Raw Materials—Control..................................		97,000
(also subledger cards, issued column, for each kind)		

(3)

Work in Process—Control....................................	364,000	
(also subledger job-cost sheets)		
Wages Payable...		364,000
(and individual employee earnings records)		

(4)

Factory Overhead—Control................................	643,000	
Service 1..	127,000	
Service 2..	94,000	
Production 1.....................................	236,000	
Production 2.....................................	186,000	
Various Accounts.....................................		643,000

(5)

Factory Overhead—Control................................	127,000	
Service 2..	34,000	
Production 1.....................................	63,000	
Production 2.....................................	30,000	
Factory Overhead—Control.............................		127,000
Service 1.....................................	127,000	

(6)

Factory Overhead—Control................................	128,000	
Production 1.....................................	64,000	
Production 2.....................................	64,000	
Factory Overhead—Control.............................		128,000
Service 2.....................................	128,000	

(7)

Work in Process—Control....................................	614,000	
(also, subledger job-cost sheets)		
Factory Overhead—Control.............................		614,000
Production 1................................	348,000	
Production 2................................	266,000	

(8)

Finished Goods...	960,000	
Work in Process—Control...............................		960,000

(9)

Income Summary...	29,000	
Factory Overhead—Control.............................		29,000
Production 1.................................	15,000	
Production 2.................................	14,000	

OUR COMPANY
Statement of Cost of Goods Manufactured
Year Ended December 31, 19X1

Raw materials used...		$ 97,000
Direct labor..		364,000
Factory overhead—actual.................................	$643,000	
Less: Unapplied...	29,000	614,000
Total manufacturing costs..		$1,075,000
Add: Work in process, January 1.....................................		100,000
		$1,175,000
Less: Work in process, December 31.................................		215,000
Cost of goods manufactured..		$ 960,000

Chapter 13

(1)

Raw Materials..	60,000	
Materials Price Variance.......................................	2,400	
Accounts Payable...		62,400

(2)

Finished Goods...	50,000	
Materials Quantity Variance....................................	1,000	
Raw Materials...		51,000

(3)

Finished Goods...	18,000	
Labor Wage Variance..	610	
Labor Efficiency Variance......................................	300	
Wages Payable...		18,910

(4)

Factory Overhead..	35,000	
Various Accounts...		35,000

(5)

Finished Goods...	30,000	
Budget Variance $35,000 − (18,300 + 16,000)....................	700	
Efficiency Variance $5 × (6,100 − 6,000).......................	500	
Idle Plant Variance $2 × 1,900 hours............................	3,800	
Factory Overhead..		35,000

Chapter 14

PAYBACK PERIOD: Cost, $41,000, divided by annual net cash flow of $7,000 equals $5\frac{6}{7}$ years payback period.

PRESENT VALUE AT 10%: $7,000 times present value at 10% of 10-year annuity of $1, or 6.144, is $43,008, which is favorable.

Chapter 17

(1) Elimination entries on January 1, 19X1:

Capital Stock (90% of Their Company).........................	45,000	
Retained Earnings (90% of Their Company at date of acquisition)....	27,000	
Goodwill..	10,000	
Investment in Their Company (at cost)......................		82,000

OUR COMPANY AND THEIR COMPANY
Consolidated Position Statement
January 1, 19X1

Assets		Equities		
Current (sum)............	$ 80,000	Current liabilities (sum)..........		$ 40,000
Plant (sum, net).........	188,000	Minority interests:		
Goodwill (per journal)....	10,000	Capital stock (10%)..	$ 5,000	
		Retained earnings		
		(10%)...........	3,000	8,000
		Stock equity:		
		Capital stock........	$180,000	
		Retained earnings...	50,000	230,000
	$278,000			$278,000

(2) Elimination entries on December 31, 19X1:

(1)

Capital Stock (90%) of Their Company).........................	45,000	
Retained Earnings (90% of Their Company at date of acquisition)....	27,000	
Goodwill..	10,000	
Investment in Their Company (at cost)......................		82,000

(2)

Retained Earnings (consolidated)................................	500	
Goodwill..		500

To amortize $500 of consolidated goodwill against consolidated retained earnings.

(3) (not required)

Retained Earnings (Their Company—since acquisition).............	8,000	
Minority Interest (10%).....................................		800
Consolidated Retained Earnings (90%)......................		7,200

To divide new retained earnings between minority and majority.

(4)

Current Liabilities.   5,000
    Current Assets.   5,000
To eliminate intercompany debt.

OUR COMPANY AND THEIR COMPANY
Consolidated Position Statement
December 31, 19X1

Assets		*Equities*		
Current (sum less $5,000). .	$119,800	Current liabilities (sum less $5,000).		$ 35,000
Plant assets (net sum).	182,000	Minority interests:		
Goodwill ($10,000 less $500)	9,500	Capital stock (10%). .	$ 5,000	
		Retained earnings		
		(10%).	3,800	8,800
		Stock equity:		
		Capital stock.	$180,000	
		Retained earnings		
		($80,800 plus $7,200		
		less $500)	87,500	267,500
	$311,300			$311,300

Chapter 18

(1)

Income Tax Expense. $24,000
    Deferred (or Accrued) Income Tax Credit. $24,000
The amount is 40% of $60,000.

(2)

Deferred Income Tax Charge.   40,000
    Income Tax Expense.   40,000
The amount is 40% of the $100,000 expense that won't be allowed as a
deduction until a later period.

(3)

Deferred Income Tax Charge.   16,000
    Income Tax Expense.   16,000
The amount is 40% of the $40,000 of rent which we have not yet
earned but on which we must pay (prepay) tax.

(4)

Income Tax Expense.   60,000
    Deferred Income Tax Credit.   60,000
The amount is 40% of the $150,000 of extra depreciation deducted in
the tax return.

Chapter 19

(1)
Pooling

Investment in Your Company Common Stock....................	360,000	
Capital Stock, par $10....................................		100,000
Retained Earnings (maximum permissible).................		160,000
Capital Paid In in Excess of Par Value (to balance)...........		100,000

To record investment in Your Company stock at its total book value ($360,000) in exchange of $100,000 par value of Our Company common, with resulting carry-forward of entire balance of Your Company retained earnings plus "capital excess" sufficient to balance the transaction.

(2)

Current Assets...	80,000	
Noncurrent Assets...	320,000	
Current Liabilities......................................		40,000
Investment in Your Company Common Stock................		360,000

To record dissolution of Your Company and recognition of assets and liabilities at unchanged book values on Our Company books.

(3)
Acquisition

Investment in Your Company Common Stock....................	400,000	
Convertible Bonds Payable...............................		400,000

To record issue of 40 bonds, par $1,000 each, in exchange for 2,000 shares of Your Company Common, recorded at market value of bonds which coincides with par value.

(4)

Current Assets (appraised)....................................	80,000	
Noncurrent Assets (appraised)...............................	350,000	
Goodwill (plug)..	10,000	
Current Liabilities......................................		40,000
Investment in Your Company Common Stock................		400,000

To record dissolution of Your Company and recognition of assets at current values plus goodwill, at assumed cost, to balance.

OUR COMPANY
Position Statements after Combination

	Recorded as:	
Assets	*Pooling*	*Acquisition*
Current assets........................	$180,000	$180,000
Noncurrent assets.....................	720,000	750,000
Goodwill............................	—	10,000
	$900,000	$940,000
Equities		
Current liabilities.....................	$ 90,000	$ 90,000
Bonds payable.......................	—	400,000
Capital stock, par $10.................	400,000	300,000
Capital in excess of par...............	100,000	—
Retained earnings....................	310,000	150,000
	$900,000	$940,000

Index

Index